JOURNEY THROUGH THE ADVENT CALENDAR

RACHEL BROWDY

To Michaela, Marshall, and Maverick,

*May the gifts of Advent and the beauty of your imagination
lead you closer to God.*

Love, Mom

beatipublishing@gmail.com
PO Box 190376
Shrewsbury, MO 63119

Library of Congress Control Number: 2022944011

ISBN: 9798985194616

Back cover author headshot courtesy of Jean Kaimann Photography.

Printed in the United States of America

22 23 24 25 26   5 4 3 2 1

CONTENTS

MAP OF
BURRA DIN

SPÉS

FIDEM

GAUDIUM

PAX

WHO IS ZACHARIAH?

"Be watchful. Be alert. You do not know
when the time will come."
Mark 13:33-37

"Zach?"

Just as he had every Thursday for the past six months since his parents died, Zachariah Labouré found himself in Dr. Reed's stuffy office, picking at the same spiderweb-shaped crack on the same ugly gray couch, staring at the same ugly brown carpet. Dr. Reed was a friend of Father Joe, Zach's uncle. Initially, Zach had refused to go to therapy. But Father Joe, the Catholic priest of St. Nicholas's Parish and School and now Zach's legal guardian, had offered to counsel Zach himself, which resulted in Zach's immediate change of heart. The only thing more uncomfortable than being forced to spend time with a stranger was being forced to spend time with an uncle he'd just met and who'd recently adopted him out of pity.

However, upon meeting Dr. Reed, Zach quickly made up his mind that he wasn't going to tell this guy anything. Everything about the short, middle-aged man with gray-speckled, blond hair annoyed him. Dr. Reed wore baggy khakis with a short-sleeved, brown and white striped shirt. The stiff fabric fell just above his ankles, revealing thick, white, cotton socks that puffed out of the straps of his brown sandals. A hemp bracelet wrapped around a peach-colored crystal hung from his wrist, and the frames of his huge glasses were dropped to the edge of his large nose. It looked like the guy had crawled right out of some cringey movie from the 1970s. Besides his irritating looks, Dr. Reed liked to sit directly in front of Zach, legs crossed, with a notepad and pen. And if Zach said anything or even sneezed, Dr. Reed would immediately begin jotting down notes, responding with a thoughtful "mmhmm." One time Zach asked to go to the bathroom in the middle of a session, and the guy even wrote that down on the notepad before giving him the okay.

But the thing that drove Zach to the brink of ultimate insanity was the drawn-out sympathetic look the guy got on his face when he was probing for information. His gray eyes would narrow. Wisps of hair would fall in front of his face as he furrowed his brows and pursed his lips. The first time Dr. Reed had made that face, Zach had had to hold back a laugh because the guy looked like he needed to use the bathroom. The only thing that made this visit different from the last was the half-hearted attempt to decorate for the holiday season. Dr. Reed had a small, sparsely decorated Christmas tree in the corner of his office as well as a plastic blue Hanukkah menorah and a brightly colored Kwanzaa kinara sitting on an end table. Zach wasn't sure which holiday Dr. Reed celebrated, but he didn't really care.

"Zach?" Dr. Reed asked again.

Without saying a word or moving, Zach shifted his gaze, making eye contact with the eccentric therapist.

"Can you answer my question?"

"What question?"

"Have you made any new friends at school? It is the holiday season after all. I'm sure there are plenty of fun things to do."

"No."

"And why is that?"

"What's the point?"

"What do you mean, Zach?"

Zach shrugged, crossing his arms.

Dr. Reed scribbled on his notepad.

Zach didn't respond. He didn't want to tell Dr. Reed that he had no desire to make new friends. He'd had friends. He'd also had parents. And if he learned anything from the day of the accident, it was that nothing was permanent. It could be taken away from you in a flash. So what was the point in trying to make new friends? Or creating a new family? From the week after the accident, while everyone was trying to decide "what to do with him," he'd devised a new plan, and that plan included himself and only himself. When memories of his parents and old friends crept back into Zach's mind, he felt a wrenching pain in his heart. One he couldn't bear. But when he thought of his new plan, he felt nothing. And nothing was better than pain.

After a minute, Dr. Reed sighed and said, "We've discussed this before, I know. But how are you feeling? Remember, any emotions you are having are completely understandable. There is no correct way to grieve, Zachariah."

Zach hated it when people called him, Zachariah. Dr. Reed did it off and on and his new teachers called him Zachariah all the time. No one in his old life had called him by his full name. Everyone had called him Zach. One of his friends in school had even called him "Zach Lab" since his last name was Labouré and after he'd gotten a 110% on a lab final exam the same year.

Zach returned to picking at the couch cushion as a memory floated to the surface of his consciousness. He remembered his mother complaining once when he had been in the car about the fact that he always had to be "messing with stuff." He had been sitting in the passenger seat of their SUV and had been rapidly clicking the window button up and down. Even though she had been frustrated, his mother had given him an exasperated smile. His dad had told her it was because his mind moved a million miles an hour, and he needed to occupy his brain to reign in his thoughts. Then his dad had patted his mother on the shoulder from the driver's-side window and had said, "Like someone else I know and love dearly." Then Zach's mom had given his dad a kiss, and she'd pulled out of the driveway to take Zach to drum practice. That was the day before the accident.

"Zach?"

Zach looked up at Dr. Reed. He'd forgotten the guy was even in the room. Zach felt a lump in his throat and a pain in his chest. He swallowed hard. There was no way he was going to cry in front of this guy.

"What are you thinking?" Dr. Reed asked.

Zach shrugged.

Dr. Reed scribbled something down in his notepad. Then he looked at his watch.

Zach perked up. When Dr. Reed looked at his watch, that meant one thing: the session was over. And sure enough, just as he did every Thursday, Dr. Reed gripped the arm of the chair and pushed himself up with what Zach assumed was supposed to be some kind of comical old guy grunt. Then he said the same thing he did at the end of every session, "Well, Zachariah. We'll try again next week."

Zach gave a half-hearted grin and walked out of the office.

The heavy-set, gray-haired secretary pulled the bright red glasses off her nose and looked up at him.

"Father Joe is waiting in the parking lot for you. Would you like a sucker?"

Zach didn't want to be rude so he took the sucker. But he didn't really want it so he tucked it into his back pocket and walked out the glass door.

A couple days later, Zach sat alone in his room, staring at his phone, trying to decide what to do. He laid on his bed alternating between scrolling through his social media feed and flipping the cover of his math book open . . . closed . . . open . . . closed . . . open . . .

HE.

WAS.

BORED.

Completely aware he had no new notifications, Zach put in his passcode anyway—1225—and began to check his social media accounts for the third time in 20 minutes. A quiet voice in the back of his mind told him to put the phone away, but he ignored it. Zach knew Father Joe didn't approve of his time spent on social media, but he just assumed it was because Father Joe didn't get it. That's how everyone his age communicated. How else was he supposed to know what was going on?

As soon as he opened the first app, Zach's heart sank. No one had commented on the recent post of himself posing with his drum set. Not even one thumbs up. And to make matters worse, a picture of his friends from his old school was first on the feed. The picture was of their yearly Thanksgiving ski trip. Zach wasn't invited this year since he'd moved so far away. Zach sighed heavily as he studied the picture. Everyone was smiling in their gear with their arms around each other's shoulders. He even noticed his friend Chase had a new snowboard and a pang of jealousy struck

Zach's heart. Sure, he hadn't exactly been that close with any of his friends. And sometimes they'd made him uncomfortable when they did really rotten stuff, like vandalizing the bathroom stalls last year at school. But they'd been the popular kids and had just let him in their group a few months before the accident. He'd only been on the Thanksgiving ski trip once. His already terrible mood dropped even further.

As he continued to scroll through pictures of the trip with rising angst, a notification caught his attention. Slightly elated, he tapped on the friendly little envelope. Then, letting out a dramatic groan, he rolled his eyes. The message was from a girl in his class at St. Nicholas Grade School. He opened the message and read:

Hi Zach! Elizabeth here.
Just wanted to say, I heard you play the drums. That's cool. Me and my
friends are starting a band and could use a drummer. Let me know.

Zach rolled his eyes again. Elizabeth was probably the nicest person he'd ever met, which annoyed him. He couldn't figure out what she was so happy about all the time. She always said "hi" to him and tried to include him in whatever lame activity she and her friends were doing. Didn't she understand he enjoyed being left alone to brood in the back of the room? Zach didn't want to be included. He just wanted to blend into his surroundings and make it through his last year of middle school with his head down. He only had to be at St. Nick's for one year, and he didn't plan on making memories. Zach ignored the message from Elizabeth and tossed his phone on the nightstand next to his bed. He huffed and stared at his stack of books on the floor.

Before his parents' death, he'd secretly, because none of his popular friends could know, loved to read. Edgar Allen Poe's dark tales and Sir Arthur Conan Doyle's mysteries were some of Zach's favorites. Zach had once thought he was a genius because he could figure out some of the mysteries before the end of the story. But he just didn't care anymore. The books were dusty. They'd been in the same pile on the floor since he'd moved into that room. Father Joe's housekeeper, Mary, a short, tiny woman with a soft face, dark hair, and gentle voice, was always encouraging him to dust and clean his own room. And so she would stop bugging him, Zach would shove things here or there, making it look like he'd tried. He didn't understand why she couldn't just clean it. Wasn't that why she was there? Of course he'd never actually say that to her face. He'd only seen her angry once so far, and he'd rather not relive that moment. When Mary got angry, Zach imagined facing down a tiger preparing to pounce on its prey.

Shoving his face into the maroon and forest green quilt on his bed, Zach let out a long groan. He picked at a loose thread on the quilt. He was pretty sure the parish quilting club had made it for him. He'd only met those women once, and that was all he needed.

Rolling his eyes at the idea of a Quilting Club, he grabbed his drumsticks roughly on his way to his drum set, stopping in front of his full-length mirror. Zach was of average height and had shaggy, curly, brown hair, a round face, and large hazel eyes. His nose was a little crooked from when he broke it skateboarding. But he liked it that way and thought it gave him more of a devil-may-care look. Annoyed that his curls were uncontrollable, Zach attempted to coerce them into place. It was useless. No matter what he did, the curls bounced back. One of his friends had suggested straightening his hair a few years ago, but Zach was firmly against it. He'd seen enough photos of failed attempts online, and he wasn't about to become part of that group of morons.

Sighing and giving up on his hair, Zach sat down in front of his drum set ready to escape. He grabbed his phone and put in his earbuds. He liked to listen to songs as he drummed along. Feeling the smooth wood of the sticks, he placed his feet in the right position and thought of his favorite classic rock song. After scrolling through his playlist, pressing play, and tossing his phone on the bed, he prepared to drop the first beat when he heard a knock at the door.

Irritated and feeling discouraged, Zach passionately but silently waved the drumsticks in the air. Then taking a quick breath, he responded in a loud exasperated tone, "Yeah?"

As the door opened, Father Joe walked in the room quietly. He was dressed in jeans and a sweatshirt, which caught Zach off guard. For some reason, he expected Father Joe to wear his black clothes and white collar all the time.

Father waved at Zach cheerfully, adjusting the glasses on top of his head. He had a kind, thoughtful face. And when his face lit up, his eyes sparkled. Anyone nearby could sense the warmth emanating from him, and he brought that warmth with him into Zach's room that Saturday night.

On hearing Father Joe's warm greeting, Zach felt a jab of guilt for being rude when Father had knocked. Father Joe shared Zach's dad's warm brown eyes and contagious deep laugh. It freaked Zach out sometimes. Lots of things were weird now.

He hadn't even remembered his dad talking about Zach's uncle much, and he'd certainly never stepped foot in a church before, much less a Catholic one. The only information Zach knew about Father Joe before meeting him was that there was a 15-year age difference between Father Joe and his dad, and that Father Joe lived hours away, which was why his parents said they couldn't see him. Zach had also heard his dad mention to his mom that he and his brother had never been close. Needless to say, Zach was unsure about his situation.

"Hello, Zach," Father Joe said.

"Hey," Zach said.

Father Joe had tried to convince him that going by "Zachariah" was "more epic," but Zach hadn't agreed. Father Joe had a quirky way of describing things. Sure, it made his homilies more interesting, but sometimes Zach was embarrassed for him. Father Joe was very confident in the idea of just being himself and that made Zach uncomfortable. Preparing for a talk, Zach reluctantly walked over to his bed.

"Mind if I sit?" Father Joe pointed to a desk chair covered in laundry and books.

"Um, yeah, sure," Zach said, cleaning off the desk chair.

"How was your first week back from Thanksgiving break?"

Zach gave a noncommittal grunt and walked back to the bed. He sat down on the edge, slouching forward, playing with his fingers as he looked down at his hands. He really didn't want to make eye contact with Father Joe. Something about him made Zach uncomfortable. It wasn't a creepy uncomfortable feeling, but more like a feeling when someone is looking at you with such intense happiness that you don't know what to do with it or what to say so you just look away. That was the way Father Joe looked at Zach on this particular Saturday night.

Apparently the grunt had not been a satisfactory answer. Father Joe continued to wait for a response. And since he was the only man in history comfortable with long silences, Zach robotically responded that school was "good."

As Father Joe sat in the chair and leaned forward on his elbows, Zach noticed two packages in his hands. Trying to pretend he wasn't interested, Zach looked around the room, waiting for Father Joe to leave. He really wanted to be left alone.

"Ya know, having your phone in your room is probably not a good idea. I mean, those things are so distracting. Mine drives me crazy. Maybe you should leave it in the kitchen? I bet it'd be more peaceful in here," Father Joe said.

Zach shrugged.

"So any new friends at school? Got any close friends? Like guys you can talk to? Mrs. Evenstar said Elizabeth has been showin' you the ropes. She's a great girl."

Zach felt his nostrils flare slightly. This wasn't the first time they'd had this conversation. Zach had never really had "close" friends. Sure, he'd had a lot of friends at his old school, but not necessarily close ones. "What did that even mean?" Zach thought to himself.

"Yeah, I have my books and drums and stuff. I don't need people—the hermit life sounds good to me," Zach said.

"I get that, Zach. But people do need people. What's on your mind?"

"Nothin'."

Silence.

Zach really hated these pauses. He felt like the silence was deafening and that Father Joe was waiting for some groundbreaking response Zach couldn't supply. It was almost like someone waiting for you to give them a present, and you realize in the silence you don't have one.

Finally, after what seemed like years, Father said, "Well, Zach, I just want you to know that I think you're doing great here. I also appreciate that you are going to counseling. I know you don't want to and it's hard, but just trying is a huge deal."

Father Joe, who liked to accent points with his hands, knocked an empty cup off Zach's desk. He always talked with his hands. In church, the readers knew if they didn't lower the microphone on the pulpit, Father Joe would inevitably hit it in his passionate reading, causing a loud boom which would emanate throughout the church, waking babies and nodding-off parishioners.

"Oops." He looked inside the cup. "Glad that's empty. Anywho, yeah, you're doin' great. Good grades, you do your chores, I mean I can't complain," he said.

Zach was unsure where this was going. When he'd moved in, he'd thought most of Father Joe's stuff was cringey; however, he hadn't wanted to be a jerk so he'd done what he was told. But he really just wanted to grow up, move out, and get away from this life as fast as possible.

Father Joe whistled awkwardly. "So I'm a little worried abouchya, man. I feel like you're holding back from life. Um almost like—like there's a spark in you that remains unlit. I know you miss your mom and dad," Father Joe paused to see if Zach wanted to add anything.

Nothing.

"But you can come talk to me anytime. You know that, right?"

Zach looked down at the floor.

Father Joe tried a different subject.

"So you've been playin' the drums for a while now. Ya know, it'd be pretty cool if you played at mass. I think the congregation would really enjoy it."

Zach just stared at Father Joe silently with surprise in his eyes. Then he looked down at his hands again. That was the last thing he wanted to do. He'd done one concert when his parents were alive and he'd been so nervous he'd tripped up the two steps to the stage and embarrassed himself in front of the whole audience. He'd been ten and had sworn off concerts ever since.

After another moment, Father Joe sighed. That lighthearted sigh followed by a quick grin was the only indication Father Joe ever gave of his frustration with raising a teenage boy. He was a bottomless pit when it came to patience. Zach even wondered how much he could get away with before this holy guy would break down.

"I get it. Do you feel like you are just floatin' through life right now?" Father Joe asked.

Nothing.

Suddenly Father Joe clapped his hands together. "Ah! What you need is an adventure! Where are my glasses?"

"They're on your head," Zach said.

"Good grief! Ha!" Father Joe grabbed them.

Zach was unamused. Father Joe's immediate change in tone and suggestion of adventure made Zach defensive. He did not want an adventure. He just wanted to be left alone. Crossing his arms, Zach managed a quick eye roll.

"So um, you have an awful lot to deal with and, erm, well, this is the time in your life when you're—"

Zach's eyes widened. If Father Joe was about to explain something about puberty, he was going to have to bail. He'd barely been able to handle learning about the "journey of puberty" from the robust religion teacher at St. Nick's in the beginning of the school year. Luckily, he'd been able to shrink down in his desk and pretend he wasn't even there. But here in the room with Father Joe, there was nowhere to hide.

Realizing what he'd said, Father Joe laughed and quickly rephrased. "Ha! No, no! Not that kind of talk." He waved his hands. "I mean you are, well, figuring out who you are but—"

Zach was relieved but annoyed. His cheeks burned red with frustration. Embarrassment trickled up his back. He just wanted to get back to his drums.

"I'm fine!" Zach snapped. "Sorry."

Zach could sense the frustration turning to tears. He breathed heavily, trying to control his feelings. He didn't know why, but lately bursts of emotion boiled to the surface every now and then out of his control. Father never reprimanded Zach for the outbursts. He would simply ignore the moment and try to smooth things out between them.

Father Joe stood, grabbed the packages by his feet, and sat next to Zach on the bed. He patted him gently on the back. Zach noticed him turning the packages on his lap.

"Yeah, that's what Mary says. Every day: 'Oh don't worry about him. He's strong and gonna be just fine, I can tell these things,'" Father said in his best Mary impression, which unearthed a quiet chuckle.

Zach perked up a bit. He had no idea Mary said those things about him. He just thought of her as the nosy lady from the Quilting Club. But he did kind of like her. Mary checked on him and constantly asked if he was hungry. She was always hiding snacks in his backpack and on his desk. The memory coaxed a small grin in spite of Zach's determination to remain indifferent.

"Well," Father handed Zach the brown packages, "I know it's not Christmas yet, but here."

Zach took the small package first and turned it over. It felt like a book and was wrapped in brown paper. He opened it and saw a worn copy of Charles Dickens's *A Christmas Carol*. He raised his eyebrows slightly in amusement and looked over at Father Joe.

"It was mine."

Zach flipped open the cover. On the inside, it read:

To: Joe
May your life be filled with the Christmas spirit!
From: Grandpa Gabe

Zach thought the message seemed cheesy, but he liked a good book. At least he did once. The thought made him sad, and he set the book on the dusty pile near his bed.

"My grandpa gave me that book. It's one of my favorites," Father Joe said.

"Thanks," Zach said.

"Go ahead and open the other one."

The second package was much larger. It was about the size of one of Zach's shoeboxes, and he had big feet. At least that's what people told him when he bought sneakers. Zach removed the paper and found an old crate. He carefully lifted the lid. Inside was a mound of packaging protecting a delicately carved tree with gnarled branches, small leaves, and an abundance of white, four-petaled flowers. Tucked among the branches were thirteen small doors. Each of the intricately carved doors had a word in cursive and a number on it. The words seemed to be in some other language that Zach didn't understand. The sculpture smelled of sawdust, and it sat on a round base with four small holes. They looked like candle holders. Zach remembered his mom changing the candle holders on their dining room table. Zach looked in the box. No candles. That's weird, he thought. If it was a candle holder, why no candles? Also, why would I want a candle holder?

"What is it?" Zach asked.

"An Advent calendar! Ya know, a countdown to Christmas!" Father said.

Zach couldn't understand why Father was so excited over a little kid's countdown to Christmas. He'd seen these countdown things before at the store, and they didn't look like this. They were usually colorful with some kind of Christmas scene on the front. Or lately, themed around the most recent blockbuster film and filled with socks. With its spring-like flowers and knotty, long branches, the tree didn't even look like a Christmas tree. Plus, the little doors looked empty, not even candy. So no chocolate and candle-less? Zach couldn't help but wonder why Father Joe was giving him old junk.

"What's with the tree? Shouldn't it be like a Christmas tree or a fir tree or somethin'?" Zach asked.

Seeing a subtle drop in Father Joe's demeanor, Zach said quickly, "It's pretty cool, I guess. I was just askin'. I mean, aren't these candleholders? Where are the candles?"

Father shifted in his seat and looked contemplative. For the first time in their relationship, Father Joe avoided eye contact. "Well, this is a different kind of Advent calendar. It's kind of a combination of an Advent calendar and the Advent wreath. Like the one we have in church with the four candles. The candles are, um, well, you'll see. They'll show up eventually."

They'll show up? What were the candles going to do? Dance into the room? Just appear one day? With a dubious look, Zach began to wonder if maybe Father Joe had a screw loose. Great, he thought to himself, he was living with a delusional old guy.

Despite his doubts, the small wooden sculpture was mesmerizing. Zach ran his hand over the tree and felt the bumps of the carvings beneath his fingers. As his hand moved along the doors, Zach jerked back. The doors were glowing. As he leaned closer, he was suddenly captivated. His hand settled on top of the biggest, most important looking door centered on the tree's trunk. The word carved into this door in fancy calligraphy was *Nativitatis*. He pinched the small doorknob with his fingers and pulled, but it didn't open. It seemed to be stuck. He pulled again. This time he heard a mysterious voice softly whisper, "Chosen."

Startled, Zach jumped and looked at Father Joe, who now held a mischievous grin.

"You okay?" Father asked.

"Yeah." A slight chill crept up Zach's spine. He looked back at the tree, assuming the feeling was nothing but his imagination. Then he stood up, hoping Father Joe would get the hint and leave. He just wanted to play the drums and get lost in his own world again.

"Thanks, Father Joe."

"Yep, hope you enjoy the gifts," Father Joe said as he walked out the door.

Zach stared at the small tree carving. He flipped door one open and found nothing inside. There seemed to be a spot for candy or something, but it was empty, just as he'd suspected. Zach shook his head. Some gift, he thought. He would have to scrounge up some chocolate and fill it himself. It was old looking and kind of retro, which he liked.

Suddenly Father popped his head back into the room, making Zach jump. "Are we still on for our bike ride after Mass tomorrow?"

Zach hesitated. He liked riding his bike, but he still didn't like going with Father Joe. He'd rather ride alone. Seeing how excited Father Joe was though, Zach gave a noncommittal grunt.

"Great!" Father Joe said. Then he closed the door and headed down the hall, whistling to himself.

Giving a great big eye roll and exasperated sigh now that he was finally alone again, Zach walked over to his drum set and sat down. Placing his earbuds back in his ears and grabbing his drumsticks, Zach closed his eyes as he started playing his favorite song, "Enter Sandman" by Metallica. He zoned out, so completely preoccupied that he didn't notice as the Advent calendar began to glow. Unfortunately, Zach had no idea what a magical and daunting artifact he had sitting right in his bedroom, and his goal of getting lost in his own world was not only literally possible but merely steps away.

In that very room was a gateway to a new realm. For inside the Advent calendar, the beautiful dogwood tree, lived the world of Burra Din. And in that moment, one portal away, the people of

Burra Din busied themselves with life, not realizing that forces of good lay in wait for Zach's arrival. Burra Din was a world in need of more than one hero, more than one good person, more than one savior, and Zachariah Labouré was the key.

PART ONE
THE LAND OF SPÉS

DOOR ONE

BENIGNITAS
KINDNESS IN THE LAND OF SPÉS

"So whatever you wish that others would do to you,
do also to them."
Matthew 7:12

After spending the rest of the evening playing the drums and binge watching the newest superhero series, Zach woke Sunday to a gentle knock on his door. Without even opening his eyes, he knew what the knock was about: church. He groaned to himself and rolled over.

"Zach. It's time to get up. Ten o'clock mass starts in about 45 minutes," Father Joe said.

Irritable and annoyed at having to get out of bed early on the weekend, Zach just lay there, pretending he hadn't heard. He missed the days of getting to sleep in every Sunday. He never had to go to church before, and he certainly didn't intend on changing that habit. However, that was one of the few things Father Joe insisted was nonnegotiable.

A second knock. This one was still gentle but slightly louder than the first.

Zach replied, "Coming."

Zach's parents had been very good people and taught Zach the importance of community. They donated to charities and volunteered for major events. His mother had even spent a month every year in Honduras, donating her time as a doctor. However, they never went to church. They hadn't even mentioned church. But now that Zach lived with Father Joe, he was getting an up close and personal experience with the goings on of Catholic Mass. Every single Sunday. The routine involved Father Joe waking him up and explaining that he had 45 minutes to get ready for Mass. But really Zach had an hour. Why the difference of 15 minutes? Well, Father Joe liked Zach to get there early to take part in the weekly rosary, and Zach despised the process. It's not that Zach hated the rosary itself. He really didn't mind it. No, Zach hated the rosary because Zach found sitting in the kneeling position listening to several old ladies repeating the same prayers over and over again in a monotone voice excruciating. And he figured he'd rather be asleep for 15 more minutes in his bed than in an uncomfortable church pew.

So Zach did what all people do in those situations. He avoided it. Also Father was usually getting ready for his second Mass of the morning and never realized Zach snuck in right before the first song. Unfortunately, on this particular morning Zach couldn't fall back to sleep for some reason. So he decided to do the next best thing. He got out of bed and walked to his drum set, sat down, closed his eyes, and played the air drums just above the instrument so as to not get caught. Zach jumped at the sound of a knock at the door.

"Zach, I forgot to mention, today is the first Sunday of Advent so I'll need your help during the blessing, okay?"

"Yeah, sure."

"See you at Mass."

"Yup."

"Rosary starts soon."

"Yup."

Ignoring Father Joe's reminder, Zach went back to playing the air drums. After messing around for a while, his phone buzzed, alerting Zach of two notifications. Checking the home screen, Zach realized it was almost 10 o'clock! He'd completely lost track of time. Zach jumped up to get dressed, smacking his foot on the side of his bed. As he hobbled over to his closet, he figured he'd just throw on some nice clothes and fix his hair. He'd have to shower later. Struggling to pull on his dark khaki joggers, Zach lost his balance. As he teetered, Zach set a hand on the top of his desk for support. However, the desk was covered in so much junk, the pile beneath his hand gave way, and Zach fell over, knocking several items off his desk. Sitting up, Zach shook his head and rolled his eyes with a groan. He put his pants on the rest of the way and pulled a white t-shirt over his head. As he walked to the closet to find an acceptable button-down shirt, Zach felt something hard under his bare foot and heard a soft crack. He looked down and saw the Advent calendar.

Hoping he hadn't broken it, Zach picked it up and examined the wooden sculpture. The detailed carving looked more intense, vividly exposing the dimensions of the tree. He ran his hand across the front in a motion similar to the night before, feeling the very small door knobs under his fingertips. Zach lifted his hand suddenly, noticing the door labeled *One: Benignitas* glowed brightly. White light trickled through the door frame; it wasn't like a bolt of lightning, more like a slow illumination. He was only a little surprised because self-glowing inanimate objects were not unheard of; however, this wasn't the glow of an LED light bulb. This was an enchanting glow that pulled at one's curiosity. So instead of surprise, Zach felt drawn to the door. Much more curious. A small voice inside Zach told him it could be magical. He tilted his head, contemplating opening the little door. But that small voice was hushed by another voice. The logical, dominant, booming voice inside Zach's head. It had to be mechanical or battery operated, right? It was the first Sunday of Advent after all. Zach reasoned with himself. Maybe it had a timer or something. Zach turned it over to check where the batteries went but found no compartment. Confused but determined, Zach stared at the little glowing door. And for one small second (for that was all it took) Zach's logical side and curious side agreed: *Just open the little door.*

Zach slowly and carefully placed his fingers on the knob, pulling the little door open. The light went out. Zach's face changed from bewildered to disappointed. Taking a closer look, Zach leaned into the Advent calendar. If he could just figure out how the little—

Then something extraordinary happened. A strong breeze blew through Zach's bedroom and he suddenly felt a strange tug, suddenly felt very warm. Not a 'whew! It's hot' warm. But a comfortable warmth that makes one sleepy. He leaned closer as his eyes drooped. And when his nose was about an inch from the small door, a flash of light burst through the bedroom, engulfing Zach! Then the magic of Burra Din grew and pulled Zach straight inside the Advent Calendar.

Lying on his back on the cold ground, Zach's eyes fluttered open. He was in a strange place. He seemed to be in some kind of forest that smelled of pinewood and cedar. The forest floor was covered in a large bed of dead, dried pine needles. But these weren't ordinary needles, and the trees weren't ordinary trees. The needles were almost the same length as Zach, and they made a very comfortable bed on the ground. Zach sat up and looked around. The needles seemed to come from the largest pine and cedar trees he'd ever seen. No, ever heard of. The trunks alone looked so fat, he imagined it would take nearly 100 adults, holding hands, arms outstretched to wrap around just one of medium size. As his eyes followed the trees' trunks up to the sky, Zach noticed a hole in the forest canopy. Beautiful rays of white sunlight illuminated the dark forest floor and reflected off the water droplets in the fog, making the forest floor seem as though it was covered with beautiful, sparkling clouds. Zach was in a daze. He couldn't believe what he was seeing. Everything around him meshed together in a vibrant, colorful blur. His senses were overwhelmed. The trees were a vivid dark green. Zach heard animals, birds, and other creatures chittering among the branches. He watched as a bird flew just under the forest canopy. The bird was such a bright orange it looked like a ball of fire whizzing across a green backdrop. The ball of fire landed on a short, brittle branch that was home to a nest.

Focusing, Zach started to piece together exactly what had happened to him. A panic rose in his chest. Suddenly it wrenched at his gut. He felt cold and hungry. He had no idea where he was. The last time he had felt this anxious and desperate was the day his parents died. He'd felt lost, and his future had felt cold and dark. It had been a lost hopeless feeling. One where your world and everything you knew crumbled around you. As if your life was respawning into a new life, a new you. But completely out of your control. The edges of his vision clouded. He was afraid he was going to pass out. Zach knelt in the soft patch of needles and breathed deeply. Remembering what his mom had told him once about anxiety attacks, Zach spoke to himself out loud, closed his eyes, and imagined slowly filling and releasing a balloon of air in his chest.

"Okay, okay, what do I know?"

He remembered when he was about four years old and was scared of the dark. His dad had run through a series of questions to help Zach rule out monsters in the closet. Zach ran through that rational reasoning now.

"What do I know? I was getting ready for church and then I was here. Right? No! I tripped and picked up that—oh no! That Advent calendar. That wooden tree, ah, ah." Zach felt the edges of his world growing darker. "It's okay. Breathe, breathe."

While Zach attempted to master self-therapy, a determined, stealthy hunter approached. The hunter didn't make a sound, carefully steadying her hand on the trunks of the trees as she traveled from branch to branch. She examined the young boy sitting alone on the forest floor talking to himself. She cocked her head. The young hunter jumped from the branches onto the forest floor without a sound. She drew a very interesting weapon, a bowshot, from her back and narrowed her eyes at Zach.

The bowshot, her own creation, looked like a collapsible crossbow. She had made the bow to increase damage and efficiency. It was much more effective than the regular crossbows used by the rest of her village. When she shot the bow, a heavy arrowhead made of special volcanic stone would rocket forward. The crossbow would then collapse behind her back, and she would quickly pull the rope attached to the arrowhead. This pull would bring the arrowhead back toward her, and she would swing the sharp metal in all directions, annihilating enemies from all sides. Gripping the homemade leather handle, the hunter contemplated the best way to capture such a strange young man.

Zach, who'd finally calmed down, stood up with every intention of finding food, shelter, and water. Then he'd figure out how to get back home. As he ran a hand through his hair, contemplating which direction to head, he felt a tingling up his spine. He froze, realizing he wasn't alone. Slowly he began to turn around.

Too late.

The hunter had unleashed her weapon. The arrowhead shot forward, and she immediately pulled it back, wrapping it around the boy's legs.

Zach hadn't even gotten a chance to grasp what was happening before his head hit the ground and his world went black.

This time Zach woke indoors. He stared at a ceiling of thick blue glass. Beyond the glass he saw a tinted scene of the forest canopy and knew he was still in a strange world. Or maybe a dream? He saw needles shifting in the breeze and daylight peeking through the gaps in the branches. It was very similar to the first time he'd opened his eyes, but this time he noticed colorful objects sitting in the trees. His vision was still blurry, so he couldn't exactly make it out. Then he realized he had no idea where he was and felt his heart pounding in his chest. Frozen with fear and uncertainty, he closed his eyes again and absorbed his surroundings. He heard people shifting and smelled something delicious, an aroma of sweet spices. He could practically taste them. Then he noticed a hint of iron along the tips of his taste buds. He licked his lips and found he'd busted his bottom lip. It was swollen and bleeding. Opening his eyes and staring at the glass ceiling again, Zach focused on the reflection of the room this time. A warm glow from a hearth illuminated two figures: one was busy at a table while the other crouched a few feet from where he lay.

"Maata! He's awake!"

A sharp pain shot through Zach's skull. He sat up abruptly, steadying himself and readying for a blow to the—well anywhere really. The last thing he remembered was something pulling his feet out from under him.

"Oh Asha, settle down. The boy is of no harm. Now, back. Back. You'll scare him, my love," the old woman said.

"But how do you know he's not working for—"

"Hush now, do not speak of such things in my home. Look at the boy and use your sense, Asha. He's harmless."

The pounding in Zach's head dulled. His eyes shifted back and forth between the women as they spoke. Zach noticed the one called Asha was very young. She had dark brown hair with deep purple and red streaks naturally running through it. She wore her hair in a very thick, long braid that coiled itself around her shoulders like a scarf and drifted down her back. Long thick eyelashes framed her big blue, eyes. Her looks took Zach by surprise. She looked human, but was she? It was as if all her facial features were enlarged, but in an attractive way. Her harsh cheekbones gave her a fierce expression, yet her eyes held a gentle sparkle, which was focused intensely on Zach at the moment. Her clothes were very odd. Tight with sharp edges, the outfit looked like a cross between a ninja suit and a medieval knight's armor. She reminded him of the elves from his favorite stories, but upon glancing at her exposed ear, he did not see the stereotypical point. Just a normal ear. She looked only slightly more intense than a human from Zach's world. She was almost like a cool animated version.

One thing was most prominent though, an intricate earring dangled just above her shoulder. This earring was made up of one long strand of white gold with a blue glass triangle attached at the end pointing toward the sky. The triangle had two white lines running across it diagonally. And what was most interesting is that the triangle on the earring was the same as the symbol tattooed on her forehead. Sharing a similar tattoo and many other traits, the other woman standing in the room seemed to be the young woman's mother. She was a bit more wrinkled and wiry. She was dressed in a flowing, colorful skirt and a loose-fitted white shirt. Zachariah immediately remembered a picture he'd seen of his grandmother from the 1960s. But while Asha held a fierce look, this woman had an aura of compassion. Zach felt safer just looking at her.

"Where am I?" Zach asked.

The women stopped talking and turned toward him.

His palms were sweating and he felt his throat go dry in the awkward silence. The old woman stepped closer.

"My name is Aachal and this is my daughter, Asha. You are in the Forest of Inspirare, dear boy." Expecting him to show some sign of recognition, Aachal waited.

But Zach, having no idea where he was, just stared at her blankly.

"Are you alright?" Aachal asked, taking a small step forward.

Zach furrowed his brow. He couldn't believe what was happening. Nothing made sense around him and a million questions were buzzing through his brain. *What is the Forest of Inspirare? Is that in Europe? I tripped in my room. How did I get here? My head hurts so much.*

"Uh, am, am I dead?" Zach asked.

Aachal and Asha shared a look. Then Aachal laughed softly and responded slowly as if approaching a scared animal, "We know you are not dead because we are very much alive. That headache you have proves you are alive as well as that blood on your lip."

Zach brought his hand to his forehead and licked his lip again, reminding himself of the cut and slight swelling. It did feel real.

Asha, impatient and wanting to be direct, for she had much to do and did not want to waste time watching over a boy, chimed in as if talking to a toddler, "You're in the Forest of Inspirare, in the Land of Spés, in the world of Burra Din. I found you talking to yourself in the woods like a bewitched monkey."

Aachal cleared her throat disapprovingly.

Asha rolled her eyes. "I found you and thought you were a trespasser or a bewitched . . . nomad, so I captured you with my new bowshot."

Zach glanced at the weapon resting perfectly between her shoulder blades. It didn't even look like a weapon and was barely visible.

"Um, so I don't know any of those places you just said. The last thing I remember is falling in my room and then picking up the Advent cal—" Zach stopped when he noticed, Asha and Aachal glance at each other again.

Aachal silently walked over to the boiling pot in the hearth and ladled its contents into a small red bowl. "Here, drink this. It will take care of that headache and calm your nerves."

Zach, still a bit wary and untrusting for obvious reasons, hesitated. He wasn't sure if he was more afraid to take the bowl or refuse it. Aachal reminded him of one of those moms who loved her children so much that she would nag them to death if they tried to argue with her.

Aachal pushed the bowl toward him again.

Zach slowly reached for the bowl.

"Oh goodness!" Asha said, hopping down from the stool where she'd been crouching. "Take it! If we wanted you dead, I would have killed you already. Why would we waste time poisoning you?"

Aachal sighed, exasperated.

Zach was surprised to find the bowl was not hot at all. He sniffed the concoction and smelled sweet spices. Immediately his head began to clear. Carefully, he took a drink and was surprised to find that the liquid was a mild temperature. He assumed it'd be boiling hot, but somehow in that short time, it had become perfectly edible. And it was more than that. It tasted amazing! The flavor was an awesome balance between sweet and spicy. He enjoyed it and, forgetting himself, he ravaged the rest of the bowl.

"Good. That's done. Now, what do we do with him, Maata?"

"Asha! He is a boy, not a snowpuff! What would Amal think to hear of such behavior?"

Asha's face burned red as she said, "Yes, Maata. I only meant, what should we do now? Take him to Amal?"

Aachal thought for a minute and looked at Zach.

Zach lowered the bowl and blinked innocently back at them.

Aachal held back a laugh.

Realizing he had soup all along his upper lip, Zach wiped his mouth with his sleeve.

"Yes, I believe that would be best," Aachal finally said. "I will pack your things and you may travel with him to Amal's. If Amal requests your help, Asha, you must do as he asks."

"Yes, Maata. But I'd rather stay here. Tend to the forest. Hunt. Can't the forest guard take him?"

"No, my dear, you must. Danger lurks in even the most unlikely places and among the most unlikely of people. And remember we are all responsible for the future of Burra Din. And if he knows nothing of this world then—" She looked back at Zach again, stopping herself. "But that is for Amal to decide. He knows nothing of the forest. You must guide him."

Setting down his bowl, suddenly feeling quite energetic and well-rested, Zach got up from the small cot and quietly asked, "Uh, who's Amal?"

Aachal glanced at Asha quickly as a change of expression consumed her face. She flickered from wary and concerned to motherly again. Wringing her hands slightly and then putting them in her skirt pockets, Aachal explained, "You say you are not from here and, ahem, we do not understand how that could be. There are stories of other realms, different realms. Ones without magic. Ones that rely purely on technology instead of strength in belief. Then there are realms between extremes that rely on both belief and magic. I do not know which you came from. I suppose the only possibility is of the prophecy, but I do not know if that is possible either. There was one like you before. One who—But we always discussed it as legend, not truth."

Zach looked confused and felt a rumble of anxiety in his belly at Aachal's uncertainty. Other realms? Magic? What was this? Some intense comic book dream? A flush of heat rose up his back as an inner storm of confusion raged within. Frustration was boiling to the surface.

Asha laid a hand on Aachal's shoulder, sensing her mother's concern.

"I'm sorry. Let me start again. Do not despair, young man. Amal is the protector of the Land of Spés. He takes care of us and negotiates defenses with the other three lands in the world of Burra Din," Aachal said.

"Burra Din? What other lands?" Zach's eyes opened wide at this notion. Other lands? In other realms? He narrowed his eyes, bracing for the answer. He wasn't sure he could take in much more of this.

"There are four lands in the body of Burra Din: the Land of Spés, the Land of Fidem, the Land of Gaudium, and the Land of Pax. These lands are each protected by a wise warrior. Amal, the Fire Wielder, protects the Land of Spés; Vera, the Earth Defender, protects the Land of Fidem; Jovie, the Ice Sorceress, protects the Land of Gaudium; and Kazuya, the Wind Whisperer, protects the Land of Pax."

Protects? Defends? Whispers? From what? Zach wondered. He felt a shiver of fear. At the talk of other realms, other lands, and the existence of magic, an overwhelming realization of how small he really was consumed him. He felt like an insignificant speck being swept away by a strong tide of existence. Curiosity and fear had taken over. Zach didn't want to be in a dangerous place. He really just wanted to go back home.

"Why do you need protection?" he asked.

Aachal and Asha gave each other that same glance again. Asha opened her mouth to explain, but Aachal put a hand on her shoulder.

"That's something Amal should share with you, dear boy. And what are you called?" Aachal asked, changing the subject.

"What am I called? Oh, Zachariah, but my friends—well, I prefer Zach."

Asha smirked and coughed out a slight laugh; Aachal sighed patiently.

Zach's cheeks went rosy with embarrassment. He didn't understand what was wrong with his name.

Aachal responded quickly to cut off Asha, certain she would say something rude. "The name is strange to us and reminds us of *chack*, which means an unintelligent creature. But of course, you are *ZZZach*, not *chack*." She placed heavy emphasis on the 'z' to express she understood the different sound.

Zach shrugged his shoulders. He didn't really care what these people called him. He just wanted to get home. Okay, he kind of cared. "Yeah, it means something like 'remembered by Yahweh.' I don't really know what that means, but apparently it's a big deal to some people. Ya know, something about God. Oh, do you have God here?" Zach felt uncertain. Did God hop realms? Did God create all the realms?

The smile disappeared from Aachal's face and Asha stopped smirking immediately. They looked at him and Asha said, "Maata! Did you hear that? The prophecy—wait, are you certain? Zzzach, say it again."

"My name is about being remembered by God or something. It's a good name in my world, I guess. If you're into that sort of thing," Zach said.

Zach stopped talking. This whole situation was completely insane. He kept wondering when he would wake up, but everything seemed so real. He'd been doing just fine at home. He was happy alone, left to his drums and solitary life. In one realm. Now he was in this crazy world and had obviously said something wrong. Heck, this was more person-to-person interaction than he'd had in months. He usually avoided people at school. He really only talked to Father Joe and Mary when absolutely necessary. Confrontation and serious conversation made him nervous. Normally this would be the point when he would simply slip away into the background. But not here. No, he had no idea where to go or how to hide here.

After a few moments of silence and apparently enough time for Zach to begin his own existential crisis, Aachal said with urgency, "You need to go now."

Her change in tone made Zach jump. Aachal bustled around, throwing items in two burlap packs.

Asha leaned over and whispered, "It is best to do what she says when she is in such a mood."

Zach was still confused as Aachal went into a back room.

"If you're going to travel with me, you will need to be tough. I move quickly and will not wait," Asha said.

She straightened her posture as she grabbed her knife from the table and slid it into a sheath on her boot. Then she walked to a row of cedar shelves on the wall of blue glass and grabbed other items. For the first time, Zach noticed the room around him. It seemed the house was a glass orb built into one of the giant pine trees. Despite the openness, the home felt cozy. The entire room was furnished with cedar furniture that matched the shelves. Forest crafts and useful tools hung from the walls. As he looked beyond the glass wall, he saw hundreds more glass homes of all different colors. It wasn't a village, it was a city! And it was the most colorful city Zach had ever seen. Vibrant orbs nestled against the giant tree trunks connected by layers of rope bridges and ladders. People casually walked or rode on what looked like four wheeled bikes, pulling carts, people, and creatures.

"Here," Asha said, shoving something into Zach's hands.

Before looking down, Zach asked, "Can they all, ya know?"

Asha gave him an impatient glance.

"Uh, see inside here?"

Asha burst with laughter. It was almost like a long cackle and ended with a snort. Zach laughed quietly.

"Zach, you are funny. Of course not. We would always be watched and they would see us without, without clothes. I would not want to live in such a place. No! You would not find me in a room such as that!"

Zach's cheeks reddened at the thought. He brushed it from his mind. Remembering Asha had placed something in his hands, he looked down, realizing the object was about three feet long. Reaching in the brown leather bag, he felt a cold metal handle. He pulled the object out of the bag, finding a sword! It was beautiful and the most exquisite thing he'd ever seen. The blade was glass. It reminded him of an obsidian weapon from a video game, but it wasn't black. This was a different color. It was the purest translucent white glass he'd ever seen. It seemed to have something engraved on the blade, but he couldn't make it out. Saateey—

"Satya," Aachal said, coming back into the room. "Excellent idea! This blade will guide you. It is true and pure. It is our treasure and you may need it. It is called Satya, or truth."

Zach was surprised. He hadn't been sure Asha liked him at all, and now she'd just irreverently given him a family treasure. It made him uncomfortable to receive such a meaningful gift.

"I couldn't take—"

"You must. The blade has been in our family since the tribes came together many ages ago," Aachal said.

"No, I don't think I want this. What if I lose it?"

Shaking her head, Aachal said, "You will not lose it. The blade has been used on many journeys, many quests. Amal will decide if the prophecy is at hand. And if the prophecy is true, you will need our dear Satya. She always finds her way home. Now, be on your way, both of you. Here Zach, this cloak will protect you in the forest. Ah! But first put on this tunic, and here are some pants. Oh yes and boots. The fabric is especially comfortable."

Zach took the clothes, boots, and cloak as he set the blade on the table. Asha and Aachal left the room so he could change. Zach was hesitant to put on the clothes because they looked like rough wool. He thought wool was scratchy, but he had no choice. He was only wearing his socks, khaki joggers, and a white t-shirt. So he pulled the long-sleeved shirt over his head and found the material had suddenly changed. The shirt felt like silk against his skin. After putting on the pants and boots, which underwent the same transformation, Zach put on the cloak, which laid perfectly on his shoulders. He moved around in the clothes, noticing the material was very light. Within seconds, Asha and Aachal were back in the room.

"Hey, they're so comfortable and fit perfectly," Zach said, still wondering how they'd transformed.

"Of course," Asha said. "Do your clothes not fit often? Do you normally wear uncomfortable clothes?"

"Uh, we have to like go to a store and pick out a size and sometimes things don't fit great or are scratchy, I guess," Zach said.

Asha raised an eyebrow. "That sounds inefficient. Why would you wear something uncomfortable that does not fit. I would not purchase such garments. Waste of time. We get all our fabric from the Village of Solis in the Land of Fidem. They provide Burra Din with the greatest material of all the lands. All the realms I'm sure."

"Asha," Aachal interrupted, "go to the pantry and fill these small boxes with food."

"Yes, Maata."

Zach watched as Asha's demeanor changed from confident to subservient at her mother's request. He missed that interaction with his own mother. Once when he'd been on a field trip, Zach had been talking to a group of friends about the time he made a ramp in the snow. He'd been explaining that the ramp was at least five feet high at its peak. His friends had been super impressed until his mom had come over and said, "Yeah and remember how you bit it when you landed, busting your nose." He and his friends had laughed. It hadn't even embarrassed him because the fact that his mom described the wipeout comically had made him even cooler.

Once their packs were filled with necessities and Aachal had finished machine-gunning Asha with her last-minute wisdom, Asha and Zach walked out through the large, wooden door. Zach paused in front of the door's colorful stained glass window. The image in the glass seemed to hold a scene from a story. As he focused on the image, a chill ran up his spine. The boy in the stained glass held a sword and stood tall against a giant wave of darkness. Zach leaned closer but felt Asha pulling at his cloak.

"Take care, my Asha," Aachal said, kissing her daughter's forehead.

"Yes, Maata."

Asha hugged her mother. Then she turned to Zach and said, "Keep up."

So the two travelers set off on their journey to discover exactly why Zach had been brought to Burra Din. But what they didn't realize was that Zach's arrival in Burra Din had not gone unnoticed. A rumbling within the land had delivered the news of his arrival to one who despised the prophecy, one who embraced darkness, one who unleashed feelings of fear and regret. And unfortunately for

Asha and Zach, that one was one of many faces that lurked in the corners of Burra Din.

Zach was in awe. The sites and sounds of the forest city were overwhelming. The trees were huge, and the glass orbs of the homes within the branches and trunks of the trees were even more magnificent up close. The bulbs of blue, green, red, gold, and silver hugged closely to the trunks but inched halfway onto a branch or two depending on their size. It was unreal. The people, weaving around the orbs on rope bridges, went about their daily routines. They looked similar to Asha with their large features, but they were just as diverse as the people in Zach's world.

As Zach and Asha walked along a wide rope bridge, people waved at them. Every now and then someone would shout a friendly hello in Asha's direction, and she'd respond with a stoic head nod. Studying the people carefully without getting too far behind, Zach found no pointy ears despite his suspicions. One thing he did notice was the abundance of calm, friendly chatter. The people would stop to talk to one another, offer a handshake, or speak a quick, kind word. No one seemed too busy to talk or distracted by technology or anything else for that matter. Heck, no one was even on their phones. Zach wondered if they even had phones. Then he remembered what Aachal had said. Some realms were dedicated to magic, others to technology, and some combined the two. Reflecting on the amount of technology in his own world, Zach secretly hoped some hidden magic could be found somewhere in his home, maybe even his room.

Following Asha's lead and pulling on his hood, Zach threw his burlap bag over his shoulder. He noticed the strap was braided similarly to the rope bridges. Anything rope-like seemed to be made out of roots or vines. Asha didn't waste any time. She led Zach to a movable platform. It reminded him of an elevator without a roof or walls. As he stepped onto the platform, Zach breathed slowly. He wasn't exactly scared of heights, but he also wasn't exactly confident about being propelled up and down by a platform, clearly made of roots, boards, and glass. Especially when the decking gave a little under the weight of each person who stepped onto it. Zach wasn't a fan. To make matters worse, Zach and Asha weren't the only two on the platform. Before he knew it, at least 20 people had boarded the now-crowded deck. The floor beneath him bounced with each movement. He gripped tightly to the railing and caught Asha's eye. She shook her head as if to say, "Chicken." Zach immediately stood up straight, trying to appear less frightened. Then with a whoosh! the platform descended. It dropped faster than Zach anticipated, causing him to fall into a large burly man, who snorted at his clumsiness. Asha pulled Zach off the platform onto a soft bed of large pine needles. Zach felt slightly woozy and tried to get his balance back.

"Ugh, I think I might puke. You ride that thing all the time?"

"All the time."

"And you like it?"

"Of course, why would I not?"

And without waiting for a response, Asha took off along the path. Zach shrugged and mocked her when she wasn't looking. He was becoming frustrated with the fact he was clueless about this new world and that Asha thought he was useless. That was probably the fifth time she'd given him that look. They walked along the base of the giant trees. Zach had never felt so small. The orbs were less prominent from the forest floor. At this level, the atmosphere was quiet, with the occasional passerby. Asha waved at each of them. Zach struggled to keep up with Asha, who was obviously not going to wait.

"Does everyone know everyone here?" Zach asked.

"Yes, of course."

"Oh."

Without turning around, Asha asked, "Do you have a maata?"

Zach, not knowing the language but clearly understanding the relationship, knew she was asking if he had a mother.

"Yes—well, I did—she isn't around." Zach wanted to avoid anything personal, especially this topic.

"Why?" Asha asked.

"She died. Well, um, both my parents did. I'm an orphan now I guess."

"Ah, what's an oarffiinn?"

Asha, interested, had finally slowed and was now walking side by side with Zach.

"A child whose parents are gone and doesn't have a family."

"Oh, that's strange. My pita died from illness a few years ago."

"I'm sorry. What's strange about it?"

Asha paused for a moment, contemplating, and then began walking again as she said, "You said you're an oarfffiinn without a maata or pita, but if I had no maata or pita, I would not be one because I am part of the forest family. We take care of each other. Do people in your world not take care of each other?"

"Yeah, I guess so. Father Joe—or um—my uncle took me in when my parents died."

"Ah see, well you are not an ooaarfffiin. You have a Father Joe!" Asha said, happy she could solve Zach's problem easily.

Zach gave her a look like a lightbulb had just finally been twisted a quarter of an inch and illuminated a truth. He hadn't thought of it that way before. Asha didn't notice his glance. She was already refocused on the task at hand.

After a few moments, Asha asked, "How did your maata and pita, or paarrents die?"

There it was. The stone that dropped in his gut every time someone asked him about his parents' death. He never elaborated on this with anyone, but for some reason he found himself willingly answering Asha's question.

"They died in a car accident."

"What's a car?"

"So it's like those carts in your village but on steroids."

"You confuse me. What is a steroids?"

"They are drugs, like medicine, you take to get stronger. But they're illegal."

"So you give your carts forbidden medicine?"

"I guess so, except we call it gasoline. And it's not forbidden." Zach felt ridiculous. How had he managed to screw up explaining a car?

"You are from a strange realm, Zach. Your clothes do not fit; they are scratchy, and you give carts medicine."

Zach laughed out loud.

Asha, offended at his outburst, said, "What do you laugh about? There was no humor. That is what you said, is it not?"

"Yeah, I did."

"So your parents died in a cart of your world?"

Zach nodded.

"I am sorry. The carts must go very fast for someone to die in them."

"They do."

He was actually enjoying this conversation. Asha didn't look at him with overwhelming pity or expect him to say anything. She didn't even try to understand his feelings. She just wanted the facts. And for some reason, Zach wanted to tell her.

"My parents were on their way home from a party when someone hit them. My mom is a doctor; she healed people in my world. My dad was a mechanic; he worked on cars—or, um, fast carts. My mom had wanted me to go along, but I hated those things and wanted to spend the night at my friend's. I wasn't with them. The doctors said my dad died upon impact, but my mom lived long enough for me to say goodbye in the hospital." Zach couldn't believe how much he was telling Asha. He'd only just met her. But he also felt really good talking about it. He felt like a weight had been lifted off his chest.

"I am sorry for your maata and pita, Zach. But I am happy you were not in that fast cart."

Without a word, Zach looked at her for an explanation.

"If you had died, you would not be here," Asha said, increasing her pace.

Zach gave a thoughtful look, following right behind.

The two maybe-almost-friends walked side by side for a while in silence. As they continued through the forest, Zach noticed fewer homes. The sky grew darker, and the noise of the forest people dwindled until an eerie quiet fell over the forest. Asha, slowing a bit, grabbed her bag and pulled out a black strap with a small metal container attached to the front. She strapped the device around her head and pulled out a small tin box.

"Are you like an adult or kid in your village? I mean you get to go hunting on your own and stuff," Zach said.

"Of course, I am 53. Once you are old enough to carry a bow, you can hunt. If you know what you are doing, you may go alone. My maata decided for me three years ago."

"Fifty-three?!"

Asha huffed with disappointment. "I know. Everyone thinks I'm older. I wish I were, but I am a great fighter for my age. I practice all the time. Why? How old are you?"

"Fourteen."

"Fourteen? You really are a bewitched monkey!" Asha said.

"Yeah," Zach said, unamused, watching Asha pull a small gem out of the tin box. She placed the gem into the device on her forehead. Immediately the metal container illuminated, looking like a miner's headlamp. Zach's eyes grew even wider.

"Well, put yours on, monkey boy," Asha said.

Zach looked in his own bag and pulled out his own headlamp device, hoping 'bewitched monkey' or 'monkey boy' did not become his new nickname. Asha helped him attach the strap to his head. Noticing the forest grew even darker, Zach tried to maintain a brave demeanor.

"How much further until Amal's?"

"Not much," Asha said.

As they ventured on, Zach noticed a flickering light ahead. Asha held her hand up. Zach stopped, peeking past her. Without a sound, Asha unleashed her weapon with the press of a button. Before Zach could blink, the bowshot was in her hands, pointed at the light. Following her lead, Zach unsheathed his sword awkwardly, making a clinking noise against his belt. Asha sighed and rolled her eyes. Slowly they stepped forward, and Zach saw a fire and two small creatures. As they approached the campfire, the creatures huddled together in fear. Zach was fascinated. The creatures were small, white, and furry, with large dark eyes. Immediately Zach thought of little yetis. Asha turned her head back to Zach slightly.

"Snowpuffs," she whispered.

"What's a snowpuff?"

"Snowpuffs are mischievous creatures who stand four feet tall and live around the outskirts of our city."

Zach, assuming they were harmless, began walking toward the fire.

"Careful, Zach! They may look innocent, but they are not. They are quick and will steal anything they can," Asha said, pulling him back by his shoulder.

Zach took a step back.

Asha stepped closer, bowshot ready.

Zach stared at them, noticing their frightened expressions. They didn't look dangerous or mischievous, he thought. They looked miserable and scared. When Asha was only feet from the creatures, the larger snowpuff grunted at her and said something inaudible.

"Can they speak? To us?" Zach asked.

"They try. I do not understand them. I do not trust them. They steal from the city. But I do not find them cowering in fear often," Asha said, stepping back and searching the forest around her. "The forest has grown more dangerous and dark as of late."

Zach noticed the small one was coughing. It could barely lift its head from the larger one's shoulder. "Is it sick?"

"Be careful, Zach. They play games. I tried to help a trapped snowpuff only nights ago and the wretched thing stole my hunting bag. I never got it back."

Zach, overcome with a desire to help the poor innocent creature, knelt down. He'd felt desperate before, but he'd never been cold and hungry. He'd always had something to eat and a place to stay. Zach didn't like choosing between his own safety and helping the poor creatures. But one more look into the little snowpuff's big, sad eyes and Zach's heart filled with sympathy. He rummaged through his pack.

"What are you doing?" Asha asked.

Without responding, Zach pulled a small cloth from his bag. In it he found a small loaf of bread. Zach tore off the end. Not even concerned with how much food he would need for the rest of the journey, Zach handed the large chunk of bread to the older snowpuff and motioned to the small one. Hesitantly, the snowpuff inched forward and then snatched the bread quickly from his hand. Zach stepped back and felt a wave of relief when the small snowpuff took a bite. A sudden sparkle filled the larger snowpuff's eyes, and its mouth slightly curved into an awkward facial expression.

"Is it smiling?" Zach asked out of the side of his mouth.

"I do not know. Why would you help these despicable creatures?" Asha asked, slowly lowering her bowshot, but not putting it away. "They do not deserve it. They steal from everyone."

Zach shrugged. "If I was cold and hungry, I would want some bread. Plus, that one's sick."

Suddenly Zach had a thought. This adventure he was on was unexpected, and yet what if he hadn't been here? What if he hadn't had the urge to help? Would it have mattered? He'd never thought about that before. He even got a warm feeling inside over the thought of making a difference. No, like real warmth; he literally felt something warm and heavy in his chest pocket as if it had been there all along. He patted at his shirt, feeling a chunk of something. Then he reached in and grabbed it. He looked down at this hand. He didn't remember putting that in his pocket. Had it just appeared? He studied the small, rough, violet cylinder of wax in his palm. As he looked closer, Zach saw a word engraved on its side: *Benignitas*. Wait! That was the same word on the door of the Advent calendar!

"What's that?" Asha asked.

"I don't know. It just like appeared in my pocket."

"Let me see."

Zach held out his hand and Asha's eyes opened wide in surprise.

"What Asha? What is it?"

"It is in the old language. The language of legend. I think that is a . . . "

"What?"

Before Asha could answer, the ground shook violently. Zach looked at Asha to gauge if the shaking was normal. She looked frightened, and Zach felt a bolt of panic in his chest. He tried to steady himself as the world around him convulsed. The snowpuffs! He turned to help them, but they were gone. The sky around them grew darker. The snowpuffs' fire went out, and Asha crouched to steady herself. Zach followed her lead and clutched the chunk of wax in his hand.

After a few moments, the ground stopped shaking. They heard heavy footsteps. A twig snapped. Asha drew her bowshot in an instant. Zach put the small candle-like treasure back in the pocket of his shirt and awkwardly drew his sword. It didn't clink this time. He was slowly getting better at unsheathing the weapon. Everything was dark and quiet again. Too quiet. Suddenly out of the darkness, a large black beast lunged from the trees. It hurled its massive body straight at Asha in a blur. Asha, who was quicker, rolled out of the way and unleashed the bowshot arrowhead at the animal, piercing its side. The animal yelped and dropped to the ground as blood rushed from the wound. Asha and Zach approached the beast cautiously. It focused its large yellow eyes on Zach and snapped. Zach, frozen in fear, stared at the beast wide-eyed. Even though the wolf-like creature was lying on its side, the beast remained eye-level with Zach and gave him a piercing glare. Jumping back, panic overwhelmed him, and he shook uncontrollably.

In a low growling voice, the beast said, "Give me the magus, boy!"

Zach jerked away from the beast.

"What?!" Asha said.

The beast fumbled, trying to stand. Zach and Asha backed up slowly as the beast rose to twice their height.

"Didn't you hear that?!" Zach asked.

"No, hear what?!" Asha asked.

"He spoke to me!"

"Fenrir doesn't speak!"

"What's a Fenrir?"

"That's Fenrir!" Asha steadied her bowshot and prepared to retract the arrowhead from the creature's side.

Lowering its neck and steadying for attack, Fenrir growled, "THE MAGUS!"

In an instant, Asha recoiled her bowshot, ripping it from the beast as it howled in pain. Zach almost fainted at the sight of the arrowhead tearing from the beast's flesh. Before Fenrir could retaliate, Asha had the arrowhead coiled around his legs. She darted around a tree and pulled, using the trunk as leverage. Fenrir tripped and howled. Quickly recovering, the beast shook and burst forward as Asha and Zach ran away. Zach struggled to keep up with Asha. His chest burned, and he stumbled as Asha gracefully hopped around the floor like a rabbit on forbidden medicine. They wove in and out of the brush, jumped over fallen trees, and lept from large rocks. But Fenrir was gaining on them. Zach could feel the beast's breath on his neck. But he couldn't turn around. He didn't want to know how close he was to death.

As Fenrir lunged at them, fangs bared, a powerful ball of red and gold light burst before its eyes and a pulsing wave of power knocked the beast back. Another ball of energy shot at its massive gray paws. Following the direction from which the magic came, Zach and Asha's eyes fell on a tall cloaked figure, spinning a red glowing ax in one hand and a gold glowing club in the other. Zach froze. What he could make out of the figure was ominous: a shadowed face and puffs of breath emanated from the hood in the cold night air. Zach was in awe; whoever this was spun his weapons with speed and skill. Fenrir jumped and the ground shook. Asha and Zach lost their balance. The cloaked figure flipped over them to shield the crouching travelers from the onslaught of fangs. Crossing his glowing weapons, the warrior generated a large ball of magic and hurled a sphere of energy forward as the beast lunged. Soaring through the air, Fenrir clashed against the red and gold orb. With his momentum gone, the beast dropped to the ground. Quickly, the cloaked figure ran to Zach and Asha.

"Come with me! More will come!"

"More?! More what?!" Asha asked.

"Not now, we must leave!" the cloaked man said.

Asha looked at Zach and said, "Follow Amal!"

Before they could move, a glowing light appeared in the forest. As the light expanded, a door appeared. Zach recognized the door immediately. It looked just like a door from the Advent calendar. Only this one held the word *Fiducia*. Amal stopped running and stared at the door. Then he turned to Asha and Zach. With fierce, glowing eyes, he focused on Zach as if really seeing him for the first time. Zach looked back at the great protector warily and watched as his large, bright eyes widened under the shadow of his hood. A rumble beneath their feet tore through Amal's moment of discovery.

"Fenrir!" Asha said.

"Hurry, through the door!" Amal said.

As they approached the magical gateway, Amal looked at Zach.

"You must open the door! Hurry! Turn the knob!"

Zach hesitated for a moment; then upon seeing the great black beast emerge from between the trees, Zach grabbed the brown rustic doorknob, turned, and pulled. As the door rushed open, Zach felt a familiar pull, and bright white light consumed the three travelers. Within an instant they were gone, leaving Fenrir alone, confused, and disgusted with his failure.

DOOR TWO

FIDUCIA
TRUST IN THE LAND OF SPÉS

"When I am afraid, I put my trust in you."
Psalm 56:3

When Zach, Asha, and Amal went through the Advent door, they couldn't see anything but bright light. They couldn't see each other. They couldn't see themselves. They couldn't see anything. But they knew they existed and were being pulled somewhere. Asha, Amal, and Zach seemed to fall from out of nowhere just feet above the ground. They dropped in a small clearing surrounded by large willow trees. Without speaking, Amal crossed his weapons on his back, clicked them into place, and walked through a neverending curtain of flowing willow branches. Zach felt a wave of relief as he realized he'd outrun a Fenrir— whatever that was—and had made it through another Advent door—whatever that meant. Brushing himself off, Zach followed Asha through the willow branches.

On the other side of the natural curtain was one of the coolest cabins Zach had ever seen. Like other cabins, it was primarily made up of logs. However, these logs were crooked and of all different shapes. The cabin was built into the base of a large cedar tree. It had two stories and leaned to one side. Large cracks ran through the cabin like veins, and Zach swore he saw the building moving up and down as if it were breathing. As they walked through the thick, red and gold, glass door, Zach was amazed by the interior of the cabin. The walls were the same as the exterior with exposed logs, and the half of the cabin that was in the tree had smoothly sanded walls. Inside were all sorts of trinkets, shelves, a small wooden table, two dining chairs, two sitting chairs, a counter, and a hearth. Toward the back of the room Zach saw stairs leading to the second story. The stairs were made out of very thick green glass, the same glass that filled the windows and the doorway.

"Amal! It's wonderful to see you! Did you see Fenrir?! I've read about him but never seen him and so close! He's huge! Can you believe this?! What was that door—magic?! Oh, Amal!" Asha exclaimed.

Amal walked over to Asha and rested a hand on her shoulder. Asha jumped, giving him a great hug. Amal, taken by surprise, laughed deeply and hugged her tight.

After a cackle and snort, Asha turned to Zach and said, "This is Amal. He's the protector of the Land of Spés. He and my maata are good friends, so I have known him for a long time."

Amal had a friendly face that lit up even when he wasn't smiling. Despite that, he still looked quite fierce and impressive. He reminded Zach of an assassin from one of his favorite video games in his deep purple cloak. Amal had dark, thick curly hair that poked out from his hood in an unruly fashion. His eyebrows and beard were also dark and curly, which made his pearly white irises all the more prominent and somewhat intimidating.

As Amal moved around the room, Zach observed the club and ax in their holsters on Amal's back. They looked like just normal weapons now. But Zach couldn't get the image of Amal flipping around with glowing weapons out of his head. It was one of the most amazing things he'd ever seen. Almost as if he'd read Zach's mind, Amal clasped his weapons and a hum of energy illuminated the ax first and then the club. Amal winked at Zach as he placed them on the table. Then he lifted off his hood and sat down.

"Have a seat, Asha, and let us get to know your friend here," Amal said.

As Asha explained how she'd met Zach, Zach carefully observed Amal. Even though he was obviously a great warrior, Zach noticed he had a gentle, quiet demeanor. He looked directly at Asha as she told her story. He listened intently to every word. And his eyes held a kindness Zach couldn't quite explain. He felt like everything would be alright now that Amal was there. And he didn't even know him. Amal was like . . . Zach wasn't quite sure how to categorize him. He thought for a moment, letting the perfect description come to mind. A gentle epic warrior. Yes, that's it, he thought. And Zach couldn't help but want to be exactly like him. Zach also noticed Amal had the same tattoo on his forehead as Asha: a triangle with two streaks. Looking down at the table, Zach found the marking on the handles of Amal's weapons as well.

Once Asha finished explaining how she'd essentially hog-tied Zach and brought him home, Amal interrupted, "Your name is Zach?"

"Yeah, Asha said it's a strange name here but it means—"

"Remembered by Yahweh," Amal finished for him.

Zach looked up in surprise. "Yeah, so you've heard of it?"

"In a sense, yes," Amal said.

"Do you know how he can get home? He is not from this world, or so he thinks," Asha explained, giving Amal a dubious look she didn't think Zach noticed.

Amal became serious for a moment.

Asha looked at Zach and shrugged.

Without warning, Amal got up and grabbed bread and what looked like spiced cheese. He placed three small cups and a jug of water on the table.

"I have much to tell, and I am sure you are hungry. So eat, I will tell you what I know," Amal said.

Asha dove into the food. Zach placed a little on his own plate but wasn't very hungry. Amal pointed his club at the hearth and within an instant a warm fire grew. Zach remembered what Aachal said about Amal being known as the Fire Wielder.

"There, that is better," Amal said. "I suppose I shall start from the beginning." He furrowed his brows and cleared his throat. "After Burra Din was created and creatures filled its corners, many people, all different kinds, began to create tribes—"

"Yes, like mine," Asha said.

"Yes, Asha, like yours. Now, the tribes lived peacefully but were unaware of the beautiful gifts they had been given when Burra Din was created. These gifts were called, well," He leaned closer to Zach, "to you Zach, they would be known as hope, faith, joy, and peace."

Zach listened intently, vigorously tapping his foot up and down under the table and flipping a piece of bread around in his hands.

"Because the people of Burra Din could not understand these four gifts at first, a young boy much like yourself was sent here from your world. He—"

"What?! He is not the first?!" Asha exclaimed.

"Hush, Asha. Let me finish. If you will be interrupting my story the entire time, we shall be here for days."

"Sorry," Asha pouted.

"As I was saying, this boy was sent here from your world, your realm. He was sent without his knowledge to guide, learn, and be

54

an example for the people of Burra Din. A tribe adopted him and taught him the ways of Burra Din's magic. You see, Zach, some realms have no magic. Those that rely completely on technology have lost all connection to magic. Therefore, the boy had to be taught. The boy successfully blended into the world of Burra Din and traveled with the tribe. On their adventures, the tribe learned through the boy as well. They came to understand hope, faith, joy, and peace. Along with the gifts, the boy shared his language and culture with the tribe. As did the tribe share their culture and language with the boy. The tribe developed uniquely because of this, different from the others, giving them much to share."

"So I'm not the first? How many realms are there?" Zach asked, tapping his foot wildly.

"No, you are not the first. As far as the number of realms that exist, I do not know. Only the creator of Burra Din and its magic know the answer to that. What I do understand is that the fates of our realm and yours are closely connected. And that you and this ancient boy somehow traveled between worlds also known as realms. But the boy could not stay long. For while time passed in Burra Din, time slowed significantly in his world, your world."

Zach shifted in his seat and switched from tapping his right foot to his left. He couldn't believe what he was hearing. Time was almost frozen at home? How could that be? Is that why he was only 14 and Asha was 53 even though they looked and acted the same age? He tried to swallow the piece of bread he'd just shoved in his mouth. It stuck in his throat, and he grabbed the water. Amal went on.

"After the boy went home, the tribe spread the gifts and knowledge across the land. And these gifts were loved, accepted, and attempted by all for a time. Despite all efforts of good, a dark power exists among us in all worlds and is known by one name in

Burra Din, *Malum*. Now Malum or the dark power wants nothing more than to possess and control the four gifts. However, what Malum does not understand is that the gifts cannot be owned or controlled because, well, they are not things to steal or possess but rather feelings or decisions and a way to live. Now that does not stop Malum from trying to destroy them. Malum hates that the gifts' powers grow. So Malum or the dark power beneath all life of all worlds covets the gifts and wants to destroy them. But the people's belief and determination to uphold the four gifts keeps the darkness at bay."

Asha let out a small grunt, confirming the story with a grave look.

"But centuries passed, and the tribes traveled and grew. Lessons were lost over time. The gifts were forgotten. And Malum grew and began to consume Burra Din. His power takes many forms, but his best-known form is a giant, monstrous, dark warrior in fearsome red and black armor. The armor is most interesting as it adheres to his body and comes to sharp points. Those who have seen him are not mistaken. He is an enemy of unique characteristics. They also say that the warrior soars above all on a formidable, armored beast known as the Dark Dragon."

Zach raised his eyebrows. He loved dragons, and even though this Malum guy seemed like the last person you'd ever want to meet, Zach couldn't help but be curious about this dragon.

"When Malum does not appear in his true armored form, he lurks about the land through the use of his dark power. And sadly, you can easily find evidence the dark power has increased: greed, distrust, violence—all sorts of dark acts. Because of this, the tribes chose protectors who took the sacred oath. A protector was chosen for each of the four lands: Spés, Fidem, Gaudium, and Pax."

"Like you!" Asha said.

Amal patted her hand. "Yes, I protect Spés. However, when the first boy left, it was said that if ever the gifts were forgotten, another would come from his world. This newcomer would journey through the land of Burra Din, discovering the gifts all over again. This would lead to the birth of a prince who would rule and save Burra Din from the growing darkness. The four lands would be reunited in a time of light and goodness."

Amal paused and looked at Zach.

Zach shifted uncomfortably. He couldn't possibly mean me, could he? Zach cleared his throat and asked, "Yeah right, you think I can lead to the prince? I'm not a warrior or anything."

"I believe this is why you are here," Amal said.

Asha jumped in her chair abruptly and said, "Zach! Show him that—um, whatever it is. It is from the legend—um prophecy. I do believe it! I do!"

Zach had forgotten all about the cylinder of wax in his pocket. He couldn't possibly still have it, right? It had to have fallen out when Fenrir was chasing them. He patted his shirt pocket and was surprised to find it. He reached in and pulled it out. Opening his hand, he presented the object to Amal. It still had the word *Benignitas* engraved on it. Amal's pearly eyes sparkled.

"Ah! Yes, Zachariah! You see?! This is the answer! This means you are here for the prophecy. For this is one of the magi. You see, magi is the term for more than one magus. There are many, and they lead to the four gifts, and the four gifts lead to the prince. They are like stepping stones in a journey. We do not know much of them. But they are signs from Burra Din that you are on the right path," Amal said.

"These little pieces of wax or whatever lead to gifts and a prince?" Zach asked.

"Yes, I can see how that would surprise you. Especially someone from your realm where technology reigns over the minds of all," Amal explained. He was not judging Zach's world. He was simply describing. But Zach knew he was right. Amal pointed to the magus and continued, "These magi come together to create a gift. You must collect three of them before a gift will appear. Once you have collected all four gifts, the prophecy states the prince will be born. The prince's birth must be drawing near, as you have been brought to Burra Din and the first magus is right before us in the palm of your hand."

Zach was shocked. He didn't know what to say. This seemed like something out of a crazy fantasy novel he'd read once. This couldn't actually be real, right? People didn't go on adventures like this anymore, did they? Asha looked back and forth between Amal and Zach. Zach, wide-eyed, sat quietly, setting the magus on the table. Amal gently picked up the magus and pointed to the engraving.

"On your journey here, you must have done something kind. Not just anything. Something without even a thought of reward or your own self-preservation. When you did that, the magus appeared. Is that the way of it?"

"The snowpuffs," Asha said.

"Yes," Zach said.

"Well, when you did and you received the magus, Malum must have sensed the awakening of the gifts and sent Fenrir to stop you," Amal said.

"Great," Zach said, rolling his eyes and dropping his head in his hands, "I mean, is that beast going to be hunting me like all the time?"

"I do not know, but what I do know is you must be very careful. For darkness is not always easy to avoid and attacks in many ways. Sometimes Malum is very subtle or he strikes when you least expect it," Amal said.

"But how do I get home?" Zach asked.

"The mysterious powers of Burra Din brought you here. Only Burra Din can decide when to send you home. How did you come to be in the Forest of Inspirare?" Amal asked.

Zach was silent for a moment. How could he explain to these two people that he'd been sucked into a small wooden tree? Wincing, he said, "Like through this tree. It's called an Advent calendar, and it has these little doors."

"Hm, I do not know of Advent calendars. I understand that according to the prophecy, doors lead to the gifts. But we did not know if the prophecy spoke of real doors or metaphorical ones. Doors on your tree seem to be the answer," Amal said. "And I do not believe you have to take on the journey. However, if you do not, the world of Burra Din may fall. Fall to greed, hate, despair, and striving. The light of Burra Din will disappear."

"Wait, you're telling me the fate of your world is up to me? Who's idea was that?" Zach asked.

"That can't happen! I will not let that happen!" Asha said.

Amal turned to her with a sympathetic look and said, "My dear Asha, you are a brave warrior, but only the prince can bring ultimate healing to Burra Din. And only one can lead us to the prince. He's been chosen."

Asha and Amal looked at Zach again. Amal gave Zach an understanding confident glance. But Asha, well Asha, looked like she was going to punch him right in the face. And Zach couldn't blame her. Here the guy she'd been calling "monkey boy" and who she thought was an idiot was now the one destined to save her entire world, her entire life. Zach just stared at them, astonished. This had to be a dream. He didn't know how to battle anybody, much less an evil force trying to conquer the world.

"Uh, I think you've got the wrong guy," Zach said, bouncing his knee up and down nervously. He stared down at the piece of cheese he rolled in his fingers. "I mean, I think Burra Din or whatever chose the wrong guy. I'm not a warrior. I can barely carry this thing around." He held up Satya.

"That is Satya. Not a thing. And you are just going to let my world die? Give up without even trying? Do not be a coward!" Asha said.

Zach's face reddened. He wasn't a coward. He just didn't know what he was doing.

Amal cleared his throat and said, "I understand your hesitancy, young Zachariah, but Burra Din chose you. No other is here. No other was given a magus. No other was chased by Fenrir. And no other has befriended Asha long enough to remain sane and in one piece."

Asha narrowed her eyes at him. Suddenly the pressure of the moment filled Zach with overwhelming despair. He was only 14 for crying out loud. He was still trying to deal with everything that had happened to him in the past six months. He had wanted to spend the rest of his life fading into the background. How could he be expected to save a world? He shook his head.

"I never wanted an adventure. I'm no hero. I'm a nobody," he said.

Amal stood to clear the table. Asha crossed her arms and raised an eyebrow at Zach. Zach avoided eye contact with her. It was like she was waiting for him to transform into some amazing warrior, or better yet just explode so she could be rid of him. Zach focused on the silence and the sound of Amal quickly scrubbing the dishes. Once they were put away, Amal sat back down. Carefully, he leaned back in his chair and folded his hands.

While stroking his beard, Amal said, "Maybe that's why Burra Din chose you, Zachariah."

Zach looked up at Amal.

"Those who take on an adventure do not do so because they know everything. The point of an adventure is to embark on the unknown, learn all you can and come out of it, hopefully, wiser. Maybe, Zachariah, just maybe you were chosen because what Burra Din needs is also something you need. Something you must experience."

Zach's eyes widened with a realization. He'd wanted to fade in the background of his own life because he couldn't escape those who knew him and his tragedy. Every day something or someone reminded him of it. But here in Burra Din no one really knew anything about him. Maybe that was why he felt more comfortable here. This was his chance. This was his opportunity to do something new. Here he could be the hero, or at least try to be. He had no idea what he was doing, but wasn't that how he'd learned the drums? He'd just sat down one day and started messing around, which had resulted in him learning more, which had resulted in him jamming out to his favorite songs. Zach grasped the magus on the table. It seemed kind of cringey, but in his heart he felt a deep desire to start this adventure. After all, what did he have to lose? He wasn't exactly enjoying his life back home. Zach had the sudden impulse to just take on the challenge despite the overwhelming expectations.

"Okay, I'll do it," Zach said more to himself than anyone else.

Asha set her hands on her hips and sighed loudly as if to say, "Finally, let's get this show on the road."

Then the magus, which had been lying lifeless, slowly began to glow. The word on the magus melted into the waxy surface and new grooves formed another ancient word.

"What does it say?" Asha asked.

"Hm, *confido*," Amal read.

"What does that mean?" Zach asked, looking up at Amal.

"Confido Cave?" Asha asked.

After the magus stopped glowing, Amal picked it up and looked at it carefully. Then handing the magus to Zach, he said, "This is what I was talking about. No one fully understands the magic of these tiny magi. They are mysterious and seem to have minds of their own. Legends connect them back to the days of Burra Din's creation. So yes, I believe so, Asha. It seems the magus approves of the acceptance of your quest, Zachariah. Excellent! Burra Din must be sending you forward. Confido Cave is a short journey from here."

"How do I get to this cave? Do you have a map?" Zach asked, slipping the magus back into his shirt pocket.

"Oh, you will not be going alone, my dear boy! Of course we will be going with you. I will show you the way," Amal said with a hearty laugh.

"You think I'm going to let a bewitched monkey save my world on his own?" Asha asked, smirking at him.

Zach let out a breath of relief, comforted by the comradery. Amal patted Zach on the shoulder.

"It's settled then. We will rest here for the night and begin our quest tomorrow, starting with Confido Cave."

After a hike through the woods, Zach, Asha, and Amal found themselves at the base of the Factum Mountains. Zach gazed up the rocky terrain to the sky. He couldn't see the peak of the mountain, but noticed several overhangs and a rocky path winding back and forth up the mountain side. Overwhelmed by the feat but unwilling to dwell on it, Zach started toward the rocky path.

"I believe there is a better way," Amal said, standing at the base of the mountain with Asha.

"Is there another path?" Zach asked.

"Do you see that ridge up there? Not the first one, but the second one with the small tree jutting out from the side? That's the mouth of Confido Cave," Amal explained.

Zach looked up. The first ridge was pretty close; however, the second ridge with the tree was not only much higher but seemed impossible to reach. The path didn't even seem to go that way. Zach looked back at Amal just to see if he was joking. But despite his pleasant demeanor, he looked completely serious.

"Huh, I don't know about you guys, but I'm not a goat, so yeah," Zach said.

"Zach, we know you are no goat," Asha said with a look that said she was not good at reading sarcasm.

Amal winked.

"Ha ha! Fire jump!" Asha said.

Amal unhooked his weapons.

Fire jump? Zach had no idea what that meant, and the fact that Asha was doing a small victory dance made him nervous.

"So uh, what's a fire jump?" Zach asked.

"Well, my boy, I will let Asha show you," Amal said.

Asha stepped forward and started to explain, "When Amal visits the city on Moon Night, our festival of the moon, all the children and even some adults get in line next to Amal for a glorious ride. The fire jump! Here, watch."

Amal knelt on the ground and crossed his weapons, the ax over the club. Energy generated from them. They glowed red and gold. Asha put one foot on the ax and one on the club, then she bent her knees.

"Are you ready, Asha?" Amal asked.

Asha crouched a little lower. She looked thrilled and full of anticipation. Amal began the countdown. Zach took a step back.

"Tree, spark, fire, blaze!" Amal said.

And with that, he pulled the weapons apart. A glowing ball instantly formed beneath Asha's feet and rocketed her into the sky. It looked like she had a jetpack attached to her legs as the ball of energy pushed her upward. When she had sailed only feet above the chosen ridge, Asha quickly parted her legs. The glowing ball exploded into tiny sparkles like a firework, and she landed perfectly on the ridge. Zach was amazed. Despite his uncertainty, he couldn't help but want a turn. "Just don't look down," he told himself. After all, he'd handled the platform okay. How much worse could this be?

"Are you ready?" Amal asked.

Zach gave Amal a wide-eyed look and said, "Sure, I guess so."

"You will manage, my boy. It is fun! Even small ones enjoy the fire jump on Moon Night," Amal said.

That did it. Zach didn't want to be considered less courageous than a small one. Probably a toddler or something, he thought. Zach swallowed his nervousness and carefully stepped on the ax and club, which were already glowing.

"Ready?"

"Yeah."

"Hurry up! I'm considering mountain hunting up here!" Asha yelled down at them.

Amal counted down, "Tree, spark, fire,"

Zach closed his eyes.

"Blaze!"

Zach felt a thrill and soared through the sky as Asha cheered for him. Feeling slightly more confident, Zach opened his eyes and saw Asha jumping up and down on the ridge, waving at him. As he passed her up, she said, "Now, Zach!"

Forgetting for a brief moment what he was supposed to do, Zach panicked and flailed his arms. Then remembering Asha, he shifted his legs quickly. The ball of energy exploded, and he sailed toward the ledge.

"Land on your feet! Your feet!" Asha said.

Zach's arms and legs were flailing about as he approached the ledge. Panic set in, and he couldn't control his body. The fear of crashing onto the ledge head-first had him leaning back. Suddenly he felt something beneath him, guiding him into the proper landing position. Zach looked down and, once the dizziness subsided, he saw Amal guiding him gently onto the ledge. Zach closed his eyes and breathed as he felt his feet land softly on the rock surface. Happy to be on land again, Zach crouched down to catch his breath. Zach looked up at Asha, elated. He'd just done something he'd never thought he'd do in his entire life. Zach brushed off his pants while readjusting his bag and sword.

"Isn't the fire jump wonderful?!" Asha asked.

"Yeah, awesome!"

"Are you two ready?" Amal said as he floated down onto the ledge.

"Amal, that was wonderful! Thank you!" Asha said.

"Ah, it is my pleasure, young Asha," Amal replied.

As the elation of flying through the sky wore off, the three travelers found themselves standing in front of Confido Cave: a boy from another world looking uncertain but more optimistic than in years, a young warrior maintaining a confident offensive stance ready to pounce, and a wise, bearded prophet equipped for battle staring into the abyss.

"How long are we going to stand here?" Asha asked, unsheathing her bowshot.

"Let us go," Amal said, readjusting the club and ax on his back.

"So we gonna use those headlamp things again," Zach asked, trying to play it cool.

"Of course! Let us put them on out here," Asha said, already placing hers on her head.

Asha and Zach attached their headlamps while Amal pulled an octagonal lantern out of his pack. With a wave of his palm, the lantern illuminated, revealing a bright orange and yellow flame. Zach's hand shook as he awkwardly placed his headlamp on his forehead. Trying to get an idea of the danger ahead without revealing that he was scared out of his mind, Zach looked at Asha.

"So, Asha, you planning on roastin' lots of beasts in there?"

Asha just stared at him for a moment and shook her head as if to say, "duh." Zach didn't like that answer, and now he really felt ridiculous for asking.

"On we go," Amal said.

As they entered the mouth of the cave, Zach was grateful to have his headlamp. The first chamber was huge, like a great hall of a castle but extremely dark. Mesmerized by the underground landscape, Zach gazed at the ceiling. It was black as night until Zach shone the beam of his gem into its arches. Long stalactites clung desperately to the ceiling, and the moisture dripping from them reflected the bright light. So despite the seemingly impenetrable darkness, small molecules of hydrogen and oxygen sparkled back at him.

"Is it not beautiful?"

Zach jumped.

"The reflection of light—is it not beautiful?" Amal asked.

Zach nodded and his headlamp bounced, illuminating more water molecules throughout the cave.

"It is interesting. It is almost as if darkness is never truly hopeless. There is always something waiting to be illuminated. Makes you wonder." Lifting a hand, Amal covered Zach's headlamp, making the ceiling dark once more. "See, complete impenetrable black, but if you add just a bit of light," Amal uncovered the headlamp and millions of sparkles twinkled on the ceiling of the cave again, "wonderful."

Zach liked the idea of something potentially hopeful waiting in the dark. Usually when he was afraid of the dark, he just assumed something evil lurked in the unknown. But he liked Amal's idea.

"Amal? Monkey Boy?" Asha said, heading down what looked like a creepy tunnel.

"Why does she call you that?" Amal asked.

Zach shrugged. "I don't really know."

"That is Asha for you," Amal replied with a light laugh.

Zach and Amal followed Asha down the tunnel of Confido Cave.

Burra Din was covered in caves, but Confido Cave was unique. For Confido Cave was an enchanted cave that had been a place of mysterious happenings for centuries. However, over time, the people of Burra Din had forgotten its enchantment, and the cave had remained untouched for decades. Within the darkness, the cave held many secrets of the early days of Burra Din and its tribes. Cave paintings covered walls of rock, beautiful gems filled its crevices, and dark, interesting creatures lurked throughout the tunnels. There was a time when the creatures were friendly and the cave was a place used for peaceful shelter. However, due to neglect over the years, as everywhere in Burra Din, an evil eked into the cave and its creatures. And this newly sinister cave was exactly where the three travelers met their first challenge.

After what felt like hours of wandering down the dark corridor, Asha stopped abruptly. The sound of crumbling pebbles falling over an edge filled the quiet room.

"Ah, this will not work," she said as she stared down a massive dark hole.

They'd come to the end of the tunnel and had two choices: venture down the deep, dark pit or head down another tunnel, smaller than the first, but far less frightening. As Amal peered over the edge of the chasm, he crouched down, and with a single touch of his lantern, he illuminated the black abyss. Now they could see that at the bottom of the pit was another room of the cave. But the edges were dark, so they had no idea where the room led.

"I choose the tunnel," Zach said.

"I am not certain," Amal said. "Do you see that light?"

"No, I don't see anything," Zach said.

Asha crouched next to him and peered down into the hole.

"Ah, yes! I see it," she said.

Asha's voice echoed off the walls. She didn't seem to understand the concept of an inside voice. Zach, confused, looked at them. He didn't see anything but a black rim around the bottom of the pit. How come they could see a light but he couldn't? Frustration was building on top of his anxiety. Zach breathed shallowly.

"'Tis daylight. That is the safest way," Amal said as he pulled a long rope from his bag.

"I don't see the light. Maybe it's just a reflection from your lantern," Zach said.

Amal and Asha looked at him.

"You mean you do not see that bright light in the corner there?" Asha asked.

Zach looked again squinting his eyes, hoping to see even the slightest sliver of daylight. "No, I don't. And why couldn't we see it before we lit the lantern. If it had been there this whole time, it would have lit up the bottom of the pit when we first got here."

"In my experience, Zachariah, when traveling through the darkness, one must follow the light even if the path is fraught with peril," Amal said.

Zach shook his head. He didn't understand why he couldn't see the light. He didn't understand why he was questioning Amal suddenly. And he didn't understand why he couldn't shake the panicky feeling consuming his consciousness. He stared down the small tunnel again, the alternate pathway. It was dark but dry and less dangerous. They could always venture down the path and see what it held, and then turn around and come back here, he reasoned with himself. And he was about to suggest just that when he heard a voice inside his head. The voice wasn't his voice. It was a negative voice with an ugly bite to it, and it said in a low whisper, "Do not follow. The pit is dark. Take the tunnel. Take the tunnel."

Zach stepped back in surprise. Amal and Asha didn't notice as Amal was beginning to lower Asha down the pit. Zach froze and listened. The voice was gone. He took a step closer to Amal and looked in the hole. He still didn't see the light. Amal, who'd tied the rope around a fat stalagmite and slowly released the slack to lower Asha, had trickles of sweat on his brow.

"Oh! Do you need help?" Zach asked.

"At the bottom," Asha said. "It is not frightening down here. Just dark."

Amal sighed with relief and pulled the rope back up the cave wall. "Are you ready, Zachariah?"

As Zach waited for Amal to prepare the rope, the voice returned. "You can't believe them. You just met them. They are leading you into danger. Go down the tunnel. Turn away! Turn away!" Zach jumped back.

"Zachariah, what is the matter?" Amal asked.

Zach felt a cold chill running up his spine. He stared wide-eyed at Amal as he watched the friendly bearded man's face transform into that of an evil demon: his eyes narrowed, deep hollow cheeks took the place of his bright ones, and he bared his teeth in a wicked grin.

"What's wrong, Zachariah?"

Zach stepped back and tripped over the large stalagmite. He fell to the ground and scurried back against the cave wall.

"Are you okay? What is the matter?" Amal asked again.

But all Zach could hear was the evil voice in his head, and all Zach could see was the dark monstrous transformation of his protector. "Run, Zzzzacccchhhhariahhh! Run!" Zach jumped up from the cave floor and bolted down the small tunnel he'd been wishing they'd take. The world around him was a blur as he ran and ran until he couldn't run any further. Once he realized no one was following him, Zach stopped and sat on a large rock. He caught his breath and took a drink from his canteen. Mid-drink, Zach came to terms with what he'd just done. He'd run away from the only other people he knew of in the ancient dark cave. He was alone and the thought filled Zach with dread as his heart began to race. He placed his hand on his chest, trying to catch his breath, and realized something felt off. Something felt empty! His pocket was empty! The magus was gone! In a panic, he checked every pocket, looked on the ground, and ruffled through his pack. Thoughts raced through his head: *How could I have lost it? It didn't fall out before! Where did it go? Should I go back and look for it? Yeah, that's what I'll do. I'll retrace my steps. I'll go back and—but what if Amal is there? Is he evil? He can't be evil. Right? What should I—*

A dark cloud slowly crept over Zach's mind as the corners of his eyes filled with tears. He pushed them back and started to walk back. After about 20 feet, he came to an intersection. He didn't remember this. He had no idea which tunnel he'd run out of! In his haste, Zach had bolted out of one tunnel and into another without even thinking. Despair filled his young heart and he sat again. He put his head in his hands, ready to give up, ready to let the darkness consume him when he heard the trickle of water. Zach perked up. Water! Where there was water, there could be an underground river. It was possible the river led out of the cave or deeper into the cave. Regardless, he wanted to check it out. He had no other options because he had no idea how to get back to Amal and Asha. Zach took a deep breath and picked himself up. He would head toward the water and make the next decision when he got there.

The corridor to the river was small and treacherous. At one point, Zach had to lie down to squeeze through a small shaft, which opened to another large chamber. He crawled out and brushed himself off. But this time when Zach looked up at the ceiling, no water droplets shimmered back. It was as if the darkness just absorbed the light instead of reflecting it. Immediately Zach felt a wave of regret. He had chosen poorly. He pointed his headlamp at the river. The river was a wide, swift, almost angry body of water. It roared through the cave and the sound was deafening. Zach felt overwhelmed and immediately decided to go back the way he came. But when he turned around, he no longer saw the cave wall. He saw a large green wall in front of him. He was confused. He felt the wall. It was scaly and wet. He followed the wall with his headlamp up, up, up, up until his light revealed the head of the largest, most intimidating serpent he'd ever seen. Zach froze and gaped.

The massive serpent was tricky. It stood very still, waiting for Zach to discover its existence. The frightening green beast looked down at him, mouth opened wide, revealing white fangs the size of semi-trucks. Immediately, Zach bolted away from the serpent. He felt a whoosh of air next to him as the serpent's head shot forward, just missing him. Zach jumped out of the way and ran faster to the wall of the cave. He saw a small dark hole and decided to take his chances with whatever was living in it. As the serpent pulled back its head to lunge forward again, Zach dove into the hole and just in time. As Zach pulled his feet into the dark crater, the serpent opened its jaws and snapped at the entrance. It continued to snap as Zach quickly pushed himself back into the dark space. And then he hit a wall. Zach turned around to find that the small hole was just that, a small dark crater in the side of the cave wall. There was nowhere to go. He was trapped.

Panic immediately set in. The serpent had stopped snapping at the wall and had laid its massive body across the entrance. There was no way out. He would just have to wait and hope that the serpent moved. But then Zach wondered, where would he go? He would have to make a break for the tunnel again without getting caught by the enormous reptile. Zach fixed his headlamp and pulled his pack around, setting it on his lap. He observed the hole that would be his home for—he had no idea how long he would be there. Water dripped down one side of the wall and trickled into a crack at Zach's feet. The ceiling of the hole was so low Zach had to crouch or sit to fully fit into the empty space. He leaned back against the dry side of the hole, feeling the cold stone against his back. Zach hoped Asha and Amal would come looking for him, but could they fight the beast guarding him? He didn't know.

Zach tried to slow down his breathing. He took deep breaths in through his nose and out of his mouth as his mom had taught him once when he'd broken his arm. He continued to breathe. Closing his eyes, he tried to think. He had his pack, his headlamp, and his sword, Satya. He opened his pack and found his canteen and food. He took a small drink and nibbled at what looked like a buttery cracker. Then he put the water and food away, knowing he had to save as much as he could. As he placed the contents back in his sack, he noticed a large scratch that reached up his arm. Examining his hands, he found droplets of blood smeared across his fingertips. Zach brought his hands to his face and found his nose was bleeding. He must have gotten a bloody nose and scratches up his arms when he dove into the dark crevice. He hadn't cared how he'd gotten in the hole; he'd just wanted to get as far away from that serpent as possible.

Zach looked out of the opening at the serpent's body. It lay still, blocking his way out. As he examined the serpent's scales, Zach noticed something unique. Each green scale was outlined by two other colors: black and red. And the scales that lay over one another were sharp and jagged. Immediately, Zach remembered Amal's description of Malum and his armor. Malum! This had to be one of Malum's pets, Zach thought. He shifted in the crevice, making sounds as the dirt and pebbles crunched beneath him. He paused as the serpent shifted. Zach leaned a little closer to get a better look at the scales. Suddenly the serpent lunged at the hole again, baring its fangs. Zach jumped quickly, backing up. This time the serpent snapped at the wall, causing the stone to shake and pebbles to fall into Zach's hair. He sat still again, afraid any movement would cause the serpent to obliterate the wall and enjoy Zach's crumpled body as an afternoon snack.

Zach leaned his head back once more and closed his eyes. He felt tears building. He had no idea what to do. He'd just have to wait until the serpent got bored and hopefully moved. But Zach was worried. He was afraid because the serpent seemed to be a pet of Malum, so it might never move. Why had he run from Amal? Why had he run from Asha? He had played right into Malum's hands. He'd walked right into danger. How was he going to save Burra Din when he willingly walked right into the evil guy's clutches. Zach dropped his head in his hands and pushed against his temples. Huddling against the cold wall of the cave for comfort and relief,

Zach sat still for hours, contemplating his fate. As exhaustion took hold, he slowly drifted to sleep.

Zach jerked awake. He hadn't remembered falling asleep and had no idea how long he'd been out. His headlamp had shifted and fallen down the side of his head. He readjusted the box onto his forehead and looked out the opening. The serpent was gone! He knew better than to just barrel out of the hole, but he couldn't stay trapped in there forever. He'd never survive. Plus he was pretty sure that serpent would eventually just tear down the wall. Slowly he crept to the entrance and peered out. He didn't see the serpent anywhere. But he was sure his headlamp would attract it soon if it was still in the large chamber. He heard the roaring river and looked in the direction of the tunnel. It seemed clear. He crawled out quietly, trying to avoid shifting dirt and rocks as much as possible. Standing outside of the hole, he decided to take one more look around before he made a dash to the tunnel.

As he turned his head, he saw it. The monstrous beast was curved against the wall of the hole just over the entrance so Zach would think it was gone even though it really hadn't. The serpent's eyes glowed red, and Zach made eye contact with the beast. It uncurved its body and its middle landed on the floor of the cave with a loud boom! Zach felt the earth shake beneath him.

Everything inside him said, RUN! but Zach didn't run. He stood there, frozen with fear. Then upon hearing a splash, Zach realized the serpent's tail was moving through the river. Its body coiled around him, blocking his path. Beginning to shuffle around too late, Zach pivoted from side to side, trying to find a way out. The serpent's coil closed in on him. Suddenly a small voice inside broke through his panic, SWORD! Zach pulled his glass sword, Satya, from his sheath. This time he pulled Satya out quickly, no clinking. As soon as he pointed his loyal blade at the serpent, Satya glowed fiercely. The center of the sword glowed blue while the outer rim flickered red and orange. Feeling a bit braver, Zach held the sword higher.

"Bah, bbback! Back!"

Each time he demanded, he felt stronger and his voice got louder. When the serpent saw Satya, it violently hissed and snapped. Venom dripped from its fangs. Realizing Satya's power, Zach pushed the sword forward. The serpent jerked back. Zach was beginning to feel braver and thought he might actually get back to the tunnel! Holding the sword steady, he shuffled to the side slowly. As he inched toward the exit, the serpent lunged at him, pushing him back from the tunnel again. Zach lost his balance and rolled down the floor of the cave toward the river. Water from the rushing current sprayed his face. The thought of falling in the river scared Zach just as much as becoming the serpent's lunch. If he fell in the turbulent waters, the serpent would snatch him up immediately or he'd drown.

Crawling forward but keeping the river in view, Zach pointed the sword once again. This time he didn't wait. He closed his eyes, jumped up, and ran forward, bellowing a war cry! He slashed at the scaly body. Satya sliced through the beast, covering Zach in blood and serpent slime. He'd slashed its eye! The beast released a deafening shriek and whipped back its giant head. Zach saw a clear path to the tunnel and bolted forward. But just before he reached freedom, the serpent whipped its tail, hitting Zach in the side and sending him flying through the air. He hit the cave wall and watched as Satya sailed across the chamber. SPLASH! His sword landed in the dark raging river. As he hit the cave floor, Zach felt a sharp pain wring up his spine. Despair took him. He'd lost his weapon, and his entire body was screaming. He slowly tried to stand as the serpent closed in on him in seconds. Zach braced himself for the final blow, feeling his knees shake and his heart pound. Holding his breath, he prepared for—

The serpent shrieked in pain! Zach covered his ears and watched as the head of the beast turned. Two lights, one red and one gold, exploded behind the scaly body. An arrowhead was ripped from the beast's back and then immediately wrapped around its neck. Amal and Asha! They'd found him!

"Yeah!" Zach jumped in the air.

Amal battled the beast, spinning his club and ax in the air. Giant illuminated orbs shot out of Amal's weapons, pelting the serpent in the head. He flipped and turned, faking out the devilish creature. The giant snake-like water beast lunged at Amal, who flipped over its head and nailed the beast in the other eye. Asha pulled tight on the rope of the bowshot, but the serpent was too strong. It lifted her off her feet and swung her back and forth. Zach heard a loud click and sharp barbs shot out from the rope, cutting into the serpent's skin. It wailed in pain but continued to swing her around. Scrambling, Zach realized he had to help. But no weapon! He ran to the river and searched the water, desperately hoping Satya had somehow resisted the flow of the raging current. No sword. Disappointed but determined, Zach desperately held out his hand and closed his eyes. He felt silly. If it worked for Thor, it could work for him too, right? Zach concentrated and called to the sword. He waited . . . and waited . . . and nothing happened. Just when he was about to give up, he heard a splash of water and opened his eyes. Satya had emerged, glowing brightly, and made a bee-line for his palm. The force pushed against him as he clutched the blade. Shocked, Zach stared at the illuminated sword.

"Mooooooonnnnkkkkkkeeeeyyyy bbbbbooooyyy!" Asha yelled as she swung around the beast, clinging to her bowshot.

Sprinting, Zach charged with his sword. Amal shot bolts of magic in front of him to clear and illuminate his path. Asha, finally gaining control of her bowshot, mounted the serpent and pulled, tightening the bladed rope around the beast's neck. Zach knew he had one shot. As the serpent swung its head back in Zach's direction, he planted his feet and steadied the sword. He had no idea how a sword the size of his arm was going to sever this creature's head from its ginormous body but he didn't care. The giant head barreled forward, fangs bared. Zach twisted out of the way and brought the sword down. Amazed, Zach watched as the blade extended into a beam of illuminated glass the length of a soccer field and sliced through the scaly green neck. Shocked at his strength and the magic of the sword, Zach watched as the serpent's head dropped to the cave floor with a loud thud; its body continued jerking in the air. Asha held on tight to her bowshot, retracting the coiled blades. As the flailing body slowed and fell to the ground, she jumped into the air and landed on two feet as gracefully as if she'd jumped from a tree branch.

Covered in serpent entrails, Asha said, "That was magnificent!"

Once the serpent's body stilled, the roar of the clashing river dwindled, and the current slowed. Zach looked around and readjusted his headlamp, which had miraculously stayed on his head. This time when the light hit the ceiling, water droplets shimmered back at him. That's strange, he thought. The darkness was less formidable now that the serpent was dead. Amal ran to them, breathing heavily and holding his weapons. Zach stared at the monstrous green head and dead black eyes, still shocked he'd been able to slice through the serpent's neck as easily as slicing through a piece of cheese. Asha placed a hand on Zach's back as she approached. Zach heard and felt the squish of liquid as her bloody palm made contact with his shoulder. He flinched, slightly disgusted.

"Ah, good job! You are stronger than I thought. Satya served you well," Asha said.

"Zachariah!" Amal said. "You have been found, my boy! Are you well?!"

"Yes! Wow! Asha, you were amazing! Did you see the sword?! It grew! Wait—how did you guys find me? I thought you were going down the pit? Why'd you come back for me?" Zach asked.

Asha's face dropped and she said curtly, "You ran off."

With a flip of a switch, Zach felt ashamed, remembering now why he'd been in that situation in the first place. How could he have thought Amal was evil? How could he let the darkness of the cave overwhelm him like that?

"I'm sorry," Zach said.

Asha stood silent.

Amal shifted his gaze back and forth between Asha and Zach and said, "There will be many challenges on this journey, Zachariah. You must believe in Asha, in the protectors. You must believe in your mission."

"Why didn't I see the light at the bottom of the pit?" Zach asked.

"That is peculiar," Amal admitted. "As soon as you darted down the tunnel, the light dwindled. The way out was gone. I hauled Asha up, and we ventured after you. We searched for quite a while. Then we came to the crossroads of tunnels. We did not know which way you had chosen. But we heard the great serpent; it carried through the corridors."

"Wait, how'd you get through the small part of the tunnel? I could barely fit," Zach asked.

"It seems we took a different tunnel. Our tunnel was quite large. More than one tunnel leads to this chamber, which is home to the great river that runs through Burra Din, the Adventurus," Amal said.

Zach walked over to the head of the serpent. "What was this thing? The scales are outlined in red and black. They're kind of jagged. Reminds me of Malum's armor from your story, " Zach said, looking cautiously at the dead creature as if it might come back to life and swallow him up.

"Great observation, Zachariah," Amal said.

"Well, I had plenty of time to think about it while I was trapped in that hole over there," Zach said.

Asha's head jerked up suddenly and she looked at the hole.

"This creature is the Leviathan. Its size concerns me," Amal said. "The Leviathan grows with the darkness of the world. If there is much darkness, the Leviathan is monstrous. If there is little darkness, the Leviathan is the size of a mere garden snake. Deadly poisonous but small."

"I would say that is monstrous," Asha said as she cleaned herself off in a small pool of water. Zach, suddenly bothered by the stench of serpent remains, decided to wash himself off as well.

"Yes it is quite monstrous. Hm, all the more reason for us to make haste." Amal walked over to a circle of rocks far from the Leviathan's remains. "I'll start a fire. We shall rest here to catch our breath. Then we must be on our way."

Once they were cleaned, Asha and Zach joined Amal. Zach felt even colder now that his clothes were wet. They watched as Amal started the fire with nothing but his club and some rocks. The fire didn't even need fuel. An extremely warm floating orb hovered above the rocks. A sense of calm embraced Zach like a warm hug. He reached in his bag and pulled out a little package, holding bread and cheese. When he was done, he threw the piece of brown packaging at the flaming orb. He watched as it burned away. Shifting uncomfortably to find a sleeping position, Zach realized how thankful he was that Amal and Asha had searched for him. He didn't want to know where he'd be if they hadn't shown up. Well, he knew. Serpent food.

"Um, uh thanks, ya know, for saving my life," Zach said, avoiding eye contact and self-consciously picking at his hands.

"It is my duty and my pleasure to protect you, Zachariah," Amal said.

Asha grunted and rolled away from him. Zach had a guilty feeling in his gut. He knew Asha was frustrated with him. She hadn't called him "monkey boy" since the battle.

"Don't mind her, she'll come around," Amal said, studying the fire.

"No, I will not. I hold grudges," Asha said.

Amal rolled his eyes and then shook his head as if to say, "No she doesn't." Zach still felt ashamed, but relieved. They really did believe in Burra Din. They'd risked their lives for Burra Din, for him. That thought gave him a warm feeling inside. He was even starting to believe in this whole mission. Zach rolled over onto his stomach. But there was something there, something like small rocks poking him in the chest. He reached under his chest expecting to pull out some pebbles but found, instead, two hard pieces of wax in his shirt pocket. He sat up abruptly with surprise and opened his hand. Two magi! One illuminated *Benignitas* and the other *Fiducia*. The magus he'd lost had returned to his pocket! And there was another one! This one had the same name as the door they'd gone through on the way to Amal's. They both had the same triangular mark that resembled Amal and Asha's tattoos. He remembered what Amal had said: "Three magi create a gift." Zach was one magus away from revealing the first gift in the world of Burra Din.

Exhilarated he'd been granted another piece of the puzzle, Zach turned to show Amal and Asha. But they were fast asleep against the rocks. He'd found two magi. Not knowing exactly where he'd end up next, Zach felt, in his heart, he was on the right path. As he clutched the magi tightly in his fist, Zach fell asleep.

DOOR THREE

VOTUM
HOPEFUL PRAYER IN THE LAND OF SPÉS

"Therefore I tell you, whatever you ask for in prayer,
believe that you have received it, and it will be yours."
Mark 11:24

When Zach awoke, he had no idea how long he'd been sleeping. The cave was incredibly dark, and their headlamps had gone out. The only light in the chamber came from Amal's fire orb. He sat up, finding Amal and Asha were already awake and shuffling around.

"Have you woken?" Asha lit her headlamp and looked directly at him.

Zach covered his eyes quickly; the light was piercing.

"Yes, Asha. Geez, you're blinding me. Could you stop shining that in my eyes?" Zach asked.

Asha chuckled and readjusted her headlamp as she mumbled something under her breath. Zach was certain he heard her say something like, "You would find better fortune blind. Ridiculous monkey."Amal relit his lantern. When he touched his club to the fire orb, it went out. Amal grabbed the orb with his bare hands as if it had never been hot. He put it back in his bag.

"I have another magus," Zach said.

"What?! Let me see!" Asha said.

Zach handed them to her, and after a quick look, she handed them to Amal.

"Fiducia! Ah, that makes perfect sense," Amal said.

"What does it mean?" Zach asked.

"Trust. You have achieved the trust magus. Now you have kindness and trust. You are learning much on this journey it seems," Amal said, handing it back to Zach.

"So only one more until I find this gift?" Zach asked.

"Yes, three magi unlock the gift, Zachariah," Amal said.

Zach put them carefully back in his pocket and wondered, "But what does that mean? How do kindness and trust unlock a gift?" Zach was puzzled. He couldn't understand how these words had anything to do with saving a world. He expected the gifts to be something like a cannon for war or gold to rule. He couldn't understand how small chunks of wax with words on them could save a world. Amal locked his weapons into place. Asha looked at both of them, waiting for their next move.

"Where now?" she asked.

"Zachariah, does the magus say anything on it besides *Fiducia*?" Amal asked.

Zach pulled the magus back out of his pocket and studied it carefully with his headlamp. It sat cold and dark in his hand.

"Nope," Zach said.

"Hm, I suppose we must find our own way out," Amal said.

"Are we going to go back through the tunnels?" Zach asked, secretly hoping this was not the plan.

"No, I suggest the river," Amal said, pulling a small box from his bag.

"We have no boat," Asha said, impatiently pacing back and forth, whipping an old bone around.

"Where'd you get that bone, Asha?" Zach asked.

"I summoned it," Asha said.

Zach stared at her.

"No! You believe all things. Haha! I got it from over there. Must be an animal bone from the serpent's dinner," Asha said.

Trying not to let Asha see, Zach shuddered off a chill. The thought that he'd almost been that serpent's dinner himself was still haunting him. Deciding to put as much space as he could between himself and the serpent's remains, Zach followed Amal over to the river. Amal set a small silver box on the bank. The box reminded Zach of a tackle box he'd seen in Father Joe's garage. It had a small latch on the side. Amal unclasped the latch, backed up a few feet, and shot a quick bolt of fire at its center. Immediately, the box multiplied into a plethora of different shapes. The pieces moved mechanically, creating a boat. Despite the fact he'd seen several magical happenings up to this point on his journey, Zach's mouth still dropped open at the immediate boat construction.

The version of water transportation that emerged from the silver box was not very large. It was just big enough for the three of them and looked like a combination of a rowboat and a canoe, sturdy but agile enough to maneuver around the large boulders in the river. The three travelers hoisted their bags on their backs and pushed the boat into the water. As it inched onto the smooth surface, each of them jumped into a wooden seat. Asha and Zach grabbed the oars while Amal stood in the back controlling the rudder. They floated with the current, heading down river. Waiting to row, Zach got a nervous feeling in his stomach and started to worry they were going deeper into the cave. What if they never came out? What if it only got darker? But as they rounded the bend of the river, a small sparkle of daylight broke through the darkness. Conveniently they saw this right before a fork in the river and were forced to choose a direction. The river had calmed down significantly since the battle with the serpent, so they gently glided along with the steady current. Asha and Zach hunkered down and got comfortable, waiting but enjoying the ride.

"Why did you run from us?" Asha asked.

"I, um, well, I thought the small tunnel was a better—" Zach stuttered.

Asha raised a warning eyebrow at him.

"I mean not a better way—but I—well, I heard a voice," Zach finished.

Asha turned to look at him. She had that annoying, doubtful look on her face that was beginning to drive Zach crazy. In his world, Zach would have written Asha off as a weirdo or someone who took too much work to like. But for some reason here in Burra Din, he wanted her to think he was cool.

Refusing to let Asha doubt his actions, Zach explained, "I was watching Amal lower you to the bottom of the hole, and I was frustrated I couldn't see the light. I started to wonder if the light was even there so—"

"We told you the light was there," Asha said.

"I know, I just didn't see it myself. I—"

"You didn't believe us."

Asha looked irritated and disappointed. Zach felt his throat tighten. He swallowed. His cheeks flush with frustration.

"It's not that. It's just, I didn't see the light so—"

"Are you the wisest person in your world?" Asha asked, completely serious.

Zach paused. "Um, no. Ha! I'm definitely not. I barely passed Algebra last year."

"You have studied Algebra. I do not know of Algebra. But have you ever studied Burra Din?" Asha asked.

Zach didn't answer.

"Then why did you not listen to us? How come you had to be certain before you trusted? We knew what we were doing. You should have followed Amal."

There was a pause. Amal cleared his throat, paying close attention to the river. He narrowed his eyes, pretending to be deep in thought. Zach knew what he had to do but he never enjoyed doing it. Usually, he just ignored these things until they went away. But Asha was not going to let that happen.

"Yeah, I'm sorry. But there was like this voice in my head, telling me to run. Then everything around me started to change. Everything looked evil."

Asha was perplexed for a moment and looked at Amal who confirmed her suspicions with a slight glance.

"Do you normally talk to yourself the way that voice spoke to you?" Asha asked.

"Um, no," Zach said.

"Then that voice was not yours," Asha stated. "Malum manipulates in fiendish ways. He was manipulating you. The evil darkness poisoning Burra Din is subtle and tricky. Malum fills you with doubt. He is not you. This is why you must let Amal and I help you. Why do you not trust?"

Zach thought for a moment. Asha was right. He'd never heard that voice before, and he'd never talked to himself in that angry, harsh way before. Asha and Amal had done nothing but try to help him since he'd arrived. Well, besides when Asha hog-tied him and called him monkey boy. And he was actually beginning to like that ridiculous nickname.

"I trust you," Zach said.

Asha gave him a look that said, "Good, that's taken care of." Zach sighed, relieved he'd waded through that confrontation. He appreciated that Asha got straight to the point and didn't play games with him.

"Hey Asha, where'd you get that weapon? It's the GOAT." Zach said.

"What is with you and goats?" Asha asked.

Zach laughed. "Oh, GOAT means the greatest of all time."

Asha's cheeks rounded as she proudly patted her bowshot. "I made it. It is the only one."

"Wow, you made that?!"

"I did. It is faster and allows for more damage and accuracy."

"Do you think you could show me how to make one of those?" Zach asked.

Asha pursed her lips, narrowed her eyes, and said, "We shall see."

Happy at the thought of having his own bowshot one day, Zach hugged his bag close to his chest, noticing the cave was much brighter. He looked out above the rim of the boat. They were coming to the cave opening, and Zach saw rushing water along with a deep forest of trees. Asha and Zach sat up straight. Asha adjusted her bowshot. As they cleared the archway, sunlight hit the boat, and Zach was blinded for a brief moment as his eyes adjusted. Asha and Zach grabbed the oars. The current picked up speed as they headed for a drop and a series of rapids. They braced themselves as the boat creaked. The fast current launched the boat downstream. Zach, Asha, and Amal maneuvered as best they could to keep from hitting ragged boulders. Water sprayed over them, and after navigating around the last rapid Asha cheered. Zach exhaled. He hadn't even realized he'd been holding his breath. The relief was short-lived. Before anyone could speak, Amal pointed. Just up ahead, Zach saw nothing but mist and a large dropoff. He turned to Asha, whose eyes were wider than he'd ever seen. Both Asha and Zach turned and looked at Amal.

"The bank! To the right!" he said.

Asha and Zach paddled with all their strength against the current, which dragged them closer to the edge of the waterfall. But as they made their way to safety, they noticed a black mass hovering over the bank.

"Look!" Zach pointed.

Hearing them, Fenrir howled.

"We can't go to the bank!" Zach said, straining his voice over the roar of the river.

Asha released her bowshot and hurled the arrowhead toward Fenrir. She missed and retracted the weapon. But before it left the bank, Fenrir snatched the arrowhead with his teeth and pulled. The large beast shuffled from side to side, dodging Amal's gold and red orbs.

"Release the arrowhead, Asha! Release it!" Amal yelled.

"Ugh! That's my favorite arrowhead!"

"Come on, Asha! Now!" Zach yelled.

Asha pressed the release button on her bowshot. Fenrir fell back against two trees, breaking them in half. He scurried back to his feet. The boat turned in circles as it soared toward the edge of the waterfall. Amal, Asha, and Zach tried hard to steer the boat to the opposite bank, but it was mostly cliff edge, leaving little space to dock. As they came to terms with their fate, Zach noticed something hovering in the mist. He squinted and leaned closer. It was brown and looked out of place.

"Look, the door!" Zach said.

Asha and Amal turned.

"Head for the door!" Amal said.

"We'll never make it!" Zach said.

He felt a pull at his arm, and he turned to find Asha making fierce direct eye contact with him. And everything slowed down. The world stood still. The chaos was silent. Zach focused on Asha. He trusted her. She was his friend.

Then the world around him came back to life. He gripped his oar with determination. As they barrelled toward the edge of the cliff, Zach felt his heart racing. They used all their strength to aim the boat toward the door. Zach felt the current working against him. Suddenly he heard a loud CRACK! His oar had broken in half. He tried to steer with what was left. But realizing it was no use, Zach gripped the side of the boat and closed his eyes as they reached the waterfall's edge. Asha screamed. And just before the boat began its descent into the foggy mist, Amal spun his club and shot a bolt of power from behind them, rocketing the vessel and three travelers through the door. On hearing the bolt of power, Zach peeked just in time to see door three. It was closed, but he couldn't turn the knob. He held his breath, hoping the boat would break through the closed door. As the front of the boat nailed the door, Zach saw the word *Votum*. Within an instant, they soared through the blindingly bright portal.

The next time Zach opened his eyes, he found himself gripping the side of the boat in a grassy field. He heard a soft breeze blowing and movement behind him. Asha and Amal were already climbing out of the boat. Zach grabbed his bag, checked for his sword, and patted his chest, finding the magi still sitting comfortably in the bottom of his pocket. As he jumped out of the boat, Zach finally noticed the scene around him. It was awe-inspiring. For miles beyond, there were beautiful green hills covered in grass and vibrant, multi-colored flowers. The landscape dipped in and out of the whitest, puffiest clouds he'd ever seen.

"Lumen Hills," Amal said. "Inhale the sweet air. Feel the freshness in your lungs! Far better than that cave."

Zach couldn't believe it. It seemed as though nothing fazed Amal. Everything they'd been through had been miraculous. Even Asha seemed surprised by most of it, and she was from Burra Din. But Amal just stayed as calm and optimistic as ever. He seemed to be enjoying every bit of their journey, finding beauty and blessings everywhere. Zach took a deep breath. The air was refreshing after the dampness of the cave and the misty river.

"Are we still in the Land of Spades?" Zach asked.

Asha face-palmed herself and said, "Spés."

"Yes," Amal replied, "if we weren't, I wouldn't be here. As a protector of the land, I can go no further than its borders."

"These are the Lumen Hills! Unbelievable!" Asha exclaimed.

"Yeah," Zach agreed.

"Not just beautiful. Watch this," Asha said, taking a few steps forward. She closed her eyes and opened her arms, palms up. "Is this right, Amal?"

"Yes, Asha," Amal said, winking at Zach.

Asha stood like that for what seemed like an awkwardly long time. Zach didn't say anything, because Amal and Asha were acting as if this was completely normal. Then suddenly out of the sky, Zach saw a small, white bird floating toward them. Only it wasn't a bird. As it got closer, it grew larger, and Zach couldn't believe his eyes. The animal landed in front of Asha and she stroked a hand down its wildly thick, white mane.

A pegasus!

Zach felt like he was going to pass out. He'd always been incredibly interested in Greek mythology, and now he was standing only feet from one of the most magnificent creatures in myth.

"Come and pet her!" Asha said as she continued to calm the elegant winged horse.

Zach walked over cautiously and stroked the creature's neck. The pegasus turned and looked him in the eyes. It snuffed loudly and brayed. Zach jumped back. Asha laughed.

"She likes you," Asha said.

Amal stepped forward to pet the pegasus.

"What's her name?" Zach asked.

"She has no name. Asha must name her, for she is her creation," Amal said.

"She made her? How?" Zach asked.

"Ah, but that is the secret of the Lumen Hills. Magic. From the depths of the Sea of Somnium to the peaks of the Gigant Mountains, Burra Din is filled with the secrets of magic. All you must do is stand and concentrate on a creature you have always wanted to befriend. If you surrender your heart and remove doubt, the wish will come true. Hence, the pegasus here."

"Sundara," Asha corrected him.

"Ah, wonderful choice. Yes, Sundara," Amal said.

At being named, Sundara winnied and nuzzled Asha. Within seconds Sundara lowered her front legs so Asha could climb her back. When Asha was settled, Sundara flew off the hill. Zach watched as they soared through the sky. He couldn't believe what he was seeing.

"You should try, young Zachariah," Amal said.

Zach nervously stepped forward. He didn't understand how this could possibly work, but heck, it was worth a shot. He had lots of ideas about what to choose. But one creature stuck out in his memory. He'd recently read that apparently the idea of dragons was not unique to European or Chinese history. No, actually many early civilizations had some sort of dragon-like beast in their mythology. For example, a Pacific Island legend says that an enormous dragon-like bird, the size of an island, dominated the sky. This bird was so enormous it could swallow the sun. This was the explanation for an eclipse, of course. It also contained sword-like feathers, mirrored-eyes, and incredibly tough skin similar to armor. This amazing beast was called a minokawa, and that is exactly what Zach wanted to summon at the top of the Lumen Hills. He stepped forward and stood where Asha had, held out his arms exactly the same way she did, palms up.

"Now what?" Zach asked, feeling ridiculous.

"Imagine what it is you want and remove all doubt from your mind," Amal explained.

"Yeah sure, sounds easy," Zach said.

But he tried to focus and picture a minokawa. He really wanted to see one, but something in the back of his mind told him this was a waste of time. How could he believe something was possible when his whole life he'd been told it was impossible? As he continued to stand there feeling silly, thinking about a minokawa while attempting to push doubt from his mind, he heard Asha in the background cheering as she rode Sundara through the sky. Zach couldn't help but laugh at Asha's hoots, picturing her having the time of her life on that pegasus. In the middle of his thoughts, a shadow covered the hill. The warmth of the sun was gone. Zach opened his eyes and his mouth fell open. Flying toward him, enormous enough to block the sun, was exactly what he'd pictured. A minokawa! A silver eagle with the tail of a dragon soared through the sky. The magnificent beast landed and proudly towered over Zach. The feathers, which shimmered in the sun, resembled symmetrical sword blades that chimed slightly with the

93

shifting of its head. The bird-like creature huffed and focused on Zach. Its eyes were fierce, and Zach was mesmerized by his own reflection, which stared back at him on their silvery surface. Despite its ability to crush Zach in seconds, the great minokawa lowered its head to the ground and huffed out another breath. Considering passing out, Zach, wide-eyed, turned back to Amal, who laughed merrily at Zach's expression.

"Go on. You created it," Amal said.

Zach, speechless, took a deep breath and walked closer to the minokawa. He raised a hand and touched its feathers. The smaller feathers near its breast was the length of Zach's entire leg. The larger feathers were longer than Zach's entire body. Even though the minokawa was not hostile and was showing signs of submission, Zach's body shook nervously. If the creature wanted to, it could bite Zach's head off with one nip.

"Um, hello," Zach said.

The minokawa let out a gentle call that echoed through the hills. Zach covered his ears as the call reverberated through his eardrums.

"What will you name it?" Asha asked.

Zach hadn't realized Asha had landed behind him.

"Ha, I haven't thought of a name yet. Just trying not to be lunch. What's your name?" Zach said.

Even though the great bird didn't speak, the perfect name immediately came to him.

"Doragon? Is that a good name?"

The minokawa stood proudly again, shadowing him from the sun.

"Doragon it is then," Zach said, feeling noble for the first time in his life.

Doragon bowed to Zach and tilted its body sideways. His great beak came to a sharp point and spikes of feathers lined his back.

"I think he wants you to climb on," Asha said.

Zach was hoping for this but frightened nevertheless. He'd never even been on a plane before, much less flown a mythical creature across enchanted hills. As he wrapped his arms around a giant feather, he was surprised to find that even though the feathers were shiny and shaped like swords, they were flexible and easy to grasp. Once he'd secured himself to the feather, Doragon turned back over and stood proud again. Zach closed his eyes as the great creature took off over the hills. The sound of the feathers billowing in the wind reminded Zach of a garden filled with thousands of lightly clanging windchimes. As he felt Doragon settle into a glide, Zach slowly opened his eyes. The view was magnificent. In the distance, the Factum Mountains with their snowy peaks towered majestically. The Adventurus River flowed at the foot of the mountain range and wound about forests of green trees and fields. The bright blue sky was an endless canvas continuously speckled with puffs of white clouds and rays of silver yellow sunshine. Doragon continued to climb. It was exhilarating.

"WOOHOO!"

He'd never felt this free, and all thoughts of anxiety were gone from his mind. Gripping the base of the feathers with his legs, Zach waved his hands in the air. Doragon let out a short eagle cry and dipped. Zach clung to a feather the length of his body. Then Doragon twisted in the air and flew upside down. Feeling like his stomach had jumped into his chest, Zach held his breath and closed his eyes. When Doragon flew right side up again, Zach slowly peeked. He'd survived! He'd been completely upside down thousands of feet in the air and HE'D SURVIVED!

"Wow Doragon! WOW! Go, go, go!"

Unexpectedly Doragon jerked to the side and let out an ear piercing shriek. Zach bolted upright and looked around. In his peripheral vision, he saw a dark mass building in the sky. It looked like a boiling black cloud. He looked down at the hills and saw Amal pulling out his club as well as Asha mounting Sundara equipped with her bowshot. Unsure what to do, Zach burrowed into Doragon's feathers for stability. The great minokawa dipped and dived to avoid the growing dark mass that seemed to be following them. Zach peaked over a mound of feathers and saw Asha flying next to him.

"Wraaaaiiiithh!" she yelled.

Wraith?! Zach had no idea what a wraith was. Was it sent by Malum? He immediately felt a wave of dread.

The billowing cloud of smoke took the shape of a black and red cloak. Within its hood of darkness, two small, red slits peered out. The wraith let out a shriek. The evil chalkboard scratch sent chills up Zach's spine and had him almost letting go of Doragon to protect his ears. As the wraith chased them, Doragon did his best to outfly the monster. Asha followed close behind, trying to cut off the wraith. Amal bolted into the sky with the rocket power of his weapons and shot giant orbs at the black demon. He flipped and twisted, but the wraith dodged his efforts and continued after Zach and his mythical eagle. An overwhelming sense of despair grew in Zach's heart. The wraith grew larger. The hood alone looked as though it could consume an entire house in one swift motion. Doragon shrieked in pain as the wraith gained on them. Doragon began to dive, and Zach saw the feathers beneath him glitch as if the beautiful minokawa was disappearing. Panic rose in his chest as Zach became certain the wraith would capture them. He clung to the feather and closed his eyes. The wind beat against him, and the tears flew off his face. This was it. He was definitely going to die.

Within an instant, he felt like he wasn't holding onto anything anymore. He opened his eyes and looked for Doragon's feathers. The minokawa was barely there; he was almost invisible. Zach was free falling. The cold darkness of the wraith began to wrap around him. Gold and red orbs flew past him. Out of the corner of his eye, he saw Asha nearby, dipping up and down. She released her bowshot into the wraith to no avail. Zach clutched his arms around himself as his heart hammered in his chest. But just as he was beginning to pass out, the world around him disappeared, and he saw Asha. She was sitting next to him in the boat calmly saying, "Malum fills you with doubt. He's not you." Amal appeared behind her nodding in agreement. "He's not you."

An explosion of strength and awareness shot through Zach. This was Malum! He had to stand up to Malum. Zach's eyes shot open. He believed in Doragon, the awesome minokawa, once more. As he strengthened that belief, determined not to die, Doragon returned! Zach felt the plate-like feathers once again and grasped them quickly. The wraith jerked about, folded in on itself, and shrank in size. With another loud call, Doragon spun in the sky and headed straight for the receding black mist. The wraith shrieked and billowed away quickly. Zach thrust a fist into the air.

"Yeah!"

With the wraith out of sight, Doragon returned to the hill where Amal was locking his weapons into place and smiling proudly. Asha landed, speaking soothing words to Sundara. Doragon turned to the side gently. Zach let go, dropping to the ground.

"Thank you, Doragon. Thank you!" Zach said, hugging the creature.

Doragon bowed and with a clinking of his feathers, took flight straight into the sun. After a gentle headbutt with Asha, Sundara followed the great eagle into the sky.

"HOLY COW! Did you see that? That was the most amazing thing! What was that thing? What's a wraith?!" Zach was brimming with excitement.

"That was a wraith, Monkey Boy! You did it! Malum tried to stop you, but you did not let that evil monster win! No you did not!" Asha said.

Amal walked over and patted Zach on the back. Zach laughed and jumped around. Realizing his chest pocket was heavier than before, Zach reached in, expecting another magus. And he was right! This time he pulled out three magi. The third one read *Votum*.

"Ah," Amal said, "prayer. This is a special prayer, a wishful prayer. A prayer from the heart that reveals a great desire. Burra Din is grateful you shared your heart this day."

"Huh, this is a prayer?" Zach asked. He'd always thought of prayer as something boring, something memorized and recited without feeling. This was a new idea to him. Could he really pray about something he truly wanted? Well, here in Burra Din he did, and it seemed Burra Din listened.

After traveling through the Lumen Hills for hours, they decided to set up camp under a rock overhang jutting from one of the larger hills. Zach was thankful the grass was much more comfortable than the hard cave floor. He sat on his blanket and ate the soup Amal had boiled over the fire from the contents of his seemingly bottomless bag. Normally Zach didn't like soup, but today the soup was a great comfort. He was starving and coming down from the past two days of excitement. He slurped and realized that while adventuring was completely unpredictable and often dangerous, he was beginning to enjoy it. In less than 48 hours, he'd arrived in a new land; followed around a girl who he clearly annoyed; met a sorcerer; found out he was the chosen one; collected three enchanted waxy rocks; fought a giant serpent in a cave; a wolf with some type of vendetta and a wraith; fell over the side of a waterfall; and flew a magical creature. This was awesome! And stressful. He suddenly felt exhausted. But then a discomforting thought trickled into the back of his mind: Malum. He knew very little about his so-called enemy.

"So what's with Malum? Where'd he come from?" Zach asked.

Amal furrowed his brow as he concentrated on ladling more soup into Asha's bowl and said, "Malum is a mystery, really. Many stories exist regarding his creation; however, no one is quite sure."

"Mmmm, soup," Asha said quietly to herself.

"What are the stories?" Zach asked, rolling his eyes at Asha's oblivious demeanor.

"A smart choice, Zachariah. Understanding the enemy is vital to turning the tide of war," Amal said.

"Alwaysss imp . . . ortant to know your . . . enemy," Asha said with a full mouth.

Amal stroked his beard. "Ah yes, what I know should help you."

He pulled a small glass bottle from his bag and twisted off the stopper. Then he poured its contents into his hands and tossed them into the air above the fire. The sparkling material formed shapes and played out the story Amal shared.

"In the beginning of time, Burra Din and all worlds were part of an ultimate soul. One that contained the power to create or destroy anything. This soul was an omniscient soul, for it would instantly know the entire fate of its creations: past, present, and future. When the soul decided to create the universe and all that it entails, the soul was broken into pieces. These pieces became the worlds we see before us today and all the creatures in all the worlds. But there was something about these pieces of soul that made the creation even more fascinating. These pieces of soul—"

Sssssluurrrp. Sssslllluurrrp.

Amal paused. He and Zach looked at Asha. She was slurping the last bit of soup from her bowl.

"What?" Asha's eyes stared innocently over the bowl.

Amal continued, "These pieces of the ultimate soul had free will. Each piece harbored a portion of the ultimate soul within them, but could do with their lives as they wished. Now, the great soul preferred they do good and make the universes and worlds places of life and goodness. But not all souls did as they were expected. There was a group of them that were envious of the ultimate soul's power to create, so they conjoined and developed into the second most powerful soul. They were determined to absorb all souls in creation to become the most powerful and defeat the one ultimate creator."

"Okay, but wouldn't the evil souls that came together be more powerful since the, uh, good guy's soul is all broken up?" Zach asked.

"Ah, you would think so. But the power comes from what each living part does. If there are more good living parts in creation, then the ultimate soul remains powerful. But if the collection of evil souls begins to turn those souls, then the balance of good and evil shifts."

"So where does the massive evil viking come in?" Zach asked.

Amal, confused, tilted his head.

"Oh yeah, wrong world. Vikings are like extreme warriors with epic armor and weapons. So you guys don't have Vikings? That sucks," Zach said.

"We do not, but I want to hear more about these brave warriors. Are their weapons as formidable as my bowshot?" Asha asked.

"The Vikings would definitely want you on their team, Asha," Zach said.

Asha sat a little taller.

"But yeah, where does Malum come in?" Zach asked again.

"Ah, when the gifts were forgotten and evil began to infiltrate Burra Din more than ever, great battles occurred. The evil attacked outright and fortunately lost. But the evil did not disappear. The evil darkness of Burra Din rejoined in the form of an ancient warrior who was and still is connected to the darkness of all worlds. The tribes declared the evil warrior Malum and celebrated their victory and the shift of fortune to the side of good. After the four gifts were lost and the protectors were chosen, Malum returned. But this time the attacks were more subtle, whispering into the minds of creatures and people, slowly encouraging them to switch to a life of evil. You see, Zachariah, Malum must slowly turn the hearts of the good people of Burra Din before a full-out attack. He wants his power to grow. As such, we battle evil more personally than before. Malum creeps into our minds, giving our doubts power, such as you experienced in the cave and in the sky."

"But Malum attacked us with Fenrir, the wraith, the snake monster, I mean, Leviathan. That doesn't seem very subtle," Zach said.

"Yes, your arrival and finding of the magi forced evil's hand. Malum is more desperate now. If you discover the gifts and lead us to the prince, Malum's grasp over Burra Din comes to an end. Malum will still exist, but the prince is predicted to bring ultimate victory over all evil forever. Burra Din will be saved. And the cycle of salvation will spread through all the realms, all the worlds."

Amal's light show above the fire exploded into a tiny firework spectacle. One spark shot upward and exploded into a brilliant, sparkling star. Then one after another, more stars exploded. At this point, Asha had abandoned her bowl and had become completely engrossed in the story. She'd rested her chin on her hand and was smiling to herself. Her expression of wonder made it easy to see the reflection of the fireworks in her eyes. Suddenly embarrassed he was so enamored by Asha, Zach quickly shifted his gaze to Amal.

"So no pressure, huh," Zach said.

Amal laughed. Zach rested his head on the rock wall. Watching the fire, his eyelids grew heavy. And just before he drifted off to sleep, Zach felt the comforting warmth of optimism consume his mind. Zach felt like he could do just about anything with Asha and Amal by his side. Feeling kinda cheesy but enjoying it, Zach had found true friends for the first time.

. . .

Zach felt very cold. Shivering, he sat up, rubbing his eyes. It was still dark. He looked around. Amal and Asha had disappeared and the orb of fire was gone. Fear consumed him. He rubbed his eyes again. A fog settled over his vision. Nothing was clear. He couldn't focus. Panicking, he turned in all directions as his heart raced. He was just about to shout out for Asha when—

He woke up. But the nightmare wasn't over. When Zach opened his eyes, there wasn't fog this time but a black veil floating in front of him. The wraith! The creepy wraith had returned and locked its haunting gaze upon Zach. He glanced beside him, looking for his friends. Asha was stirring, and Amal was lying still. But his eyes were open! He winked at Zach. A wisp of relief that he wasn't alone calmed Zach's nerves.

The red slits in the hood narrowed as the wraith hissed, "Theeee maaagggiiii."

Zach crouched and clutched the magi in his pocket. Before he could respond, a ball of magic shot from Amal's club, knocking the wraith across the field. Asha jumped awake and whipped on her bowshot, which unfortunately was useless when fighting the wraith. Amal planted his feet in a warrior stance as he spun his weapons. They glowed, creating gold and red circles of light in the darkness. Zach scurried back a few feet to stand near Amal. He clutched his brightly glowing sword, Satya. Despite the darkness, the moonlight held steady, illuminating the wraith's whereabouts. The three travelers wielded their weapons, bracing for attack. To their surprise the wraith contracted back into a black ball. Asha let her bow down, and Amal let his club drop slightly. Zach, still completely freaked out, held his sword steady.

Suddenly the small black ball started humming. It hummed so loudly, the travelers had to choose whether to hold their weapons or cover their ears. When the humming reached a deafening level, the small black ball exploded, and the wraith reappeared. The swirling black fog consumed the entire field. Before they had a chance to stop it, the wraith shot between Zach and his friends, dividing them. The wraith circled Zach and created a massive black cyclone around him. Amal and Asha tried to fight the increasing winds but were blown back. The world around them erupted into chaos. Trees were pulled from their roots, the grasses whipped, and the pools of water trembled. Within the cyclone, Zach froze, overwhelmed by fear. He heard the chaos around him but no wind blew inside the black tornado. He tried to look through the swirling wall, but all he could see was more darkness. He'd been separated from his friends. The cyclone started to shake and images of Zach's life played out before him against the cloud of the wraith. The moments of his life the wraith had chosen to replay were some of the worst moments Zach had ever experienced: his friends in second grade laughing at his love for reading, the day in sixth grade he'd cried in his room and promised to change everything about himself to fit in, and of course the day his parents died.

Zach watched himself grasping his mother's hand and sobbing as she spoke her last words to him. He had never spoken a word about this to anyone. His father had died immediately in the car accident, but his mother had held on. The entire scene was replaying right in front of him. Zach was horrified. He watched as his mother cried out Zach's name as the first responders pulled her from the vehicle. He watched himself being rushed to the hospital. He tried to close his eyes. Reliving this was pure torture. But he couldn't. Even when he shut his eyes, the vision of himself walking into that hospital room remained. With a tightening in his chest, he watched the events unfold.

A short, kind nurse guided Zachariah gently to his mother's side. The room was filled with beeping monitors and tubes that traveled in and out of her. Zach immediately wanted to run away, and he almost had when he heard his name. Zach's heart broke at the sight of his mother's twinkling eyes beneath her frail and bruised body. And there, in the dark unfamiliar hospital room, he had said goodbye to his mother as he absorbed the loss of his father. His heart had been completely torn from his chest that day. And now he was being forced to relive it. Despair clutched his heart. Zach felt weak. His knees buckled, and he fell to the ground. He no longer crouched in a cyclone. It seemed the wraith wrapped around him in a spherical shape, consuming every inch of him. Zach couldn't breathe. His heart was racing again. This was worse than the dream. He wanted to go back to sleep, he wanted to go home, he wanted to be with his friends again.

Wait! My friends!

Zach, eyes closed, tried to escape the frightening scenes around him. He thought of Asha and Amal. He thought of their help. He thought of everything they'd been through. Zach pictured himself outrunning Fenrir, defeating the serpent, soaring through the sky on Doragon, watching Asha unleash her bowshot, hearing Amal's laugh, and then he thought of Father Joe. He thought of how Father Joe was there for him. Zach imagined him laughing and talking to parishioners.

Suddenly Zach felt a small rise of power and the twisting in his chest subsided. He could do this! He could take down the wraith himself. No! Not himself but with his friends. They weren't in the cyclone with him physically, but just thinking of them made him stronger. Opening his eyes, Zach stood tall and unsheathed his sword. Satya illuminated. He lifted the glass blade high in the air and let out a loud yell as he drove his glowing sword into the dark mass. Surprisingly, the sword felt as though it hit something hard despite the ghost-like nature of the wraith. He heard a loud shrieking but did not relent. Zach pushed his sword further into the darkness. The thick matter thinned out and swirled more slowly. Zach pulled the sword back and stabbed at the wraith again. Finally, the wraith pulled away from Zach and drifted before him. It floated around chaotically like a popped balloon. When it was no bigger than a golf ball, the wraith disappeared into a burst of light. The winds stopped, and the world around Zach calmed once more. Immediately he searched for Amal and Asha. They came running from the nearby woods, jumping over fallen branches and debris. As they reached Zach, the three of them clasped hands and embraced. They were overjoyed to see each other. Asha machine-gunned Zach with questions.

"Monkey Boy, you defeated the wraith! I can't believe it! How'd you do it? Was it hard? How'd you figure it out?"

Zach laughed and Amal patted him on the shoulder.

"I'm proud of you, Zachariah. To defeat a wraith is no small feat. You must have had great hope in your heart."

"Well, I couldn't have done it without you," Zach said.

At that the magi glowed. Zach pulled the chunks of wax from his pocket and held them in his hand. The three magi began to melt right in his palm.

"What's happening?!" Asha asked.

Amal looked down at Zach with pride and a bit of sadness.

"What is it?" Zach asked.

"I must leave you here, Zachariah," Amal said.

"What?! No!" Asha cried.

"My dear Asha, you will do well without me. You both must continue on and find the other protectors in the three lands. They will help you. They will help you defeat Malum. I know you can. Collect the magi, restore the gifts. I have hope," Amal said.

And with that Amal's arms spread wide and streaks of light shot out from his body. A content look washed over Amal's friendly face as he became one solid beam of light. The beam of red and gold floated above Asha and Zach. The magi in Zach's hand melted together and formed one cylinder of wax. The three engravings disappeared. Zach looked at Asha. They both watched as Amal's spirit floated above them. Slowly a wick formed within the wax. The beam of light shot down into Zach's hand, illuminating the newly formed deep purple candle for a brief moment. As the candle's glow receded, a new word appeared on its side: Spés. Just beneath the word was the tattoo marking, or symbol, of the Spésian people.

"The gift. I am with you," Amal said.

Zach looked at Asha.

With tears in her eyes, Asha said, "Hope."

PART TWO
THE LAND OF FIDEM

DOOR FOUR

PATIENTIA
PATIENCE IN THE LAND OF FIDEM

"You also must be patient. Keep your hopes high,
for the day of the Lord's coming is near."
James 5:8

Amal was gone. Zach knelt on the ground staring at the candle in his hands. The violet cylinder of wax was little consolation for the loss of his friend. He was silent. Asha stood next to him, tears streaming down her cheeks, clutching her bowshot strap. She was a silent crier, but Zach couldn't bear watching the tears fall from her eyes. All he could think about was how unfair this was. They'd done it. They'd defeated the wraith and done exactly as Burra Din had desired. Then as a reward the magi had melted together into one giant piece of wax that looked like a candle—a candle! How was a candle going to help? Then to top it all off Amal had disappeared and floated inside it. How the heck was that supposed to help him defeat a delusional, ancient, evil Viking with a vampire fashion complex? "This sucks," Zach thought. They had been much better off with Amal. Zach was just starting to get the hang of this.

"He's not gone," Asha said as she knelt next to him.

111

Zach looked up at her.

"He's not," Asha said, helping him up. "We can do this."

"How Asha? How on earth—or whatever—" He threw his hands in the air, clutching the candle. "How can we possibly do this without Amal?! It's not fair! Why did he have to go? Is he dead? Where'd he go? Did he know he was going to leave? Why didn't he tell us?!"

Asha shook her head.

"What?" Zach asked, irritation rising.

"Zach, I do not know how to answer any of those questions. But whatever happened must have been right. Amal was smiling. He was proud, Zach. He was proud of you. You did it. And that in your hand is the first key to saving Burra Din. Can you not feel it?"

Feel it?! Zach didn't feel anything but hurt and sadness. He felt betrayed. He'd gotten close to Amal, and then Amal had just disappeared. This was exactly why he wanted to live the hermit life. How could he possibly be happy about some candle in his hand? He'd never felt comfortable letting out his feelings before, but he couldn't stop himself.

"This?! This Asha?! How on earth can this help? It's a candle! Yeah, right. The next time Fenrir shows up, I'll just wave this in his face. I'm sure that will keep him from swallowing me whole." Zach waved the candle in front of her face and said in a mocking tone, "Oh yeah—Oh hi, Fenrir! What's that? You want to bite my face off. Oh, you can't because I have this candle!"

Asha's tears dried up and her jaw set. She'd had enough. Within seconds, she unleashed her bowshot, wrapped its rope around Zach's legs and pulled him down. He landed hard on his back, and the candle flew into the air. Asha caught it with one hand and held it over his face. Zach looked up at her from the ground.

"Zach, I have no idea what this candle does. But I know it is a gift, and if you want to get home and save Burra Din—I still believe this mission should have been given to a great warrior—then get up off your butt and stop whining like a baby or I'm going to start calling you far worse names than Monkey Boy. Now, get up!"

Taken by surprise and slightly embarrassed he'd lost his cool in front of Asha, Zach got up. His cheeks flushed with hurt pride. He rolled his eyes at her and silently walked over to pick up his pack.

"Where then? Where do we go now, Asha?"

"I do not know. But we need to get on the move before Fenrir catches up with us."

Zach grabbed the candle from Asha and put it in his bag. He was so angry and distracted by their argument, he didn't notice the glow of the candle as he shoved it in the side pocket.

"What's the deal with this Fenrir anyway? Why does he follow us? Why doesn't he just give up? I mean, it's not like he's the only creature Malum's sent after us."

"Actually, he probably is," Asha said.

"What? Where did all those other things come from?"

"Well, Fenrir is the loyal servant of Malum. The others work to destroy good in the world but are only a part of the darkness. They act on their own, I understand. But Malum rewards Fenrir."

"So he's like a pet?" Zach asked.

"What is a pet?"

"An animal that lives with you that you take care of."

"Hm, are not all animals pets then? You take care of all animals, do you not?"

"I don't know. I don't like cats," Zach said, fiddling with the strap of his pack.

Asha grunted and readjusted her bowshot. And the two travelers hiked together along the Lumen Hills comfortably discussing the idea of a pet.

After hiking south for what seemed like hours, Zach finally asked, "Where exactly are we headed?"

"Well, Amal said we must look for other protectors, which means we must leave the Land of Spés and find another land. The Land of Fidem and Vera, the Earth Defender, is just south of here. I really should have spent more time studying maps with my maata," Asha said.

"How much longer until we're out of the Lumen Hills?" Zach asked, unsure whether he could climb one more steep slope.

"We need to reach the river as soon as possible. The river will lead us to the Land of Fidem. And seeing as we only have two legs each, walking seems to be the only way of getting there. Unless you have any other bright ideas, Monkey Boy."

Zach stopped walking and grinned mischievously at Asha. Realizing what Zach had in mind, Asha bolted to the top of the hill and hooted. She held out her arms and within seconds Sundara returned. Zach followed suit and watched as Doragon blocked the sun with his massive body. Zach and Asha climbed onto the two creatures and bolted into the sky. Sundara coursed around Doragon, weaving in and out of his path as the pegasus was merely a tenth of his size. Doragon huffed in delight as he made wide circles and twirled upside down. Asha and Zach cheered on their creatures as they played in and out of the clouds. Once they reached the border of the Lumen Hills, the creatures landed near the Adventurus River's edge.

"Why can't they go any further?" Zach asked.

"The hills' magic created them. They can only exist within the hills," Asha said, stroking Sundara's mane and giving her a hug.

Zach patted Doragon on the side and when Doragon lowered his head, Zach said, "Thanks."

The two creatures flew into the endless blue sky. Zach turned and looked upon the river once again. It was wider, slower, and clearer than before. They could hear the great waterfall in the distance. Trying to think ahead, Zach began searching for large logs. He wanted to make a raft. Heck, if Huckleberry Finn could figure out how to construct a raft out of logs, he could too. Noticing one sticking half out of the water, Zach began to pull at the dead piece of wood.

"Why are you pulling at that log?" Asha asked.

"I'm going to use this log to make a raft," Zach said.

"Oh, that is an idea. How many logs do you need?"

"I'm not really sure. I've never done this before."

He pulled harder at the log. He clenched his teeth, held his breath, and tugged. It seemed to be stuck in the mud.

"Would ya give me a hand?" he asked.

Asha shrugged and walked over to help him. After pulling with all their might, the log finally came free, sending chunks of gray river silt into the air. Asha had stepped back just in time, but Zach was covered in the slimy mud.

"This is a messy process," Asha said, holding back a giggle.

"Yeah," Zach said frustrated and sweaty, wiping the mud from his eyes. "Do you have any other suggestions?"

Asha brushed a small bit of mud off her sleeve. "We could just cross the river downstream. There."

Zach squinted and saw a bridge.

"Asha! If you knew that bridge was down there, why didn't you say anything?" Zach asked.

"You were determined to make that raft," Asha said.

"Seriously?" Zach asked.

Asha laughed, letting out a cackle and snort. Zach couldn't help but chuckle himself. It was impossible not to laugh when Asha snorted.

"You're impossible," he said as he knelt down, washing off his face and hands in the water.

"Me?! Oh yes, I am the difficult one," Asha said as she started toward the bridge.

Zach followed close behind.

As soon as the travelers had crossed the large wooden bridge, a heavy wind picked up. The wind was so strong Asha and Zach could barely walk in a straight line. If they wanted to talk to each other, they had to yell. After steadying himself the best he could, Zach reached for Asha and pulled her close.

"Wheeerrreee aaarrrre weeee?"

"Veeellloooxx Plaaaiiinnnss innnn thhhhheeee Lllaaanndd offf Fiiiddddeemmm," Asha said over the roar of the wind.

Getting an idea, Zach held up a finger and struggled to pull a rope out of his bag. Remembering a trick from rock climbing with his dad, Zach tied the rope around his waist and held it up. Asha grabbed the rope and wrapped it around her waist, tying it tight. Then Zach walked in front as Asha held on to his shoulder, guiding him. They headed south, looking for shelter from the wind. After walking for half the day, Zach was about to give up and suggest they head back to the river when Asha pointed to a small flower patch. It was the strangest thing. The winds violently whipped around them, and the tall grasses of the plains danced energetically. However, the flower patch stood quiet and almost still. Just a slight breeze blew through the beautiful, multicolored flowers like a breath of fresh air. Asha pointed in that direction.

As they got closer to the football field–sized flower patch surrounded by grassy plains, the wind blew even more violently.

But the full hundred yards of flowers swayed gently as if behind a wall of glass. And just before they reached the garden, they saw a woman standing in the middle of the field, her back to them. She stood like a deer, sensing something in her presence. Slowly she turned, noticing the two of them. They froze. But when they stopped moving the wind pushed them North, and they slid across the field slowly. The woman walked closer to the garden's edge, motioning them to enter the field. Asha started walking toward her. But Zach stood still. The rope between them tightened. Zach gave Asha a look that said, "We don't know her." Asha rolled her eyes and pulled Zach along.

As soon as Zach dropped one foot in the garden, a gentle breeze replaced the thrashing violent wind. Zach could hear again and noticed the large field was full not only of flowers but also of small honey bees that buzzed about collecting nectar. Though Zach and Asha's presence didn't alarm the honeybees, they took careful, slow steps regardless. Taken aback suddenly, Zach found the woman who'd been standing yards away was now right next to them. She reminded him of a gentler Amal. She had the softest caramel skin he'd ever seen and flowing brown hair that came down to her waist. Her large, brown eyes were gentle and kind. And in her hand she twirled a rose that she carefully and expertly clasped between thorns. This had to be a protector, he thought to himself. She was beautiful.

"Hello," the woman said.

"Hello," Zach said with a goofy look on his face.

Asha gave Zach a look as if to say, "Why are you acting like that?"

"Are you friends of Amal?" the woman asked.

Zach and Asha looked surprised.

"How do you know Amal?" Asha asked.

"You must be Asha," the protector said.

She bent over to caress a small purple tulip. In doing so, she coaxed a tiny matching butterfly from its resting place. They watched as it danced across the field of flowers and landed on another violet flower. The woman began to walk slowly among her flowers. Asha and Zach followed her.

"These are my charges," she said as she motioned to the field of flowers. "I am the protector of the Land of Fidem. I am Vera."

She stopped and turned to them. Her beautiful red lips spread wide in a wise yet childlike grin. Zach couldn't stop staring. When she made eye contact with him, his cheeks flushed and he quickly looked down at his feet. Vera looked back over her field.

"Miss, um, I mean, Vera, what's *Fidem* mean?" Zach asked, remembering that the candle in his bag was named Spés. That could only mean one thing. The next three magi had to form a candle named Fidem, right?

"Ah, I could tell you, young Zachariah, but you must find the meaning yourself," Vera said.

"Does it not mean 'belief,' or something like that?" Asha asked.

Vera laughed quietly at Asha's persistence and impatience. "Yes, something like that."

Vera turned and began to walk slowly away again. Her long, light-blue dress billowed in the wind. As she pulled her flowing hair over her shoulder, Zach noticed a mark just beneath her ear on the left side of her neck. The tattoo looked just like Amal's and Asha's mark, only turned to the right.

"Vera, where did Amal go?" Asha asked.

Vera's face suddenly grew serious and her eyes became watery. "I'm sure you two are quite hungry and in need of rest. Let us go to my home in the garden, and we shall discuss things further."

As she turned around, Zach looked at Asha who shrugged.

They walked quietly to the edge of the field. Vera turned and looked at Zach as if expecting something. Zach averted his gaze. He had no idea what she wanted him to do. Even though he knew she was good, there was something more mysterious about Vera. Amal was optimistic and straightforward, with a bright sparkling light in his eyes. Vera, on the other hand, was quiet, with a current of gentleness flowing through her. It was almost as if she knew the future or had an idea the future was good. She was extremely content.

"Zachariah, are you ready?" Vera asked.

"Ready for what?" he asked cautiously.

"Whaaaat are we waiting for?" Asha asked.

"Zachariah," Vera replied.

Zach, surprised, shook his head.

"Zachariah, are you sure you are ready? Think about your journey. Are you ready to continue your adventure?" Vera asked.

Zach contemplated what she said. He was nervous but definitely ready to get going.

"Yes."

Behind Vera, a door appeared. This door had the word *Patientia* carved on the front. Turning, Vera gestured for Zach to lead the way. He carefully walked forward. The door was right on the edge of the garden. He reached for the doorknob, stopped, and checked that Asha and Vera were behind him. Then he turned the knob and pulled the door open.

When they arrived on the other side, Zach and Asha found themselves in the most beautiful garden they'd ever seen. Flowers went on for miles, and flowering trees stood like shepherds protecting a colorful flock of symbiotic vegetation. Mesmerized, they followed Vera and watched as the flowers leaned away, creating a path for her. At first Zach and Asha couldn't see Vera's house. However, once they were almost face to face with the front door, they realized her house was in the earth. The enchanted field of flowers had small, sloping hills. Vera's house was built within the largest of these hills. The roof was covered in flowers, and little windows poked out of the green grass. The wooden door was unique. It was shaped like a rose, and the details were carved into its face. At the center of the door was a large iron knocker that resembled the tattoo on Vera's neck.

As she opened the door, the plants around her house burst with energy. It was almost as if the plants were her pets, and they were happy she'd come home. Vera entered the house with Zach and Asha closely behind. Once they were inside, the magic of the land was even more obvious. Intricate patterns of green vines held up the walls of the house. The wooden beams accented the vegetation, and every so often a little yellow or blue flower emerged. Vera's kitchen table was circular with rose patterns all over it. In the center, where one would normally find a vase, a vine curled up the legs of the table and poked through a hole where blooms of roses erupted.

"Welcome to the Gardens of Gratia. Come now, make yourselves at home," Vera said as she walked to the kitchen counter.

Asha and Zach walked over to the table, and before they could pull the chairs out to sit, the chairs moved. Zach looked up at Asha and then down again at their seats. The vines were pulling the chairs out for them! They carefully sat down, and the vines pushed their chairs in gently. Vera returned to the table with an intricate teapot and three cups. The tea set was white and blue porcelain, with little cups shaped like tulips. From across the table a small vine placed a porcelain plate of what looked like flower-shaped sugar cookies with purple icing in front of them. Zach was starving and snatched one quickly.

"Please tell us what happened to Amal," Asha said as everyone settled.

Zach felt a lump in his throat. He slowly set his cookie back down and tried to swallow the bite in his mouth.

"Yes, I am sure you are both very concerned and miss him terribly," Vera said.

Tears threatened the corners of Asha's eyes, and Zach set a hand on her shoulder.

Vera continued, "Burra Din chose us as protectors, and the time is coming when Burra Din will no longer need our protection. Zachariah's arrival has proven that."

"It's my fault?" Zach asked.

"No, my dear. Not your fault. It is a wondrous thing, an awesome thing. Burra Din's creatures need reminding of the world's ancient gifts, and it is your job to reveal them. However, once these gifts are revealed, a prince will come who will save Burra Din for all eternity by ruling through compassion and grace. Protectors will no longer be necessary."

Zach remembered the candle in his bag. He reached into his pack and pulled it out. He handed the candle to Vera. Her eyes grew wide as she clasped the rustic violet candle. She drew it close to her and read its inscription. Her eyes filled with tears.

"Oh, Amal," she said tenderly, "it is beautiful. Zachariah, your presence in Burra Din has started a chain reaction of events that have been foretold in the—"

"Prophecy," Zach interrupted, rolling his eyes. He'd heard this before and was becoming frustrated. He wanted to bring Amal back. He didn't want to watch Asha suffer; he didn't want to suffer.

"Can we bring him back, then? Isn't there some magic to bring him back? He turned into light and then the light went into, well, that." Zach pointed to the candle. "What is it? Is it a gift?"

Vera handed Zach the candle again and said, "It is. Yes, the gift of hope, and it is your job to keep it safe until you discover the others. You discovered the first three magi. They have formed to make the first gift, hope, or Spés."

Zach couldn't understand how the candle was a gift of hope.

"Amal will return," Vera finally said. "Actually, he has never left."

Asha looked up at Vera, wiping away her tears. She hadn't wanted anyone to see her crying.

"What do you mean?" Asha asked.

"Amal is always with you. His spirit united with the gift of hope from the land he was destined to protect. All will be well in the end."

Asha seemed to agree with Vera but Zach wasn't convinced.

With a snarky glare, he asked, "We only have one of these and a lot more to go. How do you know 'all will be well'?"

"Zachariah, can you see into the future?" Vera asked.

"No."

"I cannot see into the future any more than you can," she said.

"Exactly! So how do you know it's going to be okay? Without Amal, we can't defend ourselves, we can't—"

Zach stopped as the house shook. He looked around and then up at Vera. She had a concerned look on her face, one of sorrow. Zach was pretty sure her mood affected the environment around her. Great, he thought. He didn't want to see what happened if she got angry.

"Zachariah, I understand you suffer. Losing Amal is difficult. But suffering and loss are a part of life. Nothing remains forever. And worry will not change what comes to pass. If you do not know the future, is it better to assume the worst and spend your life anxious, dwelling on suffering? Or to hope and truly believe in the ultimate outcome? For then your days are full of contentment.

For what can you do to prevent the future from coming? It will come, will it not?"

Zach sat silently and looked down at his hands. He'd spent the majority of his life worrying about what people thought of him and how he could prevent bad things from happening. But bad things still happened.

"Do not be too hard on yourself, Zachariah," Vera said. "It is natural to fear the unknown. But to hope—" Vera paused as Zach and Asha looked at her "—is courageous! Hoping for a brighter future is the first step. You should be very proud. Come now, let me show you something."

Zach and Asha followed Vera to an oval picture window. They looked out at her beautiful land as she said, "This is only part of the world I protect. However, you are welcome to stay here and help me tend to the gardens while we wait to discover the next step in your journey."

"Wait, you don't know where we're supposed to go?" Zach asked.

"Amal did not know either, Zach," Asha reminded him. "We had a magus by then, remember?"

"Yeah, but you're a protector. Don't you have any clues or anything?" Zach asked.

Vera paused and looked out among her garden. "You may stay here until Burra Din believes you are ready. You will know when it is time."

Zach wasn't sure he liked Vera. Amal was happy and seemed to have answers for him. Well, okay, not really answers, but at least some kind of guidance. Vera, while gentle and beautiful, was mysterious and didn't seem to be in a rush to do anything. Zach just wanted to get on with it. He didn't want to wait around any longer. He wanted to get the supplies they needed, rest, and head out. Not knowing where they'd go or when they'd go was like torture for him.

"Zach," Asha said.

"Huh?" Zach asked, realizing they'd had a full discussion while he was thinking.

"You're shaking the floor," Asha said.

Zach looked down. He'd been bouncing the heel of his foot up and down the whole time. It increased as the intensity of his thoughts increased. He remembered his mom saying the same thing to him when they'd gone out to eat one night after he'd gotten three A's on his report card.

"Vera requested we help her in the garden while we wait," Asha said.

"Oh, um, yeah, I guess," Zach said, shrugging defensively. He really didn't want to help in the garden. He wanted to fight a beast or do something that felt like he was truly saving Burra Din. Amal's world had been a series of extreme events: boom, boom, boom! Zach didn't like the idea of slowing down, having time to think.

"That's wonderful," Vera said. "You may stay here with me and sleep in the library."

Vera gestured to a room off the side of the picture window. The cozy space was filled with bookshelves made of vines and roots. There was a small round window and flowers poking out between crevices. As the vines came to life, they reformed to create cots on the side of the room. Then roots slowly traveled through a side door, laying pillows and blankets on the cots. Zach looked back at Vera, wondering if she was controlling the plant-life. But Vera maintained her calm demeanor as the vines and roots settled back into the house once more.

"Many thanks to you, Vera," Asha said, walking into the transformed room and setting her bowshot on the cot.

"Thanks," Zach said, brooding.

"You are very welcome," Vera said. "We will soon discover what Burra Din has in mind for our Zachariah."

For the next few days, Zach and Asha spent each moment as Vera did. They woke early to the sound of birds flitting around the windows at sunrise, had a meager breakfast of honey and toast, and then made their way to the gardens outside Vera's house. They gently trimmed, planted, and watered according to Vera's instructions. Vera would disappear for hours throughout the day, explaining she had to tend to the gardens in other parts of the Land of Fidem. Zach and Asha weren't exactly sure how she got there, as they never saw her leave or arrive. She just seemed to disappear and reappear. At the end of each day, Zach and Asha were usually covered with dirt and would take showers where the amount and temperature of the water was dictated by a hovering vine. It was not generous, but afterward Zach felt clean enough. He would have given anything to stand in the shower longer. His muscles were sore from hauling wheel-barrel loads of soil back and forth. The last time he'd done manual labor even close to this was when he'd helped his dad spread mulch in his mom's flower beds. The day hadn't been so bad. He and his dad had debated the best rock bands and laughed as his mom went on a rant about wearing sunscreen and hats outside. But she'd gotten the last laugh. They'd gone in at the end of the day completely sunburnt. Memories like these flooded his mind every day in Vera's garden.

In the evenings, they would enjoy a hearty stew made from the vegetables they'd harvested, tell stories, and go to bed. Well, Asha and Vera told stories. Zach would usually stay silent. He didn't like how the garden reminded him of his parents. He didn't like dwelling on the memories. And he felt like they were wasting their time. So Zach brooded. But no matter how much he brooded, the answers did not come. This went on for almost two weeks. Then one day, while Zach and Asha were watering the flowers just outside the front door of Vera's cottage, they heard a quiet voice.

"Hello."

Zach and Asha turned to find a small boy standing directly behind them. He looked similar to Vera in that he had a gentle demeanor and soft, beautiful dark skin. Once again, Zach glanced at his ears—no points. Zach was certain someone in this world had to be an elf.

"Hello, what do you want?" Asha asked bluntly.

The boy jumped, and Zach stepped closer. Clearly, Asha was scaring him. She wasn't the warmest creature.

"Hey little man, it's okay. You lookin' for Vera?" Zach asked.

The boy looked down at his feet. When he looked back up, his eyes were full of tears.

"Way to go Asha, you made him cry," Zach said.

Asha gave Zach a dirty look but shrugged her shoulders.

Zach wasn't sure what to do. As he opened his mouth to say something, Vera appeared by his side.

"Oh, my poor Barii, what's the matter?" Vera asked.

Barii ran to Vera and wrapped his arms around her. She knelt down and lifted his chin saying, "Oh, oh, oh, my sweet child, come inside. It will be alright." Vera led the boy into the front door. "Asha and Zach, come along with us."

Once Vera calmed the boy down with some warm tea, she asked him once again, "Barii, what is wrong, my sweet child?"

The boy looked up at her with big watery eyes and said, "Maata is sick. I cannot help her. Can you help me?"

"Yes, explain what is the matter," she said, taking one of his hands.

"She coughs all night. It wakes me up. She shakes in the night. Pita is hunting and does not know she is sick. I do not know when he will be back. I told her I was coming here. I told her I would get help. Can you help me?" Barii pleaded. Tears streamed down his cheeks as he tried to control his sobs.

"Does she have a fever?" Vera asked as she walked around putting ingredients into a small container.

"Yes, she is very sweaty, Vera. She's so sick. So sick," Barii said.

Zach, feeling sorry for the little boy, scooted closer to him. A memory of his mother in the hospital bed resurfaced. Zach felt tears stinging his eyes.

"I will make the medicine immediately, my love," Vera said.

Zach, suddenly feeling overwhelmed with compassion for the little boy who looked no older than six, said, "I had to sit by my mom when she, um, when she was sick too."

He didn't want to explain the whole story to Barii. He told himself it was because he didn't want to scare the little guy. Barii looked up at Zach, wiping his eyes.

"Do you like music? When I was your age, my mom—or maata—and I would rock out, or um, sing in the car," Zach said.

Barii perked up. "Yes! I sing to my maata. She loves it when we sing."

"Do you play an instrument?" Zach asked, trying to keep Barii's mind off his mother.

"Yes, I play the atenteben!" Barii said, wiping his cheeks.

Zach had never heard of that instrument before. But when the little boy pretended to play it with his fingers, Zach thought of a flute or clarinet immediately.

"That's sick. I play the drums. We could start a group. Hey Asha, you sing?" Zach asked.

Asha gave Zach a disgusted look. Zach laughed.

Barii looked confused and said, "My atenteben is not sick. My maata is sick."

Zach grimaced at his own choice of words. "Oh, I didn't mean that. When something is, uh, exciting or, uh, impressive, people say 'that's sick' in my world."

"That is confusing," Asha said.

Zach shook his head.

"That's sick," Barii said quietly to himself, letting out a little giggle. But his smile faded quickly as he said, "Did your maata get better?"

Zach had hoped Barii wouldn't ask that. He was trying to figure out a way to explain what happened to his mom without scaring Barii when Vera said, "Here now, this medicine should help your maata. Mix the medicine with warm water and have her drink it three times a day. It is from the garden and is fresh. It will help her rest."

The little boy jumped from the chair and hugged Vera.

"Will my maata get better?" Barri asked.

Vera paused, knelt beside the boy, "Burra Din will take great care of your maata. All will be well in the end."

Uncertain but happy to have the medicine, the boy headed out the front door.

"Barii!" Vera called after him.

Barii turned around.

"I shall send you home," Vera said.

Zach and Asha followed as Vera guided Barii to a small flower in the corner of her garden. It was an exotic flower of many different colors. Zach thought of his tie-dyed t-shirts as Vera handed Barii a petal.

"Think of home, Barii," Vera said.

Barii closed his eyes, and Vera placed the petal in his palm. Within seconds, Barii, the medicine, and the petal were gone.

"That's sick," Asha said slyly.

Zach laughed. Then looking at Vera, Zach said, "Is that how you travel?"

Vera nodded, folded her hands, and walked back to her cottage. An uneasy feeling had Zach contemplating another question.

"Vera," Zach asked, "do you really believe that Burra Din will take care of Barii's mom? What if she doesn't get any better?"

Vera stopped walking and turned to Zach. With watery eyes, she spoke gently, "I tend to the garden. It heals people and gives them light in the dark. When a flower or herb dies, it does not hurt the garden, and it is not fully removed. The dead plants become nutrients for the living plants, giving them the energy to thrive. Burra Din takes care of us the way I tend the garden. Suffering and change is essential to the beauty of life. Burra Din will take care of Barii and his maata. Burra Din will prevail."

Zach, worried he'd offended her, followed Vera silently back to the cottage. Something she'd said had triggered a realization within Zach's mind. He felt something he hadn't felt in a while. He felt content. Watching Vera use the plants to create medicine gave Zach hope for the boy and his mom. He realized now that Vera's garden was essential to the Land of Fidem, and while it wasn't an epic battle or wild adventure, he was perfectly happy helping her provide hope for the people. Now when he dug in the dirt as sweat dripped down his forehead, he would think of Barii and understand the importance of his work. Zach may not have been able to save his own parents, but he could help here. He also really wanted to believe that no matter what happened, Burra Din would take care of the good people. And if this was where Burra Din wanted him, he would wait. It annoyed him.

But he would wait. And in that moment of acceptance, Zach felt something he hadn't felt in a while, a small weight in his chest pocket. Surprised, he pulled out the purple piece of wax engraved with Vera's triangular tattoo and the word: *Patientia*.

DOOR FIVE

HUMILIS
HUMILITY IN THE LAND OF FIDEM

"For all those who exalt themselves will be humbled,
and those who humble themselves will be exalted."
Luke 14:11

Vera, Zach, and Asha sat at the table staring at the magus, the ominous piece of purple wax.

"I am very grateful you discovered the magus in the gardens. This is the first of the Land of Fidem. You collected three in Spés before a gift appeared. Now you have the first of my lands. Burra Din must believe you are ready," Vera said. "When you received the magus, was any information revealed?"

Zach was so excited he'd discovered the next magus, he hadn't even thought of that. His shoulders dropped.

"No, it didn't," he said. Thinking over his time in the gardens, Zach shrugged. "It's okay. I'm sure we'll figure it out."

Zach had barely gotten the last word out of his mouth when a beam of light ripped through the atmosphere and another door appeared. The word *Humilis* was carved beautifully across the top of the door.

"Seems we are ready," Asha said.

Zach jumped up, excited to finally be on his way. He and Asha packed their bags as Vera grabbed her high-collared coat and flower print bag. Initially Zach hadn't been sure he liked Vera, but regardless he was relieved she was coming along. Seeing her in action when helping Barii gave Zach a sense of security. The three of them stood in front of the glowing door, waiting.

"Ready?" Zach asked.

"Always," Asha replied.

Zach turned the knob, and light filled the room as the three travelers walked through the door.

Zach heard the rush of water before he'd even opened his eyes. Adventurus River? He found himself standing in a clearing near a large, shallow creek. Vera watched as Asha walked over to examine the body of water.

"This is Innoxius Stream," Vera said.

"We could just walk across it," Asha said. "It's shallow."

Asha grabbed a stick and poked around at the bottom of the stream.

"We may consider using the bridge up ahead," Vera said.

Asha's face fell a bit. Clearly, she would have found it more fun to ford the stream herself.

"Yeah, maybe this waxy rock has some answers," Zach said, pulling the magus out of his pocket and holding it in his palm. He concentrated on it. The wax sat cold and unmoving. He rolled it in his hand.

"Yep, I got nothin'," he said.

His eyebrows furrowed in frustration. How could he do his job of saving Burra Din when he didn't even know where to go? He knew he had to be patient, but he was feeling the pressure. The sadness in Barii's eyes, losing Amal, and experiencing the darkness lurking across Burra Din so far increased Zach's desire to help and help fast. He was starting to feel the journey was ultimately up to him. The magi arrived when *he* did something, the doors appeared after *he* did something, and the prophecy explained what *he* was expected to do. It was all up to him, right?

"Let us travel to Fides village. We may check on Barii and his mother," Vera suggested.

"That sounds good. Maybe if we head there, we will get a sign or something," he said.

Zach was also curious about Barii and his mother. They traveled along the bank of the stream and came to a simple wooden bridge. It was made of planks and didn't even have a railing. The stream itself wasn't very deep, so the bridge existed merely to keep travelers dry. Vera and Asha started to cross the bridge when suddenly Zach froze.

"Hey! Do you guys hear that?"

Before they could respond, Zach heard a low growl and a rumbling voice, "The magi! The gift! Give them to me!"

Asha spun around quickly and jumped next to Zach, wielding her bowshot. They looked into the trees near the stream and saw the massive black beast. Zach looked back at Vera, who slowly turned around. Her eyes glowed brightly, and Zach noticed their color was gone. They were now a pearly white. She looked terribly awesome as her hair blew in the wind. She trembled with power, and an aura of light illuminated her body. The ground quaked beneath them. Asha and Zach held their hands out to steady themselves. Zach knelt down. He not only felt the ground shaking but watched as the grass elongated, braiding itself into a rope, and slithered along the ground like a snake.

Fenrir lunged from the woods but immediately whipped back mid-air. Asha and Zach watched as a great rope of grass and branches wrapped around Fenrir's leg, pulling the beast into the woods. Fenrir clawed the ground, but he was no match for the power of the enchanted forest. Zach turned, realizing Vera was controlling the rope of grass. She was still standing on the bridge in a trance, eyes glazed over and wind whipping through her hair. Suddenly a bolt of power shot from Vera and into the ground. In an instant, the rope pulled Fenrir up by his hindlegs and whipped him in the air. The howling beast spun in circles and was hurled miles away. The fading howl blended in with the sounds of the forest shifting back to sleep. Asha and Zach stared at Vera, who was now standing on the bridge calmly, eyes returned to normal.

"I do not believe he will be a bother to us. Malum must be nervous, for Fenrir has not been seen in the Land of Fidem for many years. He must be kept from the village. Let us go," Vera turned to cross the bridge.

Zach stood wide-eyed. He was still in shock from the scene he'd just witnessed.

"Come along, Monkey Boy!" Asha said, prodding him.

Realizing he was being left behind, Zach rushed forward. They crossed the bridge and followed Vera into the treeline. The forest was full of thick brush and vibrantly green trees. They reminded Zach of the big oak tree right outside Father Joe's house. As they entered the forest, the vegetation moved once more, creating a welcoming pathway as Vera entered the woods. When they made it through the tunnel of branches, they came out on the other side to a bustling village. Zach was mesmerized by the sight. The variety of activity was almost overstimulating. The people of the Land of Fidem were of all shapes and sizes, similar to Vera and Barii. The homes were large and triangular. The sides of each roof came down to the ground and were lined with perfectly trimmed hedges and accents of flowers. Each home had an intricately decorated front door and a small balcony on the second floor. The houses were trimmed with woodwork that wrapped around their frames in a floral pattern. Memories of gingerbread houses filled Zach's mind. Only his family made their houses out of maple cookies because Zach never cared for gingerbread. Before they'd taken more than two steps into the village, a man wearing what looked like a fancy military uniform of black, silver, and gold welcomed them.

"Vera," he said in a booming voice, "it is lovely to see you!"

Zach couldn't help but be impressed at the man's demeanor. He was a large, round man with a great black beard and short black hair. Zach's eyes were immediately drawn to a large, intricate topaz bracelet that wound all the way up his arm.

"Hello, Eadrich! I hope everything is well with you and your family," Vera said.

"Yes, of course. And who is this with you?" Eadrich asked.

"This is Asha from the Land of Spés and Zachariah, who is new to Burra Din," Vera said.

Eadrich's jovial attitude faded slightly when he looked at Zach but returned when he approached Asha.

"My dear Asha, the hunter. Yes?" Eadrich asked.

"How do you know of me?" Asha asked.

"Ah, Barii told us tales of visitors to Vera's gardens," Eadrich said.

"It is good to hear his name," Vera interjected. "Is his maata well again?"

"Yes, she is better than before," Eadrich said.

"That is most wonderful news. We are on our way to visit her and Barii. I hear his pita is hunting. It seems the hunters have been gone for an unusually long period," Vera inquired. "The hunters are usually back by the end of this season, are they not?"

"Ah, you know how hunting goes. There is no telling how long it takes. Let us concentrate on this young man," Eadrich said, turning his heavy gaze on Zach.

"Yes, this is Zachariah," Vera said.

"News has traveled that the warrior of the prophecy has arrived," Eadrich said, studying Zach's face. "I suppose I see it in him as well."

Then giving Zach an appraising look, Eadrich bowed slightly.

"The prophecy describes a boy, Eadrich. One who will reveal the four gifts," Vera said.

"Ah, yes, of course! He looks most knowledgeable," Eadrich said.

Asha gave Zach a glance that said, "Something about this guy seemed off." Zach agreed. The guy was giving him an eerie feeling.

"Uh, thanks," Zach said.

"Come! We must celebrate your arrival. Follow me, and I will lead you to the great hall," Eadrich said.

Vera, Asha, and Zach followed Eadrich through the bustling marketplace where they were selling all sorts of goods. Zach saw colorful toys, elaborately decorated food, and an abundance of diverse clothing. He gazed over the different colors and materials as they passed. Then one particular stall caught his attention. It was a shop covered in topaz. When he made eye contact with the plump, rosy-cheeked shop owner, she held up beads, encouraging Zach to come closer. Zach felt awkward. He didn't want to ignore her, but he also needed to follow Vera. After a moment of hesitation, he thought a quick visit wouldn't hurt. He walked over to the stall. Without speaking, the lady placed the beads around his neck. Then she touched her heart.

"For you, the hero."

Surprised at being called a hero, Zach froze for a moment, blushed, and looked away. He concentrated on the topaz beads like they were the best gift he'd ever received.

136

"Thanks," he said.

"Now go!" the shopkeeper said pleasantly, waving him off.

Jogging quickly, Zach caught up with Asha and Vera. The more he thought of the shopkeeper's words the more Zach realized the shopkeeper was right. The woman had called him a hero and well, he technically was one. Feeling proud of his mission, Zach's normal walk turned into a slightly arrogant swagger. If these people believed in him, thought he was a hero, why shouldn't he be one?

Asha gave him a funny look.

"What?" Zach asked.

"Nothing," Asha said with narrowed eyes.

Zach felt like she was studying him.

When they got to the great hall, it was just that. A great hall. Shaped like the rest of the homes, the hall had intricate edging but no front wall. The front was completely open. Inside were rows of seats and an empty platform.

"We will celebrate your arrival tonight at a festival in your honor, Zachariah! Are you pleased?" Eadrich asked.

"Eadrich, that is not necessary," Vera said.

Zach, on the other hand, was enjoying the treatment. In the time it took them to walk up the steps of the hall, two beautiful young women had run by and given Zach what looked like pastries as well as kisses on the cheek.

"Huh?" he asked in a daze.

Asha rolled her eyes.

Realizing Eadrich was waiting for his response and ignoring Vera, Zach said through a mouthful of buttery pastry, "Yeeosh, that shounds (gulp) good."

"Excellent! It is decided!" Eadrich bellowed, walking to the corner of the hall and lifting a large mallet. He hit what looked like a huge, golden gong three times. After the third time, the village erupted into cheers, and Eadrich puffed his chest.

"Ah, the village is in agreement! The festival is tonight!" Eadrich said.

Amidst the cheering, they hadn't noticed Barii appear at Vera's side.

"Vera!" Barii said.

"Barii! What a joy to see you! How is your maata?" Vera asked. She leaned down and hugged the small boy.

Barii glanced at Eadrich, who gave the boy a stern look, and then Barii looked down at his feet.

"She is well," he said.

Vera studied Barii with concern, noticing the exchange between him and Eadrich.

"Vera, join Barii today. He will be tending the garden. Our crops have not been producing much as of late," Eadrich said.

"I must stay with Zachariah, I am afraid. We have important business to carry out per the prophecy," Vera said.

Barii opened his mouth and then closed it, noticing Eadrich's glare.

"Ah, yes, I understand. But do you not have time to tend to your people? Zachariah will be fine. Asha, the fierce hunter, is here to protect him. He shall be safe," Eadrich said, winking at Asha.

Asha responded with a suspicious glare.

"I'll be alright, Vera. These guys seem safe. They understand the prophecy," Zach said, wanting her to go for some reason.

"Exactly!" Eadrich boomed.

"Very well. I will return soon. Come now, Barii. Let us see these crops," Vera said.

As soon as Vera left, Eadrich clapped his hands and two men appeared.

"Ah, yes! Please take Asha to the armory. She will be perfectly pleased to see the advanced weapons we have created. Let her have her choice of any weapon she desires," Eadrich said.

"I have the greatest weapon of all. I mean no offense, Eadrich. But the Fideans are not known for weapons. My weapon is perfectly effective," Asha said, standing stoic next to Zach and patting her bowshot strap.

Zach felt his face flush. Asha was being rude and for some reason he cared.

"Asha, go," Zach said out of the side of his mouth.

Asha shook her head. "I will not go. My job is to protect you."

Eadrich let out a hearty laugh and said, "Yes, Asha! You would say such a thing—and right you are! But trust. We will tend to Zachariah. Now go! Pick out your weapon!"

Zach watched Asha whip Eadrich a look that said, "You don't know me." Then she looked imploringly at Zach. Zach hardened his facial expression.

"No," Asha said, "I will not go."

"Asha!" Zach said sharply, "This is MY mission. It is MY responsibility. You can't protect me. I have the—"

"Don't!" Asha yelled.

Eadrich's eyes grew wide, eager to hear what Zach had to say.

Zach was mad that Asha had cut him off mid-sentence. He was the chosen one, after all. She had to listen to him.

"Go, Asha! I don't need you," Zach demanded. He wasn't really even sure why he felt so angry at her.

"You are not yourself, Zach."

Zach scoffed at her. He felt Eadrich's hand on his shoulder and grew stronger. He was sick of Asha pushing him around and acting like he was an idiot. He wasn't an idiot. No! He was almost a man in his world and he was the hero of this world.

"Go, now!" Zach finally yelled.

But Asha didn't move. She planted her feet stubbornly. With a grunt from Eadrich, the two men placed their hands on her shoulders. Zach watched as Asha's eyes inflamed with rage. Her shoulders heaved as the guards increased their grip. Zach looked at her, emotionless.

"Go, Asha."

Asha's face transformed from fierce to hurt within seconds, and she reluctantly followed the men out of the great hall. Zach watched her go. A small part of him, a mere whisper in his mind, triggered a tiny flame of guilt. He brushed it away.

"Now, let us walk up to the stage so we may set everything up to your liking for this evening's grand celebration," Eadrich said.

Zach followed Eadrich, watching villagers carry up a wooden throne carved similarly to the houses. The floral edging came together at the center of the headrest, where a triangular symbol of Vera's tattoo sparkled in white gems. Zach nonchalantly glanced at Eadrich's neck. No tattoo. That's bizarre, he thought to himself. He looked around at the villagers setting up for the evening's ceremony. No tattoos. All the people in Amal's land had had the same tattoo Amal had on his forehead. In this village, none of the people seemed to have Vera's marking. A red flag? He wondered. Maybe. Should he ask to go and find—

"Here, Zachariah! For a hero!" Eadrich exclaimed, pointing to the throne.

The sight of the magnificent chair erased all suspicion from his mind. Zach thought it was awesome! Every time he'd played video games or watched epic movies, he'd wished to be the powerful ruler directing soldiers into battle. Here in the village of Fides, his wish was coming true. Slowly he approached the throne. He'd never felt this way before. He didn't just want to sit on the throne, he deeply coveted the powerful seat. As Zach ran his fingers along the delicate carvings, he imagined all the people in the hall celebrating him. And a dark voice within him encouragingly whispered, "You're the hero."

Oddly, the boy, who rarely sat still and often tapped his foot to a constant beat, rested upon the throne the entire day, watching the Fideans prepare for his festival. Throughout the decorating process, Eadrich had taken Zach's cloak and Satya, promising to keep them safe. Then he'd presented him with an elaborate green and gold robe. Before Zach even knew he was hungry or thirsty, the village baker and pub owner brought him food and drink. Zach was loving it. He'd never been treated like royalty before. Zach couldn't believe this was happening to him. But the longer he watched the people work, the more he changed. He sat up straighter. His gentle demeanor became fierce and direct. As things were brought to him, he no longer said please or thank you. When anyone approached him, Zach would lift his nose slightly in the air to ensure they knew he was better than them. For the first time in Zach's life, he felt powerful. And why shouldn't he? He was the one who would save Burra Din. The lives of these people were in his hands. They should bow before him. Zach contemplated his plans for the village.

Eadrich approached Zach's throne, making his way through the workers. Then he bowed before Zach, "My good hero, the hall is almost prepared. Are you happy?"

Zach paused and avoided eye contact with Eadrich. After waiting a few seconds longer than normal to emphasize his control, Zach responded haughtily, "Yes, I believe I am."

Eadrich looked up and clapped his hands. "Wonderful! It will start within the hour."

Zach gave one royal jerk of his head and sat back on the throne. He slouched to the side and leaned on the armrest. Thoughts raced through his head. *See, I don't need Asha. I don't need . . . what was that protector lady's name again? Does it even matter? Look at the people who love me. I'm the hero. I will save Burra Din eventually. I deserve this. It's a good thing to take a break every now and then—Wait, who's that?*

141

Zach looked through the crowd and saw a young woman placing flowers in a vase. For the first time since he'd arrived, he stepped off the stage. The crowd of workers parted for him as he walked down the aisle. His large robe trailed behind him. The young woman's beauty was mesmerizing. She had long, black hair and skin the color of caramel. Her topaz earrings dangled from her ears and laid gently on her smooth, bare shoulders. Zach was beginning to enjoy the fact everyone wore topaz jewelry. It matched his necklace and made him feel like a leader of a united people.

"What's your name, girl?" Zach said, uncharacteristically.

The young woman bowed her head and spoke softly, "Lena."

Eadrich, who was suddenly behind Zach, cleared his throat gruffly.

"Lena, my hero," she corrected.

Zach stroked his necklace.

"You will sit with me during the festival," he said.

"Yes, my hero," Lena said as she continued to look at the ground.

Eadrich clapped his hands and a smaller, less decorative chair was placed next to Zach's throne. Zach turned around and walked back up the aisle. Eadrich and Lena followed closely behind him. After reaching the stage, Eadrich clapped his hands again and all the workers exited the building. The hall was empty save for Eadrich, Lena, and Zach.

"My hero, we shall start the festival. All we ask is that you sit and enjoy yourself. We hope the festival brings you joy," Eadrich said with a bow.

And at that, the festival began. Musicians beat drums in the corner of the room as groups of people, led by ribbon dancers, paraded into the hall. The first group was the shopkeepers. They were dressed in long, blue robes with a sigil of a market stall embroidered on their front pockets. They entered the rows with their hands in a prayerful position. Their families, also dressed in blue, walked beside them. Zach noticed the woman from the shop who'd given him the topaz necklace. No one showed any kind of emotion. They all bowed as one and then sat in their rows. The next group to enter was dressed in green and had a sigil the shape of wheat on their robe pockets. Farmers, Zach realized. He was delighted by the uniformity of it all and watched as group by group the people filed into the great hall of Fides. The fact these people came together because of him had Zach standing even prouder. Once all the people of Fides had entered the hall, the dancers split into two groups and knelt in front of the pews. Eadrich, dressed in a white robe with the sigil of the sun on his chest, walked to the front of the dais and held his hands out. He clapped once and everyone let out a low grunt.

"The prophecy has begun! Our hero is home!" Eadrich said.

The crowd cheered.

"Let us show our hero Fidean gratitude by having him sound the ceremonial gong!"

The crowd cheered. Three men wheeled the gong to the front of the room. Zach, who normally hated being in front of people, walked confidently to Eadrich and grasped the large, heavy mallet. He held it high and paused. The crowd cheered. Before he brought down the mallet, Zach saw within the intricate decorations of the gong an image of a young man standing up against a wave of darkness. The image was exactly like the one in Asha's front door's stained-glass window. Zach cocked his head. Something suddenly felt wrong. He began to lower the mallet. Staring at the mallet, he felt a twist of uncertainty in his heart. He didn't want this, did he?

"We shall praise our HERO!" Eadrich exclaimed.

Zach immediately forgot his thoughts and crashed the mallet against the intricately decorated metal. A loud GONG rang out, and the crowd cheered. Eadrich bowed and motioned for Zach to return to his throne. As he sat down, Eadrich raised his hands and addressed the crowd once more.

"We shall praise our hero in true Fidean style!"

He clapped his hands to signal the guards. Four men, dressed in green uniforms consisting of what looked like parachute pants and a high-collared military dress coat, walked to Zach and hoisted him up onto their shoulders. The guards' cylinder hats were decorated with colorful feathers that tickled Zach's arms as they carried him about.

With his hands held high, Eadrich addressed the crowd, "As our hero is carried out of the great hall, we must show him our gratitude! Lift your hands in praise! Then we shall feast and be elated with the knowledge that our hero has arrived!"

Zach was beaming. People clapped and cheered as he was carried through the crowd. He waved and turned to each side of the hall. Some of the Fideans reached up and shook his hand. Zach had never felt this way before. He was famous! The people loved him! But as the guards approached the exit, Zach realized something was wrong. The men carrying him weren't turning around. No, they were carrying him out of the great hall. Zach didn't understand. Didn't he get to eat the great feast? Where were they taking him?

"I demand you put me down!"

Zach tried to jump from their arms. The men gripped him tighter and marched through the main street. Zach struggled. His robe fell to the ground as they entered a cold, dark building. He managed to get free for just a second, clawing to gain his balance and run away. But the men were much stronger than he was. One guard overpowered him and slapped him. The slap wasn't just painful; it was shocking. Zach had never been hit before. His cheek burned, and he was embarrassed. Zach fell to the ground, tears welling in his eyes. Roughly, the guards drug him down cold stone steps. His head hit the nose of a stair, and Zach felt the warm blood dripping down the side of his face as his vision blurred. Anger at feeling so weak replaced the shock.

"But I'm the hero! I must fulfill the prophecy!"

The guards stared blankly ahead. It was as if they didn't even hear him. Zach pleaded for them to let him go. He noticed they each had a small topaz nose ring. They lifted him and tossed him into a small cell. The guard who slapped him slammed the cell door. Without a word, the guards marched back up the stairs. The dungeon door banged shut. Zach's hip hurt from landing on the solid rock floor, but he shot right up and ran to the cell door. He reached out toward the guards, pressing his face against the cold metal bars.

"I'm the hero! You can't do this to me!"

He shook the bars, but they didn't budge. Resting his burning cheek on the cold metal for relief, Zach heard an angry, familiar voice.

"You're no hero."

He turned, and in the cell next to him, bowshot gone, Asha sat in the corner, wringing her hands with rage.

"Asha! What are you doing here? I thought they took you to get weapons? What'd you say to them?"

Asha's eyes grew wide, and Zach saw tears building. She stood up and walked over to the cell. She motioned for him to come closer. Zach sensed her rage and was afraid to get too close. He walked toward the wall their cells shared and stood a safe distance from her, clenching his fists.

"It's your fault!"

Asha glared back at him.

"What did you say, Asha? Did you tick them off? Is that why we're in here? Everything was fine. I bet you opened your big mouth and ruined everything. Why can't you just leave me alone?"

Asha widened her eyes in surprise. Then slowly, she backed away from the bars, shaking her head. Zach watched as Asha walked to the opposite corner of her cell, curled up in a ball, leaned against the wall, and turned away from him. He wasn't sure, but he swore he heard her crying. Despite a very tiny pang of guilt festering in the bottom of his stomach, Zach was pleased. She should be sorry, he thought. She was so mean to him and he was the hero. She should start treating him like one.

For the rest of the evening, Zach and Asha sat in silence. Zach built small pyramids out of pebbles. Sure this was all some big misunderstanding, Zach waited by the cell door. Asha didn't move from her corner; however, Zach didn't hear her crying any longer. Now she sat braiding and unbraiding the bottom portion of her hair. Achieving a five-tiered pebble pyramid, Zach sighed and leaned back against the door of the cell. The cold stone floor reminded Zach of his old house. The one he'd lived in with his parents. The house was literally old. It had been built in the 1800s and had a stone foundation. He'd liked it down there as a kid because it reminded him of a dungeon. Who knew one day he'd be sitting in a real one? Zach remembered helping his mom with laundry in that basement. And once, when he and his dad had been eating breakfast, they heard Zach's mom scream from down the stairs. They'd rushed down to find out what was going on and found her standing as far away from the dryer as possible, holding out a broom. On the end of the broom, a black snake was coiled around the bristles. Snakes loved the cold stone basement, and this particular snake had found its way into the dryer. From that day on, his entire family had opened the dryer door a bit more cautiously. He laughed to himself.

"Why are you laughing?" Asha asked with disdain in her voice. "Like you care."

"You are very angry with me. I do not understand the change in you."

Zach swallowed hard. He didn't really understand it either.

"I don't know. You think I'm an idiot," Zach said.

Asha looked down at her hands.

Zach crossed his arms defensively and rolled his eyes.

After a few moments, Asha said, "I am sorry."

Zach looked up at her in shock. Had Asha just apologized?

Asha let out an exasperated sigh, got up, and walked toward the bars they shared.

"Do you want my apology? Or shall I take it back?" Asha asked, softening her voice slightly.

Zach could tell this was very difficult for her. It looked like she'd swallowed a bee. Without moving, he relented, rolled his eyes, and gave in resentfully.

"Thanks."

Furrowing her brow as if she were calculating something, Asha stepped closer and said, "Come here."

Zach stepped forward cautiously, and when he was just within Asha's reach she snatched the topaz necklace and pulled him against the cell wall. Then she said in a quiet, angry voice, "You are not Zachariah!"

With that, she ripped the necklace off him, and the beads tumbled to the floor. Then she gave him a hard shove, and he too fell to the floor. Zach blinked at Asha. Suddenly an overwhelming sense of shame encompassed him. The events of the day flooded his memory. He realized what he'd said and—oh no!—what he'd done all day. He put his head in hands regretfully. Tears fell from his eyes, stinging his swollen cheek and revealing another small cut.

"Asha, I'm so sorry," Zach said.

Scrambling, Zach walked over to her with his arms spread wide.

"Ah, there you are! There's my Monkey Boy!"

"What happened to me?"

"Those jewels. I think they are enchanted or cursed."

Zach was silent for a moment and then murmured, "Where's Vera?"

Asha lowered her head and said, "I do not know. She went with Barii. I know it was a lie. I believe Eadrich is in charge, and he—"

"Eadrich is in charge," a loud voice boomed from up the stairs.

They heard slow, heavy footsteps descending. Eadrich stood in front of the cell door with a wicked look on his face, hands clasped in an arrogant manner. Neither Zach nor Asha spoke. It was useless. Asha glanced at Zach as if to say, "Malum is obviously controlling him." From behind his back, Eadrich revealed the candle from Zach's bag. Zach felt a drop in his stomach. The gift! The magi! He'd completely forgotten all about them. He quickly touched his chest and felt the newest one in his pocket. Relief spread through him.

"No!" Asha exclaimed and ran to the bars of her cell. She pulled at the cell door but it didn't budge.

"Oh, Asha. These bars could hold you for an eternity," Eadrich said, shaking his head at Asha's foolishness. "But we are not that cruel." He clutched the candle and paced slowly back and forth as if preparing for negotiation. "No, we will not make you suffer for an eternity. Your death shall come swiftly. You see, Asha," Eadrich stopped in front of her cell door, "You killed the hero. Zachariah is dead because of you. You shall be publicly executed for this heinous act at dawn."

"What?! No!" Zach cried out. "I'm alive, you can't do that!"

"Not for long," Eadrich said. He waved the candle in front of Zach's face and then placed it in his robe pocket. He lifted his hands in the air to summon the guards.

The same four guards marched in unison down the stairs of the dungeon and turned perfectly in front of Asha's cell. Asha backed up to the farthest corner. Zach demanded that they stop, but no one flinched, no one cared. Asha put up a fight. She punched one of the guards directly in the nose, and while that one recovered, two of them grabbed her arms. As they drug her to the cell door, Asha kicked a guard right in the gut. He bent over and wretched all over the floor.

"Let her go!" Zach intervened. "Let her go! Take me! It's my fault!"

Finally after a serious scuffle, the fourth and largest guard pushed Asha across the cell into the bars. She smacked her head and crumpled to the floor. Now that she was unconscious, Asha looked frail and small. Zach felt sick. He'd never seen her like this. Tears streamed down his face. And despite Zach's protests, the large guard picked Asha up and threw her over his shoulder. Blood dripped from the back of her head to the cold, stone floor. Zach felt like the world was moving in slow motion. Once the guards had left the room, Eadrich pulled a small paper sack from his pocket and threw it at Zach.

"Eat. We need you alive for a bit longer," Eadrich said. And then he walked up the stairs, leaving Zach alone with a moldy lump of cheese, nothing to drink, and a wrenching pang of guilt.

. . .

Asha was dead. He just knew it. Even if she managed to come back from that head wound, Eadrich had said he was going to publicly execute her. Zach had tried for hours to break through the cell bars. He'd tried with everything he had and all his strength.

149

He'd even created a contraption out of fabric, rocks, and a random stick on the ground. It was a total failure. Then in desperation, he'd spent an hour simply pounding on the bars and screaming, hoping someone would hear him. But no one did. It was over.

Plus, Vera was gone. Eadrich had probably sent her and Barii right into a trap. Zach felt hopeless. He sat in the corner far from the cell door, flipping the strap of his shoe back and forth. Watching the leather spring back each time, Zach sighed. He was starving. But just the thought of eating the cheese made Zach want to throw up. He was pretty sure his tear ducts were dried out from all the silent crying he'd been doing since they'd dragged Asha away. The blank look on her face after she'd crumpled to the ground was now tattooed in his memory. They hadn't given him any water. He was so thirsty. And he couldn't sleep. He didn't want to sleep. Thoughts of nightmares loomed in the back of his mind. Time was also a complete illusion down in the dungeon. He had no idea how long he'd been there. This reminded him of the cave, which reminded him of Amal. An overwhelming sense of anxious uncertainty filled him. Zach dropped his head in hands.

But the sound of footsteps returning had Zach looking up at the cell door. He didn't get up. But Zach's ears perked up. These footsteps were heavy but sounded faster. A cloaked figure appeared in front of the cell doors. Zach didn't move.

"Who are you?" Zach asked.

Before he could get out another question, he recognized the sword of glowing glass illuminating the side of the mysterious person.

"Satya!" Zach said. He jumped up. Who was this person? How'd they get Satya, and how was it glowing? Then Zach heard a loud laugh and a snort. Hesitant relief built within him as he asked, "Asha?"

Lifting the hood, Asha laughed and snorted again.

"What?! How did you—Asha!"

Asha held up a finger to hush him.

"You think you are the only one who can summon Satya? She is my family's, after all."

Asha held the sword and slashed it through the cell lock. Zach jumped out of the way just in time. In true Asha style, she hadn't warned him to move before illuminating the sword further and slicing through metal. After she'd sheathed Satya, Zach pulled the cell door open. He rushed through the doorway and immediately hugged her. Then suddenly aware of the show of affection, Zach jumped back, face flushed. Asha stared at Zach, surprised, and then a very small smile appeared at the corner of her mouth.

"Sorry, I thought you were dead."

Asha gave Zach a look as if to say, "Me? You're joking, right?"

"You were unconscious when they took you away. How'd you get away?" Zach asked.

But before she could open her mouth, they heard a shout from the top of the stairs. Zach and Asha ran to the back of the small dungeon, but there were no other ways out. They stood trapped against the back wall as the four guards appeared at the bottom of the steps. Then the guards moved aside, and Eadrich stepped forward.

"Asha, you are a worthy foe. But alas, once we remove that sword from your grip, your execution will be at hand."

Eadrich raised his palms. But just before he clapped them together, the ground beneath their feet shook. Eadrich lost his balance and fell against the wall. Zach and Asha knelt on the floor and covered their heads. Just in time, too. At that very moment, a huge root broke through the dungeon floor and split into four smaller roots. They quickly snaked along the ground and wrapped themselves around Eadrich's arms and legs. Four of the fattest roots Zach had ever seen burst through the walls of the dungeon and wrapped themselves around the guards. Amidst the settling dust and debris, they heard swift, quiet footsteps approaching. Zach looked up from his crouched position and was relieved to find Vera descending the stairs. Barii was right behind her, holding her hand proudly.

"Ugh! Do not come any closer!" Eadrich said. Except this time it wasn't Eadrich's voice. No, the voice that emerged from Eadrich was dark and gravely. Zach recognized one of the most frightening voices he'd ever heard. Malum.

"How did you get out of the cursed field?!" Eadrich asked.

"Yes, Malum. You cursed the field to trap me in an endless maze of crops. However, you forgot one thing about the protectors."

Eadrich narrowed his eyes.

"Our gifts cannot be contained," Vera said.

Without saying another word, Vera walked toward the trapped demon. Zach and Asha ran over to join Barii. Barii hugged Zach tightly around the waist. Asha, Zach, and Barii stood back as Vera calmly confronted Eadrich, who was now clearly transforming into Malum, the demon-like creature. His eyes were an endless black, and when he opened his mouth Zach saw nothing but darkness. Eadrich's skin was even turning black, with red veins protruding from his face like some kind of creepy road map. Vera began to shake, and her white aura reappeared. She reached forward and gripped the topaz bracelet that wound up Eadrich's arm like a snake. She touched Eadrich and he cried out in pain as his skin sizzled. Vera gripped the bracelet tighter and then wrenched the beads from his arm. The beautiful string of beads broke. As the gems hit the floor, they disintegrated into a puff of black smoke. A sweaty, pale Eadrich lifted his head, he no longer looked evil. He had a confused look on his face and was out of breath.

"Vera? What happened?" Eadrich asked.

The roots carefully placed Eadrich back on the floor. When realization of his actions hit him, Eadrich's face transformed from surprise to despair.

"Oh Vera, I am ashamed. What has happened to my Fideans?! What have I done?" Eadrich fell to his knees, dropping his head in his hands.

Vera walked over to Eadrich, helped him off the ground, and hugged him tightly. As they broke their embrace, Vera looked into Eadrich's eyes deeply as if to say, "All is forgiven." A single tear fell from Eadrich's tortured face. Zach was shocked at how quickly Vera had forgiven everything Eadrich had done. He watched as Vera wrapped an arm around Eadrich's shoulders.

"Come, my friend, we shall cleanse the town. All will be right."

As they walked through the village, Zach watched as topaz jewelry disappeared in puffs of black smoke and awareness filled the Fideans with shame. Some dropped to their knees, some cried out in pain, and others merely stared blankly ahead. Listening carefully to Eadrich and Vera's conversation, Zach overheard them discussing the source of the problem. The old woman who'd given Zach the necklace had come across a mound of topaz in the nearby woods. She'd celebrated and immediately brought the topaz back to the village. She'd claimed the topaz was a gift and would bring the village good fortune. Then, she'd begun making jewelry for everyone, giving it away. But as each person had acquired their handmade piece of jewelry, they'd slowly changed. Malum had entered each of their hearts. And those, young and old, who'd caught on and had refused to accept the jewelry grew very sick from the insecurity, except for one little boy.

"Barii! How come you didn't get cursed? Why didn't you get sick?" Zach asked.

"I didn't need one. I already have good fortune," Barii said.

"Oh yeah?" Zach asked.

"Yes! Burra Din takes care of me. I have no need for topaz. Plus, jewels are silly!"

Zach was a little jealous of Barii's confidence.

"How's your maata?" Asha asked.

"She's much better now! Vera said the sickness that poisoned my maata and the crops was fear." Barii paused as if trying to remember exactly how to say it. "Fear of the sickness of Malum." Barii started skipping ahead casually and said, "Do not worry! Vera cast him out!"

Once the entire town had congregated on the edge of Consano Lake, Vera stood in front of the people and said, "My beautiful Fideans, you have been plagued by the sickness of Malum. Come forth and cleanse yourself. Feel no more shame. This will prepare you for the prophecy to come. Thus Zachariah will continue his journey and—"

"I can't," Zach said nervously.

He'd realized that, on his own, he'd made a grave mistake. He'd walked into two of Malum's traps willingly. Everyone looked at him. Vera grew concerned. Zach cleared his throat.

"Um, I keep screwing up. I can't do this alone." Zach gave Asha a charming nervous look. "Will you help me?"

Vera gently patted Zach on the back approvingly. Asha jumped and gave him an unexpected hug. Barii clapped his hands and jumped up and down. The Fideans cheered.

"Yes, Zachariah! We will help you," Vera said.

Then she lifted her hands high in the air, and the crowd watched as streams of flowers shot from the forest over the lake. They exploded in the atmosphere like fireworks. As the petals settled along the still water of Lake Consano, the whole village jumped into the water. They splashed around playfully, celebrating the renewal and healing of their village. Zach watched as one by one, their ancient tattoos reappeared to match Vera's marking. Zach spent the next hour splashing and playing in the lake with Asha and Barii. When they'd had enough, they decided to head up to the village bonfire to get warm. As Zach wrung out his clothes, he noticed a familiar weight in his pocket. When he reached in, he gripped his fingers around a second chunk of wax.

DOOR SIX

MOLLITIA
RESILIENCE IN THE LAND OF FIDEM

"Be strong and courageous. Do not be afraid;
do not be discouraged."
Joshua 1:8

"You found it!" Asha exclaimed as she ran out of the water.

"How'd you know?" Zach asked.

"I saw you reach into your pocket. That makes two, right?"

"Yep, uh, *Humilis*," Zach said, struggling with the pronunciation. "Just like the door."

"Interesting. It seems we only need one more before . . . " Asha glanced at Vera, who was wrapping Barii in a big, fluffy towel. Zach's face dropped.

"Yeah, I guess so."

Vera and Barii walked over to Zach and Asha.

"Are you ready to join the village bonfire celebration?" Vera asked.

"Barii! I will race you to the top of the hill!" Asha said, and without waiting for a response, she took off.

"Hey! No fair!" Barii said, running after her.

Zach chuckled, watching Barii fight to catch up with Asha. Vera walked next to Zach in silence.

After a few moments, she said, "You found another magus, I presume."

"Yes," Zach said.

"That is wonderful! Why do you seem disappointed?"

"I'm not disappointed, just, um, I don't really know."

Vera remained quiet.

Zach continued, "Well, last time we found three magi, uh, Amal, he's gone. Will you disappear too?"

Vera contemplated as she walked slowly up the hill. When they were still a ways from the bonfire crowd, Vera stopped walking and turned to Zach.

"To say I would not miss my time in Burra Din would be a lie. It saddens me—as I'm sure it did Amal—to leave such a beautiful world. But there are two things you must remember and that I hold dear to my heart."

Zach looked up at her.

"I am overjoyed to rejoin the spirit of Burra Din and, most importantly, my passing through this world means the prophecy is coming true. The prince will save Burra Din, and Malum will be defeated for good."

Zach sighed and caught himself before he rolled his eyes. This all sounded cheesy, too good to be true.

"What is it, Zachariah? This is truly good news," Vera said.

"Yeah, that all sounds great but—" Zach was afraid he'd offend Vera.

"But what?" Vera encouraged.

"But how do you know this prince will actually come? I mean how do you know this kid is gonna defeat Malum for sure."

Vera said nothing. She gently took Zach's hand, lifted it, and placed it on his heart. Then Vera hugged him and gave him a gentle kiss on the forehead.

"It's that easy, huh?" Zach asked, cheeks flushed.

"Hope, my hero. Remember what Amal taught you," she said as she walked over to join her people.

Zach watched her go. Even though he felt a bit irritated with the fact Vera never seemed to give him straight answers, something about her made him feel safe. Watching Barii attempt to talk Asha into dancing had Zach heading toward the bonfire when suddenly, a beam of light caught his eye. The new door's edges illuminated, and the word *Mollitia* appeared across the top. Within minutes, Zach had found Vera and Asha. By the time they'd collected their things, changed into dry clothes, and returned to the door, a significant crowd had gathered. The crowd split to make way for the three travelers. One of Barii's friends, ignoring the boy's warnings, was pulling at the doorknob. However, the door didn't budge.

"Hey! What're you doin'?!" Zach said, pretending to be angry.

The boy jumped back and scurried away. Barii laughed and ran over to Zach.

"Can I go with you?" Barii pleaded with big bright eyes.

"I don't think so, little man. It's too dangerous. I'm not even sure I'm old enough for this job," Zach said.

Barii looked down at his feet, disappointed. Zach knelt down next to him.

"You know what? Your job is more important."

Barii looked up at Zach.

"You have to take care of your village—ya know—like you did before. Without you, we wouldn't have even come here or known about the sickness of Malum. So keep up the good work and keep spreading the, um, well—"

"The light," Vera interjected.

"Yeah, the light in your village," Zach said.

Zach shook Barii's hand to make it official. Barii giggled. It was a custom he'd never experienced before. Fideans usually bowed. Feeling slightly foolish now, Zach pulled Barii in for a hug and then picked him up. As his giggle turned into a roaring laugh, Zach tossed him to Asha, who caught the boy in a friendly embrace. Then Eadrich worked his way up to the front of the crowd and bowed to Zach.

"Dear Zachariah, I do hope you return one day to Fides. I wish to make more happy memories. I am dearly sorry for how I treated you all," he said.

"It wasn't you," Zach said. "Don't worry about it."

Zach glanced at Asha, who winked at him. Vera embraced Eadrich, and the three travelers walked to the door. As light filled the atmosphere, the Fideans gasped and erupted into cheers. And the three travelers ventured through the bright doorway.

On the other side of the door, Asha, Vera, and Zach found themselves in a shockingly different atmosphere.

"Are you sure this is still Fidem?" Asha asked.

They arrived on an island in the middle of Consano Lake; except the eastern part of the lake was very different from the western part. The lake in this area was pitch black. The freaky water looked more like tar than refreshing H^2O. The dark island was not much bigger than Zach's room. It was covered in dead grass and three trees with less than a handful of green leaves each. But the strangest thing of all was that the water didn't seem to move. The lake was completely motionless.

"Yes, this is still very much my land," Vera said sadly. "I have been unable to reach this section of Fidem. I did not fully understand why until now. No, this is far worse than I imagined. My garden has been transformed into a wasteland. This must have disconnected the land from my direct protection. Oh, my poor people!" Vera's eyes filled with tears. "I was here only weeks ago. I tried to reach them only days ago and was unable to appear here. My poor people."

Zach looked beyond the lake to the shore. No one stood on the beach despite the fact small huts littered the land beyond. The huts reminded Zach of those he'd seen in a *National Geographic* magazine. But this place didn't look like the paradise he'd wished to visit one day. The entire village was creepy and desolate.

"What was this land?"

"This was Solis, and it was a beautiful place filled with wonderful people. I cannot believe this," Vera explained.

"I have heard such stories of Solians," Asha said, still in shock. "Great things."

"Hey Asha, are these those guys you were talking about that make these clothes?" Zach asked.

"They provide Burra Din with the most high-quality fabric," she said proudly. Then looking at the deserted beach she added, "At least they did."

"Where should we go?" Zach asked, watching Vera go pale.

No one answered.

Zach walked closer to Vera and said gently, "Vera?"

Vera looked devastated, almost hopeless. Zach was starting to panic. If Vera was freaked out, that meant they should be freaked out too, right?

Quietly, Vera breathed deeply and said, "It seems your journey is dependent upon the protectors. We shall head to the border of my land. Burra Din will reveal the plan in good time."

"A boat," Asha said, pointing to the far side of the small island.

The boat looked rough. Green paint was chipping off the sides, and it seemed to be partially buried in the sand. Zach walked over and started to scoop sand out of the boat with his hands. Asha helped. Vera concentrated, and a branch from a nearby tree extended to the boat. It wrapped itself under the small vessel and lifted it out of the sand. Zach and Asha sat back and watched as sand poured out. The branch held the boat in the air and then carefully placed it right in the water? Sure, water. And it receded back to the tree. Then they heard a loud thump. Vera had collapsed! Zach and Asha rushed to her side.

"Vera!" Zach said.

Vera slowly opened her eyes again.

"Are you okay?" Zach asked.

"Weak. The land is . . . is dying. I am dying. Shore."

With panic in his eyes, Zach looked up at Asha. She was already putting stuff in the boat.

"We have to get her to shore," Asha said.

They picked up Vera and set her in the boat. She seemed more frail with every passing moment. The veins along her body turned black as dark circles encased her eyes. Zach could no longer look at her. It was as if she was slowly turning into an extremely convincing Halloween decoration.

"Don't touch this water," Asha said. "It looks like death."

Zach looked down and saw that the water now lapped up against the boat, but in snake-like tendrils instead of the usual small waves. Zach got a chill up his spine as he stepped into the boat. No leaks; that's a good start, he thought. Vera settled into the middle of the boat and rested her head on the seat. Asha and Zach started to row across the lake. The tar-like substance made the short journey a difficult one. Their oars stuck and had to be pulled out of the liquid as the boat inched along. Within the first strokes, Asha gave Zach a worried glance as Vera's labored breathing became louder. Zach tried to row faster, but it seemed the shore was getting farther away and the black liquid felt thicker. On his next stroke, the oar seemed to be stuck. Zach pulled at the oar but it didn't budge.

"Why have you stopped?" Asha asked.

"My oars stuck on something," Zach said, leaning over the boat and cautiously peering in the liquid. He jerked. Someone was staring back at him.

"Whoa! What is it?!" Asha asked as she balanced herself on the rocking boat.

"Someone's in there. It's, it's . . . " Zach leaned closer. The person peering back at him from the water looked familiar—dark and evil—but familiar. Zach leaned even closer.

"Zach, don't lean! You're tipping the boat!" Asha yelled.

"Zaaaccharii—" Vera begged in a soft voice under her labored breathing. "Stttoopp, Zzzaa—"

"The water is death!" Asha said and reached for Zach to pull him back from the edge. But before she could grab his shoulder, the blackness wrapped itself up the oar and pulled Zach overboard.

"Noooo!" was the last thing Zach heard as he entered the tar-like substance. He panicked and kicked his legs. He struggled against the dense liquid. He felt like he was falling slowly, slowly, slowly to the bottom. He stopped. He was stuck. Still holding his breath, he felt compelled to open his heavy eyelids.

He was face to face with himself! But this wasn't Zach. This was someone evil, lurking beneath the surface of the lake. He watched as the evil version of himself pointed. Zach shifted his gaze. In the distance was a flashing image of the lush forest village of Inspirare, then the Lumen Hills, the Gardens of Gratia, Fides village, and all the beautiful scenes of Burra Din he'd experienced so far. He looked back at the evil version of himself and was repulsed by the darkness of his eyes and the twisted grin on his own face. This couldn't possibly be him, could it? Then the evil Zach laughed maniacally as the scene of Burra Din melted behind him, and the sounds of muffled screams filled Zach's ears. He tried to cover his ears, but his arms didn't move. The evil Zach focused his dark eyes on Zach and blinked. When he reopened them, Zach saw dark holes where his eyes had been and a shrieking laughter escaped the evil version of himself. Zach felt weak and sick. He felt himself slowly fading.

"Zach! Zachariah! Monkey Boy!" Asha yelled.

Zach slowly opened his eyes. Once he realized where he was, Zach shot up and asked, "Whaaa—what happened?"

"Oh! Thank Burra!" Asha said.

Vera let out a sigh and continued to breathe slowly.

"You were barely overboard and sinking so slowly. But I could not get you out! You just sat there stuck!" Asha said, still staring at her hands.

"Huh? I was deep under wa—or whatever that stuff is. I saw, I saw," Zach couldn't explain it. Had it been real? It felt real. He felt like he'd seen a ghost. The pictures haunted his mind. He couldn't tell Asha what he'd seen. Would he do something like that? Could he turn that evil? Evil enough that all of Burra Din fell, causing the death of countless wonderful creatures?

"What, Zach? What did you see?" Asha asked.

Vera touched his arm lightly, and warmth spread through Zach's body. The fear that was starting to consume him disappeared. He felt stronger. But when he looked at Vera, she was no longer awake.

"Oh no!" Zach scrambled to her, rocking the boat. "No! No! No! Vera! We need you! Vera, wake up!"

Asha grabbed Zach's shoulders and shook him.

"Zach! We have to get her to shore. She is still breathing. See?"

Zach looked down at her and saw her chest rising and falling ever so slightly. He grabbed his oar and started rowing. Visions of his mother before her death crept into his mind along with visions of his father slipping away into darkness. The warmth Vera had shared with him started to subside, giving way to another feeling, a cold of regret and sorrow. By the time they reached the shore, Zach felt exhausted and stretched thin. Asha jumped out and pulled the boat onto shore. Then she helped Zach pick up Vera. They carried her to the closest hut. The door was gone, and inside the hut sat abandoned furniture. They laid Vera on what looked like a bed of palm branches.

"What now?!" Zach asked.

"I do not know," Asha responded desperately.

Zach felt very cold. He was still covered in black liquid. Visions of his mother's death were surfacing from his memory and mixing with the present reality of Vera's sickness. Zach sat down and put his head in his hands. He retreated within himself and felt despair take over.

"Zach? Are you cold?" Asha asked, hugging herself.

Zach didn't respond. He couldn't even hear her.

"Zach! I am so cold," she said. Asha sat on the ground and started shaking violently. "Zach, are you there?! It is dark! Zach, I—" Asha stopped speaking and laid on the ground.

Zach couldn't look at her. He couldn't go on. What he'd seen in the lake had confirmed it; he couldn't do this mission. It would consume him. It would turn him evil. He would be the end of Burra Din. What if he had arrived to prevent the prophecy? What if he was accidentally helping Malum? What if all this time he thought he was here to help but really he was here to cause more problems? What if? What if?

"Zachaaarrriiiaahhh. Zachhhaaarriiiahh."

A voice? Within Zach's consciousness, he heard the voice again. Whose voice was that? It sounded so familiar. It sounded like—

"Mom?! Where are you?" Zach's heart jumped, and tears filled his eyes.

"Zachariah."

"Yes, Mom! I'm here, Mom! I'm here! Mom, I miss you so much. Mom, come back! Mom!" His heart was breaking at the sound of her voice.

"Be still, my baby."

"Mom, are you okay?! Where are you?!" He felt like he was searching through a fog.

"I'm wonderful. All is well. But you must fight, my love. Stand and fight. The light is within you, Zachariah. It runs through you. You are not alone. Never alone. Be hopeful!"

Her voice was fading.

"No, Mom, don't go! Mom!" Zach pleaded.

"I love you. Never alone."

Zach woke and found himself curled in a ball on the floor of the hut. His cheeks were wet with tears. He felt warmth inside him again and a hum of energy. He looked around to find Asha on the floor unconscious and Vera on the bed of palm branches barely breathing. It was up to him. He had to fight. Zach jumped up and ran out of the hut. He searched everywhere and found whatever life was left on the desolate beach. It took longer than he wanted, but eventually he found something he thought Vera could use: a handful of green leaves, two small, dull flowers, and a handful of lake grass.

When he reentered the hut, Vera was barely alive. Zach jumped at a crash of thunder. He looked outside. Twisting clouds and a wall of rain charged forward in their direction. He looked up, finding the roof had a huge hole in it. He braced himself for the cold water. And as the storm raged, Zach split what he found into two handfuls. He put one handful in Asha's palm and one in Vera's palm. Then he held both of their hands and waited. Nothing happened. What was he thinking? He scolded himself. He didn't know what he was doing. Why would he think this would actually work? He squeezed their hands and prayed.

"Please, please, please Burra Din. Please, please, please."

Zach repeated his plea over and over. When the sky opened up above him and rain poured through the roof, the weight of his seemingly failed attempt crushed his optimism. Zach dropped his head. There was no one to help him, no one to save them. He was all that was left. Looking down at the small lavender petal, Zach remembered. He remembered Vera's power and that it came from Burra Din. Zach wasn't alone; he just had to trust. Truly trust Burra Din would help him. A surge of determination filled him, and he screamed into the storm, praying with every fiber of his being. Zach held on tight to their hands. A bright flash of lightning filled the sky as a loud crack of thunder shook the earth. And then suddenly, as quickly as the storm had arrived, the rain, thunder, and wind stopped. Zach slowly opened his eyes. He saw Asha first. Eyes wide open, she started to smile.

"Thank you, Monkey Boy," she said quietly.

Zach's heart jumped. He looked at Vera. The color was coming back to her face, and she was beginning to breathe normally again. After a few moments, she too opened her eyes. The ground beneath them brightened as if the sun were shining again. But it wasn't just the sun. The village around them came to life as if a great curse had been lifted. Vibrant color filled the village, and the sun shone brightly on the beach.

"Do you hear that?" Asha asked.

Zach listened. He heard the lapping of waves against the shore. The water! Zach ran out of the hut and saw the lake was once again a beautiful blue. When he turned around, he saw Vera standing just outside the hut with Asha beside her.

"What happened to this place?" Zach asked.

"The sickness of Malum must have taken hold here first. This must be why Burra Din decided it was time for you to come. Parts of our world are falling, but not for long! You have done it, Zachariah! You have brought life back to this land. Now! Let us continue this work," Vera said with new energy.

As she walked along the beach, parts of Solis that had been dark turned vibrant and beautiful again with a mere touch of her fingers. Zach walked over to the boat they'd taken. He stuck out his pointer finger and touched its edge. Immediately, the boat turned green as if the paint had never been chipping. It was magnificent. Zach looked at Asha, and she laughed.

"This is awesome!" Zach said.

They ran around the beach, touching anything dark and threatening. Immediately those things came to life. Colorful singing birds returned, and a giant golden fish shot out of the lake, making a great splash as it returned to the water. Zach had never felt so wonderful in all his life. But where were the people of the village? The Solians? Asha must have read his mind, because she called for Vera.

"Where is everyone? Will they come back?"Asha asked.

Vera walked to Asha and Zach, leaving a trail of large, magnificently exotic flowers behind her across the beach. She said, "All we can do is repair the damage here and hope the beauty of life calls them home. We cannot force them to return. They must listen to their hearts and the call of Burra Din."

For the next few days, Asha, Zach, and Vera tended to the land of Solis. After rebuilding the village each day with hard work and a little magic, they spent the evenings around the campfires telling stories. Zach usually listened to Asha and Vera tell stories of their lives in Burra Din. But one particular evening, Asha asked, "What's your world like, Zach?"

Zach widened his eyes and let out a deep breath. He didn't really know how to explain it or compare it to a world like Burra Din.

"Um, well, it's different from here. Obviously we have beaches and stuff, but it's different from Burra Din. There really isn't magic. I mean there was maybe at one point, but not any more," Zach said, remembering Amal's words. Some realms rely purely on technology while others rely purely on magic.

"No, magic?" Asha asked, confused.

"Not really. People are pretty busy. I mean, it's not that it's bad or anything, it's just not magical," Zach said. He didn't hate his world, but he couldn't help but wish they had at least a little magic.

Asha and Vera watched the fire silently.

"Maybe the magic is hidden," Asha finally said.

Zach's ears perked up.

"Hm, that is possible," Vera confirmed. "Sometimes, like in Burra Din, the gifts, or in this case magic, have been forgotten for so long, they are buried deep down. I bet you could find it, Zachariah."

Zach blew out a breath and widened his eyes.

"Maybe, but I think I better finish this quest first," Zach said.

Asha and Vera laughed lightly at Zach's facial expression. As Zach stared into the fire, he thought that maybe, just maybe, if he returned home one day, he would look for that magic.

The next morning, Zach opened his eyes to find a small child staring down at him. Not much really surprised him anymore.

The child had long blond hair, deep blue eyes like the lake, dark skin, and a tattoo on her neck to match Vera's.

"Hey," Zach said. "Where'd you come from?"

"I'm Livi. This is my home. Why are you sleeping outside my home?" she asked.

Zach heard chatter around him. As he sat up, he saw at least 20 children running around the village. "Nice to meet you, Livi! I'm with Vera," Zach looked in her direction. She was surrounded by children, handing each one a flower. "We helped rebuild the village."

"Oh, thank you!" Livi cried out and jumped on Zach. Zach laughed and hugged her. "Where is your, um, maata and pita, Livi?"

"They will not come. They do not believe Solis is healed. They are afraid. But I said, 'yes.' I said, 'Maata! It is done! It is healed. Burra Din tells me so!' She thought I was just being a silly child. She said, 'yes, dear.' But I knew, so I ran here with my friends, and we all started shouting and all the children ran here."

"That's pretty impressive. How'd you know for sure?" Zach asked.

Livi looked him square in the eye and said, "Burra Din told me, of course."

"Nothing like the faith of a child," Vera said.

At the word "faith," Zach felt a shifting in his pocket. He touched his chest, and even though there were still only two magi, they felt very warm. Then someone tugged on his shirt. A small child no older than three or four who looked just like Livi held something up and encouraged Zach to take it. Zach opened his hand, and the little child placed three rose petals in his palm.

"A gift!" Livi said excitedly. "This is my brother, Tubi, and he must like you. Rose petals are so special here."

Tubi scurried back to Vera and held her hand. He buried his face in the side of Vera's dress.

"Why do their maatas and pitas not come?" Asha asked, surrounded by children now. She held her arms in the air as if puppies were jumping up on her.

Before Vera could answer, Livi crossed her arms and pouted, "They do not believe us. We told them it was safe. Burra Din told us so! They do not listen. They are angry and afraid, Vera! We ran away, and they did not follow. They did not come with us. I do not understand!" Frustration filled Livi's eyes with tears.

Vera walked to her, gently hugged the young girl, and said, "Asha, take the children to the huts and help them find something to eat. Zachariah and I must find the rest of the village."

Asha just stared at Vera. Zach unsuccessfully tried to hide a laugh, which turned into a cough. He could tell Asha was more comfortable hunting and fighting wild beasts than leading a large group of children.

"Yeah, Asha. Show them your bowshot," Zach said.

Asha glared at him.

"Oh, Asha! Tell us your hunting stories and about your village in the forest!" Livi said, grabbing Asha's hand. Following his sister's lead, Tubi grabbed Asha's other hand. They pulled her away toward the huts along the beach. As she reluctantly followed, she narrowed her eyes at Zach, who shot her a toothy grin.

"Let us go into the woods from where the children came. Livi said the people are hiding in the caves along the cliffs," Vera suggested.

Zach followed Vera, who seemed stronger than ever now. It was almost as if the Solian children had empowered her. She walked taller and looked fiercely beautiful, with eyes full of intention. As they entered the woods, Zach felt a rush of cold wind against his skin. It seemed to be coming from the south. When he looked in the direction of the wind, he couldn't make out much as everything was covered in a dark fog. It was even difficult to make out the lines of the trees.

"Did you feel that?" Vera asked.

Zach shook his head.

"I think there's more healing needed across this land. Here, follow me," she said.

Vera walked through the woods and grazed her palm across the trunk of each tree. Color consumed them as they awakened.

Everything she touched came back to life: flowers, brush, trees, streams. Zach, hoping he still had the ability, carefully touched a dead tree along the path. The tree shook gently and green leaves began to sprout from its bare branches. Zach thought it was the coolest thing ever! He started touching everything in sight. After walking for about an hour, Vera stopped and held up her hand. Zach listened carefully to a conversation not far off.

"Alab! I must go after my children. I will not stand here and wait for the darkness to consume them. What has happened to you?"

"Ria! Do not talk to me in this way! Just because you are the high chieftain, you cannot—do not speak to me with anger! I said the children are lost! They have been consumed by Malum and driven away! We must wait—"

"Wait?! Have you no sense?! Those are my hearts running about and returning to that desolate land! I will not wait and you cannot stop me!" Ria yelled.

Vera stepped through the trees, with Zach closely behind. Ria and Alab stopped speaking and shot a look at whomever had decided to interrupt their conversation. Recognizing Vera immediately, Ria fell to her knees, crying thankful tears. But Alab stood tall and skeptical. Vera knelt beside Ria. She pulled her up and hugged her.

"My dear friend! You have returned! I knew you would!" Ria said, embracing Vera again.

Vera turned to Alab and asked, "Do you not recognize me, Alab?"

Ria and Alab looked just like Livi and Tubi, but older. Ria's long blonde hair flowed freely down her back. Two strands by her face were pulled back and braided with flowers. Her eyebrows reminded Zach of two arrows pointing to one another. Ria's looks were sharp, but her eyes were gentle and had a small twinkle to them. Alab's eyes, on the other hand, were hardened. He was one of the tallest men

Zach had ever seen. His skin was darker than Ria's, but his hair was blonder. Alab was also incredibly muscular. Zach stared at the guy's biceps wondering if he could crush Zach's skull with one squeeze. Livi and Tubi's parents were kind of scary, he thought. He would definitely clean his room if that guy told him to. Zach also noticed their tattoos matched Vera's, but Alab's looked faded.

"Oh, I recognize your looks, Vera," Alab said. "But how do I know you are not Malum playing tricks? And who is that with you?"

Vera took a cautious step forward and said, "It is good to be wary in times like these; but seek within your heart, Alab. Do you not know it is me?" She motioned to Zach. "And this is Zachariah, he is an agent of the great prophecy. It is a time to come together, not hide away."

Alab appeared unmoved. Something inside Zach compelled him to give Alab the rose petals from Tubi. But he hesitated. He really didn't want to make Alab angry. Carefully, Zach pulled the rose petals from his pocket and held them in his palm. Shakily, he offered them to Alab, watching his expression. Alab looked down at the petals.

"By Burra!"

Zach jumped. Then he looked down and watched as the petals united, forming a small rose in his hand. Alab's rigid demeanor broke, and the darkness surrounding his eyes vanished. A sparkle returned to them, and he laughed a hearty, loud laugh.

"You are here! What have I been thinking?! We must gather the children!" Alab bellowed.

Ria jumped into Alab's arms and kissed him. Zach's face burned red at the public display of affection.

"Come, Vera! Help us to spread the word to the rest of the Solians! We shall return to our village!" Ria said.

After the awakening of the Solian people, they gathered their belongings and marched back to the village. The sight was magnificent. The entire village walked cheerfully and helped one another. Those who were too old to walk were carried or rode in wagons. Ria and Alab were in the front of the people behind Vera and Zach.

"They really are a cheerful people, the Solians. It warms me greatly to see them healed again. Thank you, Zachariah, for your help," Vera said.

Zach shook his head. "I was just following you."

Vera wrapped an arm around him and pulled him in for a side hug. Zach blushed. And as the Solians returned home, Ria led her people in a cheerful but gentle song:

The light it walks among us dear
One and all relinquish fear
While in the night the darkness reigns,
Scattered stars of white remain

Children we desire to stay
For their faith is the guiding way
And while we grow let our song be sung
That our hearts remain forever young.

Ria's voice was absolutely beautiful, and Zach couldn't help but love the song. He even started to sing along. As they approached the edge of the woods and the village came into view, the children began to sing and rushed to their parents. Zach had never seen such a heartwarming sight in his life. And for the first time, this young, hardened, 14-year-old boy felt tears of happiness in his eyes. Wiping them away, he thought of a time when he was little and his mom tried to explain "happy tears" to him. He hadn't understood until this moment exactly what she'd meant. Laughing at himself, he felt the weight of a new magus in his pocket. And when he lifted it out, he read the word *Mollitia* across the side. He held it up for Vera, as her marking appeared on the wax. She sighed with relief, yet a bit of sadness lingered in her eyes. Zach could see she truly loved her people and was sad to let them go.

As they approached the beach, Asha, whose beautifully braided hair had been let loose and filled with flowers, shook her head gently. He could tell the free-flowing hair and floral arrangement were not her idea. She was so pretty. Zach's face flushed, and he wasn't sure why. Ignoring the feeling, he held up the magus. Asha cheered and ran to him. And as the village celebrated the joys of reunification, Vera, Asha, and Zach watched as the three pieces of wax became one rustic, violet candle: *Fidem.*

"Faith," Vera said, smiling with a single tear running down her cheek.

And with that Vera quietly transformed into a gentle light. The light swirled around the villagers followed by a vibrant multitude of flower petals. Then her light swirled above the village three times, gently dropping flower petals on the Solian people. Vera's people gasped and pointed as her beautiful spirit entered the Fidem candle with a whoosh and a quiet whisper: "Have faith, Zachariah. Have faith."

PART THREE
THE LAND OF GAUDIUM

DOOR SEVEN

CARITAS
CHARITY IN THE LAND OF GAUDIUM

"Each one must give as he has decided in his heart,
not reluctantly or under compulsion,
for God loves a cheerful giver."
2nd Corinthians 9:7

After spending another night with the Solian people, resupplying their bags, accepting Vera's fate, and carefully placing the second violet candle in his sack, Zach and Asha continued on their journey. Zach's chest pocket felt lighter. He was a little sad at the feeling yet proud they'd been able to acquire the second gift. He now had two candles: hope and faith. He wondered what the next candle would be and how difficult it would be to get. He got nervous meeting new people, and he hoped the next protector would be just as awesome as Amal and Vera. It was a bummer. As soon as he'd really felt like he'd gotten to know each of them, they disappeared into the candle.

"Monkey Boy! Where should we go?"

"Uh." He thought for a moment. They'd left the village intending to get to the border and go from there. Now here they were at the border of Solis Village and had no clue as to where to go next.

"We need to find the next protector. What are the other two lands again?" Zach asked.

"Gaudium and Pax."

"I don't know, do you have any idea? Does the prophecy say anything about any of this?"

"Not that I can remember, but I do not know that much about it. I was more interested in hunting than the village stories."

"Let's camp here for the night. It's getting dark anyway," Zach suggested.

Asha found a good spot to start a fire.

"Do you think Fenrir will find us?" Zach asked.

Asha shrugged and said, "I do not know, but we are ready."

She patted the bowshot resting on her back. Zach pulled the candles out of his pocket. He stared at them as Asha started the fire. He rolled the rustic candles in his palms. He missed the comfort of Vera and Amal. When they were around, he felt like they had a pretty good idea of what was going on. But he and Asha really had no idea what to do now. He knew the doors and the magi showed up in their own time. Placing the candles back in his pack and pulling out a small bag of nuts and berries from the Solian people, Zach settled in by the fire.

"Do you have friends in your world?" Asha asked as she lit the fire in one shot.

"I did," Zach said, doodling in the dirt with his fingers.

Asha sat back and looked at him, waiting for an explanation.

"I had friends, but then I moved away."

"Do you not have friends at your new home?"

"Well, not really. I don't want—I guess I didn't want new friends."

"Why not?"

"I don't know."

"That can be lonely."

"Yeah, I guess." Zach slouched a bit.

"Well, I'm your friend whether you like it or not," Asha said, staring at him.

"I believe you. I'm your friend too, Asha." Zach laughed.

"Good," Asha said.

Then she closed her eyes and drifted off to sleep next to the fire. Zach watched the flames flicker and dance about, mesmerized. His eyelids drooped.

In the middle of the night, a loud hum and a flash of light pulled Zach from a deep sleep. His eyes flickered open, and he shot up, forgetting for a moment where he was. Once his vision cleared, he realized the flash came from the giant door behind Asha. The word *Caritas* glowed in the darkness as the door sat beautifully against the landscape. A valley of trees, a midnight blue sky, a large moon, and a sprinkling of millions of stars framed the ethereal door. Zach took a deep breath and a moment to enjoy the scenery. Then he shook Asha awake. She seemed to be in a deep sleep no matter where she slept.

"Asha! Wake up!" Zach said, shaking her.

"No Maata, I'm not hunting today," Asha groaned.

"Asha, wake up!"

Alarmed, Asha flipped Zach over. He looked up at her from the ground.

"Asha! It's just me!"

Asha rushed to her feet and looked in all directions.

"A door!" she said.

Zach shook his head as he got up and brushed himself off.

"Yes, a door. Let's go," Zach said.

Asha kicked out the embers of the fire, and Zach grabbed his pack. They walked to the door, turned the knob, and disappeared.

. . .

Zach and Asha were not happy. They found themselves right smack in the middle of a blizzard. The bone-chilling wind was whistling around them, freezing exposed skin. Zach, knowing he wasn't really supposed to go back through the door, turned around anyway. The door was gone. When he'd turned back to Asha, he saw she was now in a full length snowsuit with fur insulation.

"What the heck?! Where'd you get that?" Zach asked.

Asha pointed at his pack. Zach ruffled through his bag with stiff fingers. There was no way an entire snowsuit could fit in this pack, Zach thought. But then he remembered how Amal had pulled an entire boat from his bag. So he looked for something that could possibly transform into a snowsuit. He pulled out a small box and held it up to Asha.

"No, medical supplies."

Asha shook her head and took Zach's bag. Reaching in his pack, she pulled out a small square cloth that looked like a furry handkerchief. Asha handed it to Zach and showed him how to stick it to his chest. Then she motioned for him to pull at two opposite corners of the fabric. Zach did so, and within seconds an entire warm snowsuit covered his body, equipped with a furry hood. Zach's eyes widened in surprise.

"Holy—wow! That's sick!" Zach admired the suit and asked, "Where do you think we are?"

"Somewhere in the Land of Gaudium, I think. I have heard of the cold here, but I did not know it to be this cold," Asha said.

"We have to keep moving," Asha said over the sound of the increasing wind.

The blizzard conditions were so thick Zach could barely see anything past Asha. As they walked, Zach spotted a large mound of ice with what looked like smoke billowing from the top. He tapped Asha on the shoulder and pointed. She shook her head. As they got closer, Zach realized that the large mound was an igloo, and it was ginormous! When Zach pictured an igloo, he thought of a one-room ice cave. But this igloo put those to shame. It looked like you could fit at least ten normal igloos on just one floor of this one. The igloo was arch shaped and had a large entryway with a wooden door. The windows on the sides of the ice house were round and covered in snowflake art. The smoke came out of the chimney in icicle- and snowflake-shaped puffs. Excitedly, he pointed this out to Asha.

As they reached the doorway, they heard someone behind them. They turned around. The blizzard seemed to be dying down, because they could see something coming at them. It looked like a brown blur with snow flying up next to it. As it approached at an incredible speed, Zach and Asha saw four large, furry dogs pulling a sled. The rider was bundled in a bright red snowsuit with detailed, green trim. As the sleigh reached the igloo, the large door creaked open. The sleigh stopped for a moment in front of Zach and Asha. The person waved them inside the doorway.

"Go, my loves! Go!"

Turning to Zach, Asha said, "The Ice Sorceress! Follow her!"

Once in the ice house, they found a smaller door open ahead of them. They walked down the long ice corridor and through the door. It was immediately warmer and elaborately beautiful. The foyer was huge, and when Zach looked up he saw a glass ceiling covered in snow. Around the foyer, a balcony stretched across the second story on two sides that converged at a central staircase. Open doors filled the large room off the foyer, and lines of doors off the balcony also stood open. People were bustling around in and out of the doors. They wore brightly colored clothes and were tall and thin. The men had large beards and the women had long, curly hair of all colors. The people themselves were very diverse. Some had skin almost the color of snow, and others had skin the color of night. The rest had shades between. Within the amount of time it took for Zach and Asha to absorb the scene, they heard a voice boom through the foyer.

"Ah! Hello! You've arrived!"

Zach turned and saw a tall, extremely delighted woman walking toward them. Her bright green eyes popped with excitement. She wore a burgundy suit with intricate forest green trim. She wore brown boots and let her long, straight, brown hair trail down her back. It was pulled up on the sides and revealed exactly what Zach had been waiting for this entire time. Pointed ears! He knew it! He knew somebody in this enchanted land had to be an elf! Right beneath her ear on the opposite side of Vera's tattoo sat this woman's tattoo. Although hers was turned in a different direction, it was still a triangle with two lines running through it. He searched the room, confirming the others had the same tattoo. As the woman approached Zach, she immediately lifted him up and hugged him, spinning him around. Asha backed up two steps, but it didn't matter. The woman said, "Asha!" and then lifted her too. Asha stood rigid, but the woman didn't seem to care. She swung Asha around cheerfully, and then set Asha down and helped her straighten her bowshot. The woman gave Asha a friendly slap on the back, knocking her a foot forward.

"Silly me! Here I am so excited for your arrival and you have no idea who I am." The woman opened her arms wide. "I am Jovie! And this is my land. Gaudium!"

"Who are all these people? Do they all live with you?" Asha asked.

"Ah! These are the people of Gaudium who've lost their homes over the ages to the darkness. Malum, the great fool, believes

Gaudium is vulnerable because it is cold here. But that overgrown, ridiculously muscled, ancient warrior in his absurd armor has another thing coming." Pretending to whisper, Jovie leaned in closer to Asha and Zach, holding up a hand. "Little does he know that the spirit of Gaudium is the strongest!" She let out a loud laugh. "Come now. Follow me. We will find you food and drink and have a sit by the fire!"

Asha and Zach followed her through the bustling foyer. Zach couldn't help thinking that the entire house reminded him of Santa and the stories of the North Pole. The people cheerfully said hello as Zach and Asha walked through door after door. Eventually, they came to a small room with a large fireplace and four chairs. The room was cozy and exactly what you would expect out of a picture-perfect winter cabin. Without thinking about it, Asha pushed on the center of her snowsuit and it immediately turned into a small piece of fabric again. Zach did the same, and they took a seat on the comfy chairs. Jovie wheeled a cart from the corner to the middle of the chairs. She handed Zach and Asha each a mug of hot chocolate. Zach took a sip. It was the perfect temperature. Then she offered them a plate of sweets. Okay, this was becoming more and more like the North Pole, Zach thought.

"Your room is beautiful," Asha said.

"Ah, thank you! But this is not my room. No, I just use it from time to time when I am here," Jovie said.

"Um, you don't live here?" Zach asked through a mouth full of cookies.

"No! I am not one for settling! Far too much to do," Jovie said.

"What do you do?" Asha asked.

"Why I care for my people, of course. I wander the land and bring my love and happiness to those in need. And if they need a place to stay or a place to heal, I bring them here," Jovie said.

Zach laughed along with Jovie. He didn't even know what he was laughing at, but he couldn't help it. It seemed like everything Jovie said was wonderful and exciting even though she wasn't saying anything new. He liked her immediately.

"Okay, time for me to ask the questions. I have heard you both have ventured through Spés and Fidem. How are my dear allies, Vera and Amal?! I have not seen them in ages," Jovie asked.

Zach and Asha shared a glance. Then Zach reached in his pack and pulled out the two rustic candles. Jovie's eyes brightened but filled with tears.

"Oh my! It is true! The time for the gifts has come. I knew it! Oh my dear Amal and Vera. You are greatly missed here in this land, but I cannot wait to join you in our next adventure. Oh, this is wonderful!"

Zach and Asha just kept staring wide eyed at her. They couldn't help it. Her passion and sincerity were electrifying and contagious. Zach and Asha found themselves hugging Jovie with excitement that the time had finally come for Burra Din.

"Okay, tell me about your journey so far," Jovie said, sitting back in the chair with her legs crossed. But Jovie did not sit still; one of her legs bounced up and down as she listened. Zach got a kick out of her. She seemed to be buzzing with energy and positivity. Zach and Asha sat back on their seats and took turns explaining their journey. Asha was sure to interrupt with important details. Jovie was an excellent listener. She reacted to the story in all the right ways. Zach found himself enjoying the storytelling process more and more with each of her "Ooo's" and "Ahh's." He even embellished some, hoping to get a reaction out of her.

"—then another door appeared, and here we are," Zach said.

"And what word did this door have on it?" Jovie asked.

"*Caritas*," Asha said.

"And you do not know this word?" Jovie asked.

"No, I only know a handful of words in the old language, and most of them refer to Spés," Asha said.

"Ah, that makes perfect sense," Jovie said.

"So what does *Caritas* mean?" Zach asked.

Jovie laughed loudly. "Oh no, I cannot tell you. But you will come to know the meaning very soon. And—Oh!"

Asha and Zach jumped.

"Silly me! I have a discovery to share!" Jovie said.

Jovie shot out of the chair and ran over to a small chest on the floor. She flipped open the lid and rummaged through its contents. "Aha! There you are!" Jovie returned with a stained cloth and handed it to Zach. It looked like an ancient map.

"What's this?" Zach asked.

"I found this in an old town in the Land of Gaudium. It seems to be a map of ancient Burra Din. But look here." Jovie pointed to a spot in the Land of Pax. "Do you see that spot? Right there?"

Zach and Asha leaned over the map.

"Sal-va-tor?" Asha asked.

"Yes! Salvator! That means savior, or in the case of the prophecy, the prince who will save Burra Din. I expect this is where we will find the savior in the end," Jovie said.

"Perfect! Let's go!" Zach said, standing up.

"Ah, Zachariah, you cannot find the prince without finding the gifts first. I also have a feeling I am not the only one to have found this information," Jovie said.

"You mean Malum, don't you?" Zach asked.

Jovie's face went grim for a brief moment. "Yes, I fear Malum knows this and will be waiting for us there after you uncover all four gifts."

"So you mean to tell me that after all this, we will still have to battle Malum in the end?" Zach asked as his stomach dropped.

"Yes, I believe so," Jovie said.

Asha huffed and dropped back in the chair. Zach held the map up for Jovie. She shook her head.

"Oh no, this is yours. You will need it. Wrap the candles with it and keep it safe."

Unexpected dangers were one thing. But knowing a giant evil mastermind was waiting for you in the end, that was the worst. Needless to say, Zach shoved his fears to the back of his mind. Zach carefully wrapped the candles in the map and tucked it away in his pack. Asha took a long sip of the hot cocoa and gestured to the great ice house.

"So what is this place? I mean, I have heard of the Land of Gaudium and the magic within the ice, but I have never heard of, well, this."

"This is Jovanna!" Jovie said, sitting down. "This home was made decades ago by a group of wanderers from the tundra of Gaudium and myself. As Malum has come to weigh heavy on Burra Din," Jovie paused and with a sad look shook her head. "Yes, so as the darkness has increased, Gaudium has become dangerously cold. The pastoral people of the tundra could no longer survive in their yurts, and their livestock was dying from the frigid weather. We planned a small ice house for their tribe, and when word spread throughout the land, others came who were in the same position. We expanded and worked together. They named it Jovanna, which they said was for me, but I did not and do not accept that. I said, "Let us name it Jovanna in honor of Burra Din and our hope for the future." Then we had a celebration—Oh! It was a wonderful celebration."

"What do all the people do here? They seem so busy," Zach asked.

"Of course they are! They are taking care of everyone in the ice palace and providing supplies for me to carry across the Land of Gaudium to those in need. And let me tell you, there are many in need. I am needed soon, as a matter of fact. I hear there are some issues in the Bruma Forest among the chiefs. The last thing the Land of Gaudium needs is a war. But," Jovie turned to Zach, "I hear you need the protectors on your journey. Your journey is most important, as it will save all of Burra Din. Where are you off to next?"

Zach set down his mug and sighed. "That's the thing. We have no idea. Burra Din gives us these little—"

"Magi?" Jovie asked.

"Yes, and then the doors appear. But they show up when they want. We're waiting for another sign. So, got any more hot cocoa?" Zach asked.

"Ah, yes. The doors and magi cannot be summoned. Burra Din decides when you are ready. And this ice house is full of hot cocoa. Help yourself."

Jovie sat back and contemplated this as she looked at the glowing hearth. The shadows of the fire flickered over her face. After a moment, she said, "Then it sounds as if everything foretold in the prophecy is as it should be."

"What does that mean?" Zach asked.

Jovie jumped up and held out a hand. She pulled Zach out of the chair with such energy he flew off the ground for a second.

"That means, Zachariah! That means you shall come with me!" Jovie said.

"Yes! That sounds fun!" Asha jumped out of her seat.

"Great! Let us be off," Jovie said, turning on her heels.

Scurrying behind her, Zach whispered to Asha, "Dang, I wanted more hot cocoa. Do you know where we're going?"

"Nope," Asha said, running after Jovie.

Zach laughed and chased after them.

After bundling up, retrieving supplies, packing the sleighs, feeding the dogs, tying up the dogs, and calming them down after they smelled the cookie in Zach's pocket, Zach was already exhausted and their mission hadn't even begun. According to the volunteers who packed the sled, they were headed to the Bruma Forest. Asha and Zach stood on one dogsled while Jovie settled on another. Zach could barely see through the small slit in his Jovanna-made facemask. As he was fiddling with it, one of the Jovannians came over and handed him a pair of goggles.

"Put them on," the man said.

"Thanks," Zach said.

Zach snapped them over his head. But once they were placed over his eyes, nothing changed. He assumed they were to keep his eyes warm in the cold wind, but he couldn't really see. The man jovially slapped Zach on the back.

"Good luck! She's a wild one," he said, referring to Jovie.

Zach chuckled nervously through his facemask, but it came out muffled, sounding more like a grunt. The man grunted back and walked away. Asha snorted. She was standing behind him on the dogsled with her arms wrapped around his waist so she didn't fall off. Zach wanted to turn around and give her a friendly "shut up" but he couldn't move. Jovie walked up to her sled with ease, adjusted a mysterious, intricately carved spear, snapped on her goggles, and waved at Zach and Asha.

"Ready or not—idti!" Jovie said.

Immediately, her dogs took off and a wave of powdery snow blew into the air. Zach and Asha's dogs, on the other hand, just wagged their tails. One even spent the moment, licking his rear end. Zach was beginning to panic. He didn't want to get left behind.

"Why won't they go?!" he asked.

"I do not know but we must catch her!" Asha said in his ear, pointing.

Zach looked around in a panic. He had no idea what to do. He said, "Mush!" like he'd seen in the movies, but nothing happened. "Go!"

Nothing.

Finally, the man who'd given him the goggles said, "Idti!"

So Zach repeated, "Idti!" and the dogs shot out of the doorway. Zach and Asha almost fell off the back. As they hit the tundra, the sun shining down on the ice glared back at them. It should've been blinding, but the goggles they wore protected their eyes from the light. Then Zach noticed another cool thing about the goggles. As Jovie trekked ahead of them, a red dotted line appeared after her, giving Zach and Asha the exact path behind the impulsive protector. But they didn't even need it. The dogs already seemed to know where she was. Within minutes, they'd caught up to Jovie, who had obviously slowed down for them.

Once they were side by side with her sled, Jovie lifted a fist in the air in celebration of their achievement. Then she pointed ahead and took off. Zach yelled the command, and his dogs raced after Jovie. The ride was exhilarating. Zach had never experienced anything like it before. The powdery snow billowed behind them, and they rode up and down the icy tundra. Zach felt like he was gliding across the water on a jet-ski. It was freakin' awesome! He loved every minute of it. Asha, on the other hand, continued to squeeze Zach tighter and tighter.

"Slow down! I am blind!" she yelled.

"We have to keep up with Jovie!" Zach said.

He was having the time of his life. There was no way he was slowing down. How could she not like this?! Eventually, Asha gave up, buried her face in Zach's back, and held on tight for the ride. After what seemed like only minutes to Zach, but was actually a couple hours, Jovie stopped in the middle of the great plateau.

There didn't seem to be anywhere to take shelter for their break. However, Jovie stood next to the sled and spread her arms wide. The snow around her began to swirl. Zach and Asha watched in awe as the dogs barked at the drifts of cold powder billowing around them. When Jovie lowered her hands and the snow settled, a small igloo appeared. She motioned to Zach and Asha to let the dogs off the sled. As soon as Zach unclipped the first dog, it bolted between his legs and raced into the igloo. After all the dogs were released, Zach, Asha, and Jovie followed. Inside, Jovie started a fire, and Zach watched as the smoke slowly puffed out the top of the igloo. The entire sight was fascinating. Apparently, Jovie, the Ice Sorceress, had power over the snow or maybe even water molecules, Zach thought. He remembered Aachal's description, realizing that each protector had power over an element: Amal—fire, Vera—earth, and now Jovie seemed to have power over water. Interesting, he thought, what was next? Wind?

"Your power is awesome," Zach said.

"It is all Burra Din," Jovie said.

She handed them each a small sandwich. She threw chunks of meat at the dogs, who were lying around the igloo panting. Zach rubbed one of the dogs on his belly, and the dog kicked his leg out, wagging his tail. Deciding he needed his own dog, Zach laid next to his new furry friends and snuggled in for warmth.

After their break, Asha, Jovie, and Zach hooked up the dogs and piled back onto their sleds. They hadn't gone more than a mile when Jovie pointed to a dark spot on the tundra. As they traveled closer, Zach saw that the dark spot was actually four dark spots. Once they cruised right up to the scene, the spots turned into four people huddled together. The wind was picking up, and Jovie immediately created a small igloo. As they all entered the igloo, which was a tight fit now with all the dogs and the extra people, Zach noticed the people looked very worn. An exhausted old woman dropped to the floor. She had hollow cheeks and dark circles under her eyes. Her hair was stringy and greasy. Zach couldn't help but feel a little afraid and repulsed by her. She stared at Zach, and he looked away uncomfortably. But Jovie didn't miss a beat. Nope, Jovie didn't seem to care what the people looked like. She started doling out the food from her pack and handing them the clothes from another bag. She even gave the old woman her own scarf. The woman muttered a thank you. Surprised, Zach found the four people were actually five. A man unbuttoned the top of his coat and a small head popped out of the collar. It was a child who looked about two or three. The child's hair was messy, and his face was all dirty. Scrunching his nose, Zach noticed the igloo smelled funny. It had already smelled like wet dog, but the air was beginning to carry a human stench as well. He felt a pang of guilt but couldn't help it that the whole scene repulsed him. Zach abruptly walked out of the main room. He leaned against the igloo door. It was cold, but the fresh air made him feel better.

"What are you doing?" Asha asked.

"I needed some air," Zach said.

"Those poor people," Asha said as she looked back at them.

"Yeah, they look miserable. What are we going to do? They can't come with us. They don't look like they can make it," Zach said.

"We will take them back to Jovanna, of course," Jovie said, suddenly behind them.

"But we've come all this way," Zach said, frustrated. "And why didn't they go to Jovanna in the first place? Why were they out wandering around?"

"Once they realized they no longer had food, they decided to head out for help," Jovie explained.

"That's kinda late. Why'd they wait so long?" Zach said, annoyed.

He didn't want to waste time taking care of people. Especially people who could have just fixed the problem themselves. For the first time since they'd met her, Jovie's cheerful demeanor disappeared, and she took a step closer to Zach.

"I understand your frustration, Zachariah. Helping others is never convenient. But, it seems that does not make it less important, only more so."

"Yeah, but why didn't they think? They put that poor kid in danger. They should've planned it out better. They should've tried harder," Zach said.

Jovie heaved a great sigh and set a hand on Zach's shoulder. "Everyone has a story, Zachariah. You do not know why these people decided to do what they did. And judging their choices is not your job. Your job is to save Burra Din, not decide how it should be saved or whether it deserves to be saved. You just save it."

And with that, Jovie walked back to the family. She immediately won over the child and had him giggling as she tossed him in the air and nuzzled him. Zach was incredibly impressed. Jovie had no concern for whether the child had an illness, lice, germs, or anything. She just helped. Even Asha was inspired and was teaching a boy her age about the goggles in her hands. She'd given him her scarf too. Following their lead, Zach walked over to the woman who'd frightened him earlier with a nervous twist in his stomach. She was quietly eating what looked like a cracker. Feeling awkward, Zach sat next to her. Without saying a word, he reached in his pack to find something for her. The first thing he came across were the cookies he'd snuck in his bag from the ice house. He'd been saving those for later and was excited to eat them. But something nudged him to give her the cookies. Feeling hesitant but ignoring it, Zach pulled out the entire package of cookies and handed them to the woman.

"Here, these are pretty good," Zach said.

She unwrapped the cookies and looked up at him. She gave Zach a big grin, revealing a mouthful of gums and three crusty yellow teeth. Despite the fact the woman was old and had freaked him out initially, her warm, unique smile put a twinkle in her eyes, revealing her laugh lines and crow's feet. Zach found her much more attractive. She broke off a piece of a cookie and handed it back to Zach who was surprised she would share it when she was so hungry herself.

"Thank you," Zach said.

Then the old woman laughed and bit into the cookie. She gave Zach a small hug, and they sat quietly, enjoying their sweets and watching Jovie entertain the child. Zach suddenly felt incredibly warm, and happiness rippled through his body. Then a familiar weight formed in his pocket. He reached in and pulled out a magus with the word *Caritas* scrawled across the side as well as Jovie's triangular symbol. Immediately, Zach noticed there was something different about this magus. It wasn't violet like the others. No, this magus was a beautiful shade of pink. He wondered if the other two magi would be pink too. Would Jovie's candle be pink? It made sense for her candle to be different. She was nothing like the other two protectors. The other two were calm, steady streams. Jovie was like an exciting river full of wild, yet safe, rapids. He looked up at the passionate Ice Sorceress, who was twirling the child in the air. Jovie was already looking at him. With a twinkle in her eye, she winked. Zach gently clutched the magus, waved it at her, and grinned from ear to ear.

Once the family was bundled and their bellies full, the new eight-person caravan packed everyone and everything onto the sleds. The man, mother, and child rode with Jovie while the old woman and young boy rode on the sled with Asha and Zach. Zach was worried whether the dogs could handle the weight, but Jovie had assured him that the dogs were used to serving the good people of Burra Din and saving them from the depths of cold. As they raced on, trailing Jovie, Zach noticed it was growing darker and it wasn't even night time. The winds had picked up as well. Later when they stopped for the night, Zach decided to mention his worry to Jovie.

"Is it getting darker," he asked.

"Yes, I believe it has to do with that mischievous piece of wax in your pocket," Jovie said as she set up blankets next to three of her dogs in the newest igloo she'd created.

"Yeah," Zach agreed.

That night Zach had a dream he'd lost Asha and Jovie and was wandering in the woods alone. Calling out for them, he began to cry. The cold seeped into his bones, and the darkness was blinding. He felt lost and like he was falling into a dark pit. Echoing around him, a loud deep voice rang through the darkness. "Give us the magi! The gifts are mine. You will diiiiiiiie."

Scared awake, Zach shot up and looked around. Everyone in the igloo was still asleep. Taking deep breaths, he tried to calm down. As he closed his eyes once again, the ground shook. He cocked his head. It wasn't an earthquake. No. It was more like a rumbling. The igloo shook, and the snow started to fall from the ceiling.

"Jovie!" Zach yelled.

Jovie bolted up, clutching her spear, and looked at Zach.

"Fenrir!" Asha said.

Jovie said, "To the sleds! Run!"

They quickly boarded the sleds and took off. Just in time too. Fenrir raced toward them, kicking up snow in his path. His hot breath created billowing clouds of steam from his nostrils. The great wolf sounded like a train charging down the tracks. He looked even more fierce than before. His eyes glowed, and he howled.

Jovie aimed her spear and shot streams of snow and ice at Fenrir with her powers. It slowed him down, but barely.

Luckily the lights of Jovanna shone brightly ahead. It was just a speck of light, but they could see it on the horizon of the tundra. They encouraged the dogs, and Jovie did her best to block Fenrir's path. The toddler was crying as his mother held him close. Jovie expertly switched places with the man behind her, allowing him to steer the dogs. She balanced on the boards of the sled and turned around. She held her hands in a ball shape and pushed out with all her might. A giant wall of ice erupted out of the ground, like a monstrous wide wave in the ocean. Fenrir came to a stop before crashing into it. And while he took the time to run around the magical barrier, the frightened and determined travelers bolted forward. Jovie turned and shot ice paths in front of each sled. Picking up the pace, they cruised straight into the illuminated ice house of Jovanna. As the door shut behind them, they saw Fenrir just making it around the wall. Jovie jumped off the sleds as they parked and shouted orders to seal up the house and keep watch for Fenrir. As the people of Jovanna hurried about, a bright light carved through the atmosphere, revealing another door: *Animo.*

DOOR EIGHT

ANIMO
COURAGE IN THE LAND OF GAUDIUM

"But even if you should suffer for what is right, you are blessed.
Do not fear their threats; do not be frightened."
1 Peter 3:14

After realizing quickly Fenrir would move along to find Zach and most likely leave the people of Jovanna alone, Jovie, Asha, and Zach ventured through the new door. Once on the other side, they found themselves in the middle of a thick, green and white, wintry forest.

"This is exactly where I desired to go. Bruma Forest!" Jovie said.

Zach took in the large evergreens and watched as dancing lights flickered across their branches. They reminded Zach of animated Christmas tree lights, only more mesmerizing.

"Whoa—what are those?" he asked.

"Those are wisps!" Asha exclaimed. "I have heard of them in stories but never seen them!"

She tried to get a closer look, but when Asha leaned forward, the wisps spread out further into the trees.

"They are small creatures about a quarter of the size of your pinkie. They light up this entire forest. Mesmerizing!" Jovie said.

Zach stared as the wisps danced around among the branches. The forest was a cozy escape from the bitter wind of the tundra, and the trees created a protective ceiling from the falling snow. Small breaks in the treetops revealed an enchanting sky littered with stars.

"This way," Jovie said, leading Asha and Zach on a path through the woods.

Zach patted his chest, ensuring the first pink magus was still in his pocket.

"They will stay with you. The magi know where they belong," Jovie said.

Remembering how the magus in the cave had reappeared and how they'd managed to stay in his pocket this entire time, Zach agreed. But he couldn't help but check every now and then.

"Jovie?" Asha asked.

"Yes, Asha."

"If the people are pastoralists, why have they ventured into the forest? Livestock do not do well in the deep forest."

"Well, I believe the problem is that they have very little livestock anymore because of Malum pressing down on Burra Din. What is left of the tribes have come together to live in the protection of the Bruma Forest."

Silently, they continued on the dirt path until they came to what looked like a knotty old tree. The tree was not an evergreen and looked much shorter than the rest of the trees. It also seemed almost dead. Jovie pushed against a knot on the trunk, and the tree began to shake.

"Things are not always what they seem," Jovie said playfully, trying to be mysterious.

The shaking tree grew taller, and as its trunk elongated an archway appeared. Once the tree was fully extended and had stopped shaking, Jovie motioned for Zach and Asha to follow her. They walked through the archway and were surprised to suddenly hear a bustling of children, women, and men on the other side. As Zach looked around, he was shocked to find an entire hidden village. They were still in the forest, and the trees were still full of lights, but the ground was covered in yurts. Asha turned to Zach with a surprised look on her face.

"The forest was so quiet! How did we not hear these people?" Asha asked.

Zach shrugged and imitated Jovie, "Things aren't always whaaaat theeeyyy seeeemmm."

Asha laughed, and they hurried after their protector.

The people of the village, who had Jovie's tattoo upon their necks, watched as the newcomers walked down the main road. People waved to Jovie happily and children followed her, calling out her name and frantically telling her stories. She addressed each one as they joined the group and asked them about their homes. As they approached the largest yurt, Jovie turned to the children and blew them all a kiss. The kiss traveled through the air and then grew into a giant snowflake. It was the biggest snowflake Zach had ever seen. Definitely the size of a mansion! Then the snowflake pulsed three times and erupted into smaller snowflakes, which landed on the children's noses and eyelashes. They cheered for her, and she let out a great belly laugh.

Asha and Zach followed her into the yurt. Inside, they found a different kind of welcome. For the first time since Asha and Zach had been with Jovie, people did not seem happy to see her. The room had a dirt floor and a round table in the center. Five people sat on carved stumps at the great table and stared at them.

Two were women, two were men, and one was a creature Zach had never seen before. The creature was shaped like a human but seemed to be made of the forest. The creature's head looked like a bush, and the arms sitting on the table seemed to be great roots with small branches for fingers. The creature was wearing a cloak, and the parts of the creature that were exposed were dusted with a beautiful white powdery snow. The table of what seemed to be important people stared at the newcomers.

"A yegoles," Asha whispered to Zach.

"Protector," a man at the table said solemnly.

Jovie gave the man a patient look and said, "Ah, Zakhar! Is that how you treat a friend of ages?! Come! Let us celebrate, I have wonderful news!"

"We are not here to celebrate," the yegoles said, seemingly happy to see Jovie. "We are discussing the lack of resources available. The Skotovody are too many. They are straining the resources of the—"

"The forest isn't producing as it was," said a fierce-looking woman from the corner. "A sickness has—"

"I told you. It is the sickness of Malum! It has finally arrived here!" Zakhar yelled angrily.

"You brought it with you!" said the yegoles.

"Do not speak to me in that way, you useless root!" Zakhar stood.

"I am Mir! The great leader of the Bruma forest! Do not speak to me of roots!" the yegoles said, shaking.

The table erupted in argument. It was as if Asha, Zach, and Jovie weren't even in the room anymore. Suddenly Jovie pulled the formidable white spear from her back and it glowed a pearly hue. She lifted it only inches off the ground and then stamped it hard into the dirt. A loud crack was heard throughout the room, and everyone got quiet. Jovie sighed and addressed the bickering people.

"Zachariah of the Prophecy, Asha of the Forest of Inspirare, I would like you to meet the Great," Jovie rolled her eyes, "Council of the Bruma Forest. The council is made up of the pastoral tribal leaders and the leader of the forest. From my left we have the big, burly Zakhar; the calm, steady Khorosho; the fierce, beautiful Krasota; the wise, calculating Umnaya; and the empathetic, complex Mir."

Despite the feel of the council, each member couldn't help but smirk approvingly at Jovie's descriptions.

"Now, I am sure you are wondering why I have arrived," Jovie started to say.

"We wonder where you have been," Zakhar said.

"We are here on an errand for Burra Din. The time has come! The prophecy is at hand!" Jovie said, ignoring Zakhar.

The council looked skeptical.

"Show them, Zachariah! Show them what we have," Jovie said, turning to Zach.

Zach hesitated for a moment and then realized she meant the candles. He carefully pulled them out of his pack and held them out for the council to see. Only Mir and Umnaya looked excited. The others looked unimpressed.

"We are practically starving here, Jovie, and you want us to get excited over mere candles?" Krasota said, shaking her head.

"Yes, I understand. But do not let fear and worry clutch your heart. The prophecy will heal Burra Din. The prince is coming! We will be saved! Have faith, my friends," Jovie said.

They seemed unmoved by her attempt. No one spoke. Jovie motioned to Zach, and he put the candles back in the bag.

"I see you have lost heart. That is unfortunate. For I can only truly protect you when you desire the gifts of Burra Din," Jovie said.

"You rogue!" Zakhar said.

Jovie held up a hand. "It is not my doing. If your faith is lost, my powers are lost. That is the magic of Burra Din. You must believe before the power can grow. I have nothing to prove to you, Zakhar. I know my duty to Burra Din. You know yours."

She stared at him for a long moment. Eventually he looked away and scoffed.

"I've had enough!" Zakhar rose to storm out of the yurt.

"Have a seat, Zakhar son of the Skotovody!" Jovie said, blocking the door with a wall of ice. He glared at her and sat back in his chair.

"We are happy to have you here," Mir said. "We have been struggling for a long time to try and mend this issue. Too many need of the forest and the forest is weakening."

"Yes, I am aware," Jovie said. "Why do you not come to Jovanna? We could help you there. We could work together."

"I will not join your commune, protector. The Skotovody are a proud, wild people. We do not hide indoors, tending to the needs of those too useless to work," Krasota said.

Jovie's face fell. "I can see more than faith has been lost among the Skotovody."

Clearly this was an insult. Krasota's face grew bright red, and her eyes filled with tears of frustration and rage. Mir cleared his throat as if in agreement with Jovie.

After a long awkward silence, Krasota said, "I do not have to take these insults. I—"

"I do not mean to insult, Krasota. You must know these are only truths. The goodness has dwindled among the Skotovody, but it is not lost."

Jovie's face softened. Despite Jovie's attempt to calm them down, the room erupted again in argument. This time they argued about whether or not all was lost. Someone, Zach wasn't sure who, shouted that Jovanna was their only hope while someone else suggested letting Jovie rule the Bruma Forest, for a time for surely her magic could heal the land. As the debate grew louder and louder, Jovie leaned over to Zach.

"Maybe if you appeal to them, they will listen."

Zach, shocked, looked at Jovie and shook his head. How could she think that? He had no experience running a village and knew nothing about Burra Din. Plus, the thought of speaking in public made him want to hurl those cookies he'd snatched.

"You are part of the prophecy. You may be able to gain their attention. Just speak from the heart," Jovie said.

Zach opened his eyes wider and shook his head more fervently. There was no way he was going to speak to these people. The last time he'd tried to speak in public was at a school recital. He'd had one line and when it was his turn, he'd blown chunks all over the stage. He remembered what his dad had said after the recital, "It's okay, little man. All part of growing up." Zach had believed his dad then, but he was pretty sure addressing a council of people in a magical forest wasn't an average childhood challenge.

"I understand," Jovie said, dropping her spear again. The room was silent. "Let us break for the day and return tomorrow. I think sleep and a good meal will settle our minds. We have brought supplies with us from Jovanna." Mir cleared his throat again as if to emphasize her point. "The supplies we have should help."

Zach didn't exactly understand. They had only brought three bags with them, so he wasn't sure how they could possibly have enough supplies for the entire village. But regardless, Zach didn't doubt Jovie. He'd seen too many surprising things. Jovie melted the ice blockade she'd created in front of the yurt's doorway, and they all stepped outside. The three bags sat in front of the yurt. Jovie walked over to them, reached in, and pulled out blocks made of smaller blocks. It reminded Zach of a puzzle cube his father had from the 1980s. One of those where you had to match all the colors on each side. Zach had only ever solved two sides. Jovie set the boxes on the ground, tapped each with her spear, and walked away. Within seconds, the small boxes of boxes turned into a large box of boxes and took up the entire area in front of the yurt. The Skotovody cheered, all except for a handful of people who stood behind Zakhar. They glared silently in the background as everyone started to unpack the boxes and dole out supplies.

Jovie motioned for Asha and Zach to help. Zach passed the contents of each box down to the next person, who passed it to the next person. The line continued until it reached the market, where supplies were put into piles for everyone to share.

Mir, who was incredibly tall, slowly walked over to Jovie and said, "Thank you for relieving us."

"Ah, you are very welcome," Jovie said.

Mir leaned in and spoke quietly to Jovie. But Zach was just close enough he could hear the conversation.

"Be careful this night. I believe Zakhar and his followers are plotting. They want all the power in the village so they may begin tearing down trees of the Bruma Forest for their resources. I fear he may unleash the sickness of Malum," Mir shifted uncomfortably, "if it hasn't been unleashed already."

Mir looked around suspiciously. Jovie clenched her teeth but didn't say anything. Mir walked away slowly. It looked as if he was gliding along the floor in his cloak. As Zach watched him go, something from behind a small yurt in the distance caught his eye. His stomach dropped. He grabbed Asha, who was a few feet away struggling to open another box, and pulled her with him. They took off behind the yurt. As they got closer, Zach put a finger to his lips and motioned for Asha to slow down. He pointed in the direction behind the yurt as they heard the voice of one young boy.

"You're dirt! You're so small and you're family's dead! Give us your coat. You don't need it. You're not going to live long anyway. You're too small. The dead of winter is coming for you!"

Three boys were picking on a smaller boy behind the yurt during the commotion of unpacking the boxes. The small boy was crying and had a black eye.

"No, you can't have it," the small boy said, looking down.

"What'd you say to me?" the largest boy said.

The small boy got up off the ground slowly.

"Come on, say it! SAY IT!" the large boy screamed in his face.

The two other boys stood by his side laughing. Suddenly the large boy shoved the small boy into the yurt and started pulling his coat off. Zach turned to Asha and laughed a little to himself, because Asha was already prepared for what Zach had in mind.

"Come on, Valovie! Punch him again! Make him bleed!" said a scrawny boy who jumped up and down. He seemed to be getting too much pleasure out of the fight.

"Ah, should I hit him? Or maybe I shall cut his belly!" Valovie pulled the small boy's hair and held a blade in the air. "No, not his belly. I was thinking I could—whoa!"

Asha had shot her arrowhead and wrapped the rope around the boy's legs. She pulled him to the ground and before the other two could figure out what had happened, she'd done the same to them. Zach and Asha slowly walked up to the three boys, who were on their backs, and stared down at them.

"Leave him alone," Zach said, pointing Satya, who politely remained the size of a regular sword.

"Who says?" The large boy spit at Zach.

"Oh I'm not the one you have to worry about. You see Asha over there?" Zach chuckled.

Asha, bowshot recoiled, was standing nonchalantly next to the small boy.

"I'm the reasonable one. But if I tell her you're being, well, unreasonable, she may have to get that bowshot back out and hang the three of you from this beautiful tree."

The boys glared at Zach.

"Hey Asha! This tree looks like it needs some ornaments, don't you think?" Zach said.

Asha looked up, tapping the trigger of her bowshot. Zach stepped back, and the three boys got up.

"That's it. Just walk away," Zach said.

They glared at Zach, but their gaze shifted to Asha, revealing a trickle of fear. Zach motioned for them to go away. The three boys walked off to join the group. Zach watched as the largest boy's mother came over and started reprimanding him for not helping with the boxes. Turning back to the small boy, Zach felt really good about saving the kid. Asha and Zach walked over to the boy, who was now sitting on the ground, hugging his knees.

"Are you alright?" Zach asked as he and Asha sat down next to him.

"Yes," the boy said timidly.

"What's your name?" Asha asked.

"Pavel," he said, "but my maata called me Pavie."

The boy's right eye was very swollen, and Zach noticed a tear streaming down his cheek on that side.

"Do those guys pick on you a lot?" Zach asked.

Without speaking, Pavie shook his head and more tears came down. He hid his face in his lap. Zach scooted closer to Pavie and set his hand on Pavie's shoulder.

"Why do they pick on you, Pavie?" Asha asked.

He shrugged and picked up a small stick next to his foot. Pavie looked down at it and started picking off the bark a little at a time. He sniffled.

"Because my maata and pita are dead."

Zach felt a hot streak of rage shoot through him. "Geez, that's evil. What the heck?"

"It is because I am weak. My family is gone so I just live in our small yurt alone. The village has little, and whatever I have they take from me," Pavie said, as if this were just the way of things.

"What?! No one has taken you in? No one has helped you?" Asha asked.

Pavie shook his head. Zach couldn't believe it. How come no one helped this kid out? This place was filled with people. Zach thought about how lonely he'd been when everyone had been discussing who Zach would live with after his parents died. And he'd had lots of options. He had worried about who he'd live with, not whether anyone would even take him in at all. Zach thought of how lucky he was to have Father Joe.

"How old are you, Pavie?" Asha asked.

"Twenty-two," Pavie said.

Zach laughed, he couldn't help himself. Pavie looked like he was seven in Zach's world. Pavie glared at Zach, and Zach shook his head.

"Uh, no man, I'm not laughing at you. So I'm not from this world. I'm only fourteen in my world."

Pavie's eyes widened, and he laughed too. He threw his head back, and Zach saw the little tattoo on his neck that matched Jovie's, but his tattoo seemed to be fading. The village must be getting sicker, Zach thought.

"Pavie, why don't you come with us tonight. I'm sure Jovie won't mind," Zach said as he stood and offered a hand to Pavie.

Pavie paused for a second, tossed the small stick he'd been fiddling with to the side, and pulled himself off the ground.

"Yes, that would be fine," Pavie said.

Pavie followed Asha and Zach back to the village center, where Jovie was organizing the last of the boxes. As they walked up to her, she greeted them with a wave and let out a long breath.

"Whew! The last box! Ah, hello Pavie. How are you?" Jovie looked down at the small boy. "By Burra! What happened to your eye?! Look up at me. Oh my, let me heal you."

Jovie swooped in and hugged him. Then she took his hand gently and led him to a small yurt on the far side of the village center. When they entered the small tent, they found it completely bare save for one small mat in the corner.

"Oh, Pavie," Jovie said sadly, "Who took your things?"

Pavie looked up at Jovie and his eyes filled with tears. He took a big breath and gulped, trying to keep them from falling.

"There were three boys in the village who were trying to take his coat earlier. Zach and I stopped them," Asha explained.

"I see," Jovie said.

She walked over to the small mat as a gust of cold air burst through the yurt flap, carrying one of the bigger boxes. The box playfully settled on the floor.

"Go ahead, open it," Jovie said.

Pavie walked over to the box and examined it for a moment. It was bright red with little silver snowflakes all over it. He pulled open a latch on the top of the box, and it popped open. Inside the box were all sorts of supplies and treasures. He jumped up and down with excitement and started pulling things out of the box. The items floated around the yurt and settled gently in their appropriate spots. If you looked closely, you could see the gusts of tiny snowflakes beneath the objects moving them about the boy's home. A new cot with a large blanket and a nice pillow floated through the air and replaced the dirty mat.

"What's this?" Pavie asked as he pulled out a tiny package.

"Well, how would I know? It is wrapped!" Jovie said.

Pavie beamed at her and tore through the wrapping. When he opened it, tears came to his eyes, but this time they were happy tears. He pulled out a small compass on a gold chain and placed it on his neck. He ran over to Zach and Asha and held it up for them to see.

"How did you find it?! Oh, Jovie! How?! This belonged to my family! It was lost when my, well my . . . "

"Pavie's pita and maata died hunting in the woods," Jovie explained.

She walked over to Pavie and wrapped an arm around him. The boy held the compass close to his heart. Then after a moment, he realized his entire yurt was full of everything he needed and that had been stolen from him. Pavie ran around the yurt, jumping up on the bed and then launching himself to the small chair. Jovie, Asha, and Zach couldn't help but laugh.

"Jovie! Thank you! Thank you! Look at it all! Thank you!"

"My dear, Pavie, would you mind if we stayed with you tonight?" Jovie asked. "We have treacherous days ahead, I fear, and we are in much need of rest."

"Of course!" Pavie said happily as he sailed off the chair onto the floor. Then his face dropped.

"What is it, Pavie?" Zach asked.

"What will happen when you leave? This will all be taken from me again," Pavie said.

"Oh no, Pavie, you see, I believe something about the Bruma Forest will change before long," Jovie assured him, glancing at Zach and then back to Pavie. "Also, these objects are enchanted and cannot be taken."

Pavie leaned up on his tiptoes and kissed her on the cheek.

"Oh my dear, Pavie! You have stolen my heart!" Jovie scooped him up and hugged him close. Then she set him back down on the floor and said, "Let us make dinner!"

The four of them spent the evening roasting meat over a small fire in the center of the yurt, telling stories, and watching Pavie create elaborate scenes with two toys. As they readied the room for bed, Zach unfolded a fuzzy blanket next to Pavie. He watched the boy sitting on his bed, staring at the compass. He flipped the compass open and shut.

"My parents, or maata and pita, died in an accident too," Zach said.

"Truly?" Pavie asked.

"Yes," Zach said, concentrating on unfolding the blanket perfectly, avoiding eye contact.

"I am sorry," Pavie said.

After a moment of silence, Pavie asked, "Do you think the pain in my heart will ever go away?"

Taken back by the question, Zach was speechless. He knew exactly what feeling Pavie was talking about, but he had no idea what to tell him. After a moment or two, Zach finally said, "I don't know, Pavie. I don't think it will ever go away."

Sadly, Pavie sighed in agreement.

Zach really didn't want to upset the little guy, so he tried to come up with anything to help. He remembered something he'd heard his dad tell his mom when her dad, Zach's grandpa, had died. "But," Zach continued, "I think maybe one day the pain changes into something like a memory. Like they're always with you, or uh, something like that."

Zach was trying to help, but felt like he had no idea what he was doing. But Pavie didn't care.

"I think you're right," Pavie said, lying down on the bed, clutching his compass.

Eventually, exhausted from all the day's excitement, they all fell asleep. Pavie tucked in sweetly on his new bed, and the three travelers cozied up against the fire with their blankets.

. . .

A scream in the middle of the night had all four of them jumping out of bed. Jovie grabbed her spear and cloak as she stormed from the yurt.

"Wait here," she said.

"No way!" Zach said, jumping up.

Asha agreed and Pavie followed. They didn't follow Jovie all the way, but they stepped out of the yurt far enough to see and hear what was happening. A woman was in the middle of the square, screaming and dragging the forest creature, Mir, by his shoulders. He was unconscious.

"What happened?" Jovie asked calmly as she walked over to the woman.

"I was sleeping and I heard Mir next door to me. He sounded like he was sick or something. I walked over and peeked in the door, asking him if he was alright. Then he was doubled over on the floor, ahh! He was stabbed!" The woman cried out again and pointed to Mir's stomach.

Jovie saw a green fluid pouring from his gut. She held her hand out and a ball of ice appeared. She ripped off part of her cloak and pressed it against the wound. Then she placed the ice ball inside the wrapping. Blue light from the ice ball ventured out in whisps, and Mir's body absorbed them. Two men walked over with a cot and carried Mir off to the medical yurt. For the first time since they'd been with Jovie, she looked furious. Zach was shocked and a little freaked out. She looked incredibly fearsome and somehow taller. A breeze blew through her hair.

"Who did this?!" she demanded.

"We found him! Jovie! We found him!"

Jovie spun around and found two boys who looked slightly older than Zach dragging another teenage-looking boy behind them.

"We saw him make a run for it, right after the scream. We ran after him. He—"

Before they could finish, a gust of snow wrapped around the guilty-looking young man and pulled him close to Jovie. Pointing to the medical yurt, she glared down at him.

"Did you do this?! Did you try to kill that beautiful, generous creature who took you into his forest and shared his home with you?!"

"Yes, I stabbed him! I stabbed him for my pita, for my people! Once Mir is dead, we can use the forest, but you will not let us! My pita is right. You are a demented old witch!" he sneered.

The only evidence that the insult hurt Jovie was a streak of white passion that flashed in her eyes. She took a breath and cleared her throat. Then she walked closely to him and held up his chin. His tattoo was completely gone.

"Proof!" Jovie said calmly but loud enough for all to hear. "The sickness of Malum has arrived in this village. Bol, son of Zakhar, your mark is gone!"

The crowd gasped. A murmuring of shock and doubt traveled through the village.

"Look around you! Look at your village! There is a sickness falling upon it. When one of you has lost faith, the sickness spreads. Do not let this ruin the good people of Skotovody! You are a strong people. You can—"

"You say the same things over and over again, witch!" Krasota said. "But what do you ever do about it besides bring boxes of supplies every so often. How do you truly help, protector? Tell me."

The crowd was silent. Then suddenly a CLANG made the people jump. The crowd shifted their gaze to the source of the sound and found Zach with his sword drawn, blocking Zakhar from stabbing Jovie in the back. Satya, Zach's loyal sword, glowed brightly. Sweat dripped down his brow as he pushed the blade away. Zakhar fell back from the forceful push and dropped his sword on the ground.

"Thank you, Zachariah," Jovie said.

The crowd backed up as they watched an embarrassed, red-faced Zakhar pick up his sword. He clutched the handle and nodded to his wife, Krasota, who pulled her own sword from her belt and pointed it at Jovie.

"Who here wants to prosper? Who here is tired of living upon the whims of a protector?"

The crowd stayed silent.

Krasota, eyeing Jovie and Zach, marched over to her husband and stood by his side, weapons at the ready. Jovie clutched her spear while Zach balanced his sword. Asha protectively ran up behind them with her bowshot. Zakhar's eyes shifted from Jovie to Zach to Asha.

Then putting up a hand to signal his wife, Zakhar said, "Let us put her to the test! Let us see what this 'protector' has to offer us. I believe she has lost her true power and is just a witch with meaningless tricks. She says that one is the boy of the prophecy. Let us test her declaration!"

This time a handful of the people in the crowd grunted in support.

Zach shifted on his feet and stood proud next to Jovie.

"What do you propose, Zakhar?" Jovie asked, brows furrowed.

"A challenge!" Zakhar said.

The crowd gasped.

Jovie quickly glanced at Zach and then back to Zakhar.

"We have nothing to prove to you, Zakhar son of the Skotovody," Jovie said.

Then someone from the crowd said, "If he is the one of the prophecy, he will not be defeated! Let him fight!"

The crowd roared. Some shouted in disapproval while others cheered. Zach was confused. Fight? He had to fight someone?! Zakhar?! What?! He didn't know how to fight this guy. Zach envisioned Zakhar palming his forehead, laughing while Zach attempted to swing at him, then picking him up and dunking his head in the toilet while all the villagers watched and cheered him on. In disbelief, Zach looked up at Jovie. She motioned for him to come close.

"Zakhar is challenging you in a fight to the death, Zachariah. You do not have to accept this."

"Do not fight him!" Asha interrupted.

But then Zach thought of Pavie. He thought of how Pavie had stood up to the three boys who'd been picking on him. And how Pavie stood up for himself every day. Zach could do this. He could do it for Burra Din, for Pavie, for himself.

"You do not have to accept the challenge. This is not your quest. I can fight—" Jovie tried to explain.

"I'll do it," Zach said.

Asha stepped in front of him and clutched his shoulders in desperation. "Zach, you cannot fight him. He is an experienced warrior. He is—"

"Nothing compared to Malum, right?" Zach asked.

Asha said nothing and lowered her head. A hint of a smile appeared in the corner of Jovie's mouth.

"I admire your courage, Zachariah. But please know, I cannot let him kill you. You are too important to the future of Burra Din. I must protect you. But—"

"I must fight him," Zach interjected.

Jovie raised an eyebrow at Zach's determination. "But you will fight him as you wish. I will only intervene if it seems your life is in jeopardy."

A part of Zach was screaming in the back of his mind to bail. Let Jovie take the challenge. But he pushed the doubt from his mind. He had to prove to the Skotovody people that he was the boy from the prophecy. If he was strong enough to save Burra Din, he could defeat this joker, right? Zach gave Jovie a look that said he meant it.

"Zachariah accepts your challenge, Zakhar!" Jovie said.

The crowd erupted again, shouting everything from "You're the hero!" to "Kill him, Zakhar!"

As Jovie knocked her spear on the ground, the crowd backed up to create a large circle. She squeezed Zach's shoulder supportively.

"Remember what you've learned, Zachariah. Remember the gifts."

Hope and faith. That's what he knew so far. And conveniently he felt like he would need a giant dose of both to pull this off.

"May Burra Din bless your efforts, Zach," Asha said, squeezing his hand.

"Yeah, right, Asha. If I die, you could be the hero and finally just get the job done," Zach said.

"Do not die, Monkey Boy," Asha said, rolling her eyes.

Then with a slow turn and clutching Satya, Zach found the formidable Zakhar standing in the center of the ring, sword drawn. Zach stepped forward, but before he could brace himself, Zakhar bolted toward him and shoved Zach to the ground. He placed a heavy foot on his chest and began laughing.

"This poor boy does not understand how to be a warrior! How will he save Burra Din?" Zakhar asked the crowd.

The crowd cried out:

"Slice his throat!"

"Do not crush him!"

"Kill him!"

"You're a monster!"

"Damn the prophecy!"

"He's just a boy!"

Zakhar's foot felt heavy on the center of Zach's chest. The crowd's desperate pleas for his life empowered Zach. Satya glowed, and Zach lifted the sword quickly, slicing in the direction of Zakhar's sword hand. Zakhar shifted his footing to block Zach's sword. This gave Zach the chance to scramble back up and jump back up. An overwhelming cheer erupted from the crowd.

"You can do it, Zach!" Pavie said, standing next to Asha.

Zach focused and attacked Zakhar. The dance had begun. The two fighters went back and forth. One minute it seemed Zakhar had the upper hand, and the next, Zach would pull out a slick move, saving himself and shifting the momentum of the fight. This went on for a while as Asha advised, Jovie encouraged, and Pavie cheered from the sidelines. Feeling empowered by his friends, Zach pushed forward and sliced his sword back and forth. His heart raced, and adrenaline pumped through his veins. He had no idea how he was surviving this fight. Then Zakhar slashed his sword swiftly, cutting Zach's cheek. The first real pain shot through Zach's face and blood dripped down to his chin. Trying to recover from the shock, Zach lifted Satya to block another blow, thankful the enchanted sword increased his strength. With a quick pivot to the right, he gained the advantage over his opponent. Zakhar even started to look worried. Zach was pumped. He was doing it! He could win! If he just leaned forward a bit more, he could grab the hilt of Zakhar's sword and—

"Zachariah, you are a fool!" Krasota said as she tossed a knife into the center of the circle. It flipped through the air aimed directly at Zach's back. But just before it made contact with his flesh, a bolt of ice exploded from Jovie's spear, piercing the knife and shattering it into pieces.

The crowd booed Krasota.

"Cheater!"

"Dishonorable!"

Zach was safe from the knife. But he was distracted.

"Never take your eyes off your enemy," Zakhar said with a grunt.

Zach looked back at Zakhar just in time to block a blow to his head. Zakhar shoved him hard, and Zach fell to the ground. Zakhar pinned him down with one hand while pulling back his sword for the final blow. Zach looked into Zakhar's dark piercing eyes and the Skotovody warrior transformed. Zach saw an ancient warrior covered in sharp red and black armor with a dragon-head helmet. He saw Malum! Zach froze. He was going to die. Zakhar—no, Malum—no, this weirdo from another world was about to kill him! Suddenly panicked, Zach desperately searched for Jovie. When he found her, they locked eyes and Zach felt a wave of confidence. The world slowed down. Zach turned back to Zakhar and watched as Zakhar's sword thundered toward his chest. Zach closed his eyes and thought of Amal and Vera. He felt his chest warm and pulled Satya in front of him with all his strength. Then he felt a great weight crash against his sword and heard a loud shatter of metal.

The crowd erupted into the loudest cheer of all. Zach slowly opened his eyes to find that Satya was glowing brightly and had shattered Zakhar's weapon into a million pieces. Zakhar had been pushed back by Satya's force and was lying on the ground across the circle. Asha and Pavie burst from the sidelines, screaming cheers at the top of their lungs.

"Finish him, Zachariah! Finish Zakhar, the betrayer! Finish him!" the crowd roared.

Krasota rushed to Zakhar's side. Jovie walked to the center of the dueling ground and held her spear high. The crowd quieted.

"It is tradition in this challenge for the winner to decide the fate of the defeated. Zachariah, decide Zakhar's fate."

Zach, completely out of breath, was pulled off the ground quickly by Asha. Still in shock, Zach turned to Jovie. Absorbing what he was supposed to do, Zach contemplated quietly. Then suddenly feeling Pavie's hand in his, Zach knew what he wanted to say.

"I'm no bully. Let him live."

Mixed shouts of approval and disappointment could be heard throughout the village center. Jovie brimmed with pride, Asha cheered, and Pavie jumped up and down, still holding Zach's hand. Zach's face felt hot, and he wasn't even sure exactly what had just happened. The whole thing was a blur. Asha had come closer to him, and Jovie had tears of joy in her eyes. After a few seconds, a man walked up. It was Khorosho. He silently walked to Zach, set a hand on his shoulder and gave him a look of approval. Then he took Zach's hand, held it high.

"The prophecy is upon us! Save Burra Din!"

The crowd cheered. Relief spread through Zach's body as he realized his decision not to kill Zakhar had been accepted, and immediately he felt another small weight in his pocket. This time instead of just smiling, he jumped up and down, filled with happiness. He ripped both magi out of his pocket. There in his hand was another pink magus with the word *Animo* engraved upon it. "One more to go," he thought, and then held them up as he cheered with Asha and the Skotovody.

"I found another one! Another magus! Yeah!"

Then Zach decided to show Asha how to do a victory chest-bump. She was confused at first, but once she got the hang of it, she chest-bumped Zach so hard he flew back a couple extra feet.

Laughing with Asha, he caught his balance. So for the first time in a long time, Zach didn't try to control his passion. He'd won a duel for crying out loud! He'd won a sword fight! Realizing playing it cool was completely overrated, he let it all out, truly enjoying the moment. And Jovie was proud.

DOOR NINE

MISERICORDIA
MERCY IN THE LAND OF GAUDIUM

"But in your great mercy you did not put an end to them
or abandon them, for you are a gracious and merciful God."
Nehemiah 9:31

The Skotovody celebrated and Jovie embraced Zach.
"You were inspiring. Well done, Zachariah!"

"Thanks," Zach replied, sheepishly.

"You cannot fool us!" boomed an angry voice from
behind Jovie.

Zakhar and his family, including Bol and Krasota, stood
defensively with packs on their backs. Sensing the tension between
Jovie and Zakhar, the crowd around them
quieted and watched. Jovie addressed
Zakhar with just as much kindness as
anyone she'd encountered.

"Whatever do you mean, Zakhar?"

Noticing the crowd had officially
switched allegiance to Jovie and Zach,
Zakhar stepped closer. But Zach took
a protective step toward Jovie.

"You do not fool me or Krasota! We
know you do this for power. We know you

do this in your own name to steal from Burra Din. Burra Din is lost, and you know it. The Great Spirit has put his faith in him. Burra Din is lost. You know the only way to survive the oncoming wave of darkness is to—"

"Do not say it!" Jovie bellowed.

The atmosphere around them grew dark. Surprised, Zakhar and Krasota cowered, but only for a moment. Their looks of hatred quickly returned. Zakhar placed both hands on his belt and turned to the Skotovody people.

"Don't forget, I warned you! We both did!"

And with that, Zakhar, Krasota, and their family walked out of the protection of the village and into the darkness of the forest. Zach noticed an odd thing as they walked down the forest path. It darkened and then illuminated again after they'd passed through. The small wisps tried to glow but their light was dim. It was almost as if the hatred the group carried overwhelmed their light. Turning back to Jovie, Zach pulled the second pink magus out of his pocket. As he placed it in her palm, Jovie's disappointment faded and delight filled her eyes.

"*Animo*! How appropriate!" she declared.

"I know that word," Asha said as she walked over. "My maata always says I have plenty of it." She put on her best impression of her mother. "Oh yes, Asha, we know you do not lack animo, but maybe you should think about your well-being more often."

Zach gave Asha a clueless look and shrugged.

"Courage, of course," Asha said.

"Oh yeah, of course," Zach said with playful sarcasm.

Asha rolled her eyes and shoved him.

When Asha's large, brown eyes sparkled with laughter, Zach felt a flutter of butterflies in his stomach. He didn't understand why. It was Asha. She teased him; she thought he was an idiot. He thought she could be harsh and rude. But then why did he all of a sudden feel nervous around her?

"What are you staring at?" Asha asked.

"Your big nose," Zach said and laughed awkwardly. *What?! Zach* thought to himself. *Why did I say that?* If he could have facepalmed himself right then and there, he would have. He didn't think her nose was big. He liked her nose. Didn't he? And why were his palms and armpits sweating?

Touching her nose, Asha said, "My nose is smaller than yours. And your nose is crooked."

Jovie, pretending someone was calling her, walked away. Zach put the magus back in his pocket, wiped his sweaty palms on the sides of his pants, and didn't respond to Asha. He looked over at Pavie, who was jumping off a stump, pretending to fly.

"Hey Pavie! Whatcha doin'?" Zach asked.

Asha shrugged and walked away to help Jovie.

Zach felt the embarrassment wash away. As he encouraged Pavie with each jump, Zach was lost in his own mind. He wasn't sure why he suddenly felt differently about Asha. She was pretty. Wait! No, this was just Asha. His palms felt clammy, and Zach crossed his arms over his chest. Turning to watch her explain her bowshot to an old man from the village, Zach smiled to himself. She looked like she was insulting the old guy. He probably asked a ridiculous question, Zach thought.

"Zach! Are you watching?" Pavie whined.

"Oh yeah, sorry man. How far did you jump this time?" Zach asked.

Pavie ran a few feet from the stump and drew a line with his foot. Smiling at Pavie's accomplishment, Jovie walked over.

"I just checked on Mir. He is doing better. He is sleeping but healed. He should be back to shepherding his forest in no time at all."

"I can't believe they tried to stab him," Zach said. "Why'd they do that? Why'd Zakhar try to stab you, too? You're a protector."

"When fear consumes the soul, desperation rules the mind," Jovie replied.

"So do'ya think they'll really join Malum?" Zach asked.

Jovie was silent for a moment.

"For their sake, I do hope not. Their minds may yet be changed."

"Yeah, before it's too late," Zach agreed.

"Oh Zachariah, it is never too late."

Zach looked back at Jovie confused.

"It is never too late to return to the truth of Burra Din if you are truly sorry," Jovie explained.

"What? That doesn't seem fair. Like I could run around doin' all sorts of bad stuff and then be like, 'oh, okay, yeah, I'm sorry.'"

Jovie gave a playful smirk at Zach's sarcastic scenario.

"That is not at all the same. That is not repenting from the heart, Zachariah. That is manipulation."

Zach shrugged.

"Think of it this way: have you ever done anything wrong in your life that you were so, so sorry for and knew you did not really deserve to be forgiven?" Jovie asked.

"Yeah, I guess," Zach thought about the night he'd snuck out of the house and had run down to the creek to sleep in his fort. He'd spent all day building it, and his parents had said he couldn't sleep in it. He'd been so angry, he'd snuck out. He'd been planning on sneaking back in the house before his parents woke up the next morning. But he'd overslept. When he'd gotten back, the desperate look on his parents' faces had been terrible. He'd hated himself for making them worry.

"And then you were forgiven, and you were so thankful and swore to never do it again?" Jovie asked.

Feeling guilty all over again, Zach nodded.

"Being truly remorseful in your heart grants forgiveness."

"I guess that makes sense," Zach said, still unsure if certain people in the world, like murderers and kidnappers, really deserved to be forgiven.

"One day it will, Zachariah. It will," Jovie said.

And with that, another door appeared right before them in the middle of the village square. The word *Misericordia* was scrawled across the top.

"Looks like it's time to go," Zach said as the Skotovody people backed away from the portal.

After ensuring the people of the village were headed to Jovanna and sharing a heartfelt goodbye with Pavie, the three travelers prepared to walk through the door. Only this time when Zach turned the knob, there didn't seem to be a wall full of light on the inside. The inside was dark. Zach looked back at Jovie.

"We are right behind you, Zachariah."

Stepping out of the mystical wooden door, they found themselves in a dark field near a mountain range surrounded by trees. Snow littered the ground in small, grayish-white piles. It wasn't nearly as pretty as the snow they'd seen so far. This snow was what you'd see on the side of the road after a plow rolled through, all gray and dirty. It was also frigidly cold, but a different kind of cold. It wasn't a festive cold but a dark, lonely cold. The only light came from the moon, which peeked through a layer of gray clouds.

"This is the eastern part of my land. We are at the base of the Gigant Mountains. The area has been abandoned for quite some time. You see that over there?" Jovie said, pointing.

Zach peered and saw a weaving, unmoving line.

"Is that a river?" Asha asked.

"Yes, it is frozen. But the strange thing is the incredibly deep river is completely frozen solid all the way through to the bottom. And I can do nothing for it. Darkness has consumed it," Jovie said.

"Why are we here?" Zach asked.

"That is a curious thing. But the sickness of Malum first started to take hold in the Land of Gaudium here at this river," Jovie said.

"Should we take a look?" Asha asked.

"Yeah sure, let's walk right into danger," Zach said.

Asha gave him a look.

"I'm just joking around. But seriously, that's what this whole thing's been about," Zach said.

Asha's face relaxed as she shook her head.

They walked quietly along the treeline for protection from the frigid, unforgiving wind. The land was eerie, and Zach felt like they were being watched. No more than a second after that thought, Zach heard a voice. That same voice that continually haunted him.

"Give us the magi!"

"Fenrir!" Zach yelled.

The large animal lunged from the brush. He landed on top of Asha. She wrestled him while Zach unsheathed his sword and screamed. Jovie held her spear high and tapped a ring on her finger that turned into a large, silver shield with snowflakes all over it. Yelling like an Amazon warrior, she jumped through the air at Fenrir. She launched the spear, and it grazed Fenrir's back, giving Asha the opportunity to roll out from under him and unleash her bowshot. Fenrir, gnashing his white teeth and growling, lunged at each of them. Zach swung Satya at the beast while Asha tried to either hit Fenrir with her arrowhead or wrap the rope around his legs. Jovie wrestled the beast and hurled her spear, blocking his jaws with her seemingly impenetrable shield. The battle lasted so long Zach felt his strength waning. But there was definitely something odd about this part of Gaudium. It was almost as if Fenrir was stronger than usual, and they were weaker.

"This isn't working!" Zach said.

Jovie lifted a hand, and from the light dusting of snow appeared a sled made of ice. She rushed to it. The magic was just enough to distract Fenrir, allowing Asha to get the rope of her bowshot around one of his legs, tripping him but not trapping him. It slowed him down long enough for the three of them to jump on the sled. And with a whoosh, they took off down the slight hill toward the frozen river. Fenrir scrambled up and started gaining on them.

"Ah, go! Go! Go!" Asha screamed as she held on to the front of the sled. Zach, who was hanging on to Jovie for dear life, hoped the protector had some kind of plan. As she steered the sled, they heard the approaching steps of Fenrir.

"My spear! Throw it!" Jovie yelled.

Zach looked up at her. There was no way he could throw her spear. It was huge! And he was barely hanging on to the icy sled.

"I can't!"

"You must! Here!"

She shot a bolt of magic from her palm. The magic encased Zach's feet in ice, which grounded him to the sled. Then she shoved the spear into Zach's right hand.

"I'm going to let him pass. Throw it then, Zachariah!"

"But I—"

Before he could finish, Jovie brought the sled to an abrupt stop and Fenrir, trying to catch them, slid across the ice. He stumbled over his own feet, got up, and headed straight for them. The sled tilted to one side, then the other, and settled.

"Now, Zachariah! Now!" Jovie yelled.

Zach was frozen and wide-eyed.

"Zach, you have to! Do it!" Asha yelled, readying her bowshot.

Zach closed his eyes and threw the spear with all his might. Within seconds, he heard a loud thud and a long howl. Did I hit him? When he opened his eyes, he saw Fenrir twisting on the ground and pawing at his face. The spear had gone straight through his right eye. Before Fenrir could get over the shock, Asha unleashed her bowshot and pulled on the rope. She swung the arrowhead above her head and let it fly. It twisted around Fenrir's hind legs, and she tightened the rope. Jovie, using her powers, created shackles of ice that wrapped around the beast's legs as Asha recoiled her bowshot. The ice also wrapped itself around the beast's snout. And with a giant spear sticking out of his eye, Fenrir writhed on the ground and whined in pain. As they carefully approached him, Fenrir began to growl.

"I would not do that if I were you, you foul creature," Asha said.

"Keep still," Jovie demanded.

Fenrir growled.

"Well then, you can keep my spear in your eye. I need someone to hold it for me. It is cumbersome."

She began to walk away. Fenrir whined. Jovie turned back toward the injured animal.

"I thought so."

Zach still couldn't believe how huge the dark wolf was. He made Jovie look like a child. He watched as puffs of steam billowed from Fenrir's nostrils. Jovie placed a foot on his large shoulder and wrapped a hand around her spear.

"When I pull the spear from your eye it will hurt, but your eye will seal and the pain will be gone. You will no longer be able to see. You are a dark creature so I cannot heal your eye completely." She braced herself, and Fenrir closed his other eye. "However, I'm sure the lingering magic from my spear will irk the evil in you, Fenrir, Dog of Darkness."

Then she yanked the spear from his eyeball. A loud howl echoed through the empty valley. Zach expected birds to take flight or something to happen after the loud howl. But everything was eerily still, including Fenrir, who'd passed out from the pain.

"Well, at least he won't be bugging us for a while," Zach said. "What are we going to do with him?"

"We shall find a place to rest over by the wood," Jovie said.

She waved a hand and a sheet of ice that resembled another sled appeared beneath Fenrir. As they walked over to the treeline, Fenrir, still unconscious, followed on the enchanted sheet of ice.

"Another wonderful display of swordsmanship, Monkey Boy. I am pleased you have our people's sword," Asha said, giving Zach a friendly shove.

"You weren't so bad yourself," Zach said, his face flushed.

"Monkey Boy?! What?!" Jovie laughed.

"It's Asha's nickname for me. She made it up because she's jealous of my awesomeness," Zach said, shaking his head.

Asha's eyes widened, and she threw a handful of snow at him.

"Oh, you're gonna regret that!"

Zach chased after her as they ran toward the treeline followed by a laughing Jovie and a completely unconscious Fenrir. But none of them noticed that everywhere they stepped, the land slowly began to thaw and little bright green blades of grass began to appear around beautiful white puffs of snow, sparkling in the moonlight.

After settling near the woods, Jovie made a fire from a kit in her bag. Fenrir laid on the ice sled Jovie had made with his feet shackled. Asha, Zach, and Jovie sat around the fire on the opposite side of Fenrir, keeping watch over him. Zach studied Fenrir as he breathed heavily. Zach watched the animal's breath travel in and out, creating puffs of steam from his nostrils. The evil beast closed his eyes a little tighter, furrowing his brow. Zach couldn't tell whether Fenrir was in pain or dreaming something terrible. What a tortured creature, he thought, to work for Malum. Zach shook his head. He was sure Fenrir was some type of slave dog or abused pet. He wondered how Fenrir got tangled up with Malum in the first place.

"Hey Jovie, how did Malum get Fenrir?" Zach asked.

"Ah, Fenrir was a great creature of Burra Din. One of the most magnificent creatures. He was taller, if you can imagine that. His fur was different then, too. It was black but shiny, thick, and beautiful. He was friendly and ran through the Lumen Hills with the other magnificent creatures."

"Wait! He was a creature of the Lumen Hills? Who wished for him?" Zach asked.

"Oh Zachariah, the boy who came before you, of course," Jovie said.

"What?! How's that possible?" Zach asked.

"How could a creature from the Lumen Hills end up working for Malum? Is that going to happen to our creatures?" Asha asked.

"It's a sad story," Jovie said, shaking her head. She poked at the fire with a stick. "But I suppose it is necessary for you to better understand Fenrir."

Zach and Asha waited for her to go on.

"When the boy who came before you entered the Lumen Hills, he wished for Fenrir. He even named him. You see the boy had lost his father in his world. But before he'd died, the boy and his father had studied many myths and legends together. So when he came to Burra Din, and he had the opportunity to wish for an animal, he wished for Fenrir. Apparently, Fenrir was the son of the trickster god, Loki, and a giant in Nort—or Norsedic—"

"Norse mythology?" Zach asked, excited he actually knew something for once.

232

"Yes, I believe that is the story. The boy said he wanted the creature from Norse mythology. Now the stories of Fenrir of the Norse were conflicting. In some cases, the dog was kind, and in others the dog was ferocious and evil. So when the boy created Fenrir, he chose for him to be kind. After time spent playing and tending to Fenrir in the Lumen Hills, the boy had to venture on. Fenrir missed the boy but he did not despair. Eventually, he understood why the boy had to return home."

"So what happened?" Asha asked.

"Well, when the gifts of Burra Din were forgotten, Malum realized he could slowly take over the delicate world. However, he knew the prophecy. He knew that one day a boy from another world would arrive and try to stop him. So Malum, realizing the loyalty of Fenrir and the knowledge Fenrir had of the boy, visited Fenrir in the Lumen Hills. He knew he could use Fenrir's knowledge and ability to sniff out beings of another world. He approached Fenrir, tortured him, and convinced him that the boy had abandoned him on purpose. Eventually, Fenrir accepted this and became the loyal slave of Malum, who gave Fenrir the ability to leave the Lumen Hills to do his evil bidding. Ever since then, Fenrir has changed from a proud beast to, well, this mangy creature."

"That is the saddest story I have ever heard," Asha said. "How could Fenrir give up on Burra Din and the boy?"

"Malum is convincing and relentless," Jovie said.

Asha narrowed her eyes at Fenrir. "No, you do not give up! You do not give in! He must have never truly loved the boy."

No one said a word.

Then suddenly Zach got up from his spot by the fire and ruffled through his pack.

"What are you doing?" Asha asked.

"Getting these." He held up the two candles: Hope and Faith.

"Why?" Asha asked with a rising panic in her voice. "What are you doing, Zach?"

Jovie's expression immediately changed to one of surprise and concern.

"We have to save Fenrir," Zach said.

"What?" Jovie asked. "I am not sure if that is possible. Fenrir pledged his loyalty to Malum when he gave in. It is a binding contract I am afraid."

"It can be broken, right? Burra Din is a land of magic. You yourself said it's never too late. Surely, Burra Din can break an unjust contract. It wasn't Fenrir's fault. He lost someone close to him. He was manipulated. He was convinced the boy who left never loved him. That's not fair! How could Burra Din let him suffer?!"

Zach raised his voice, and Fenrir's eye cracked open. But he didn't move. Jovie took a step toward Zach.

"Zachariah, Burra Din did not do this to Fenrir. Fenrir did it to himself. He let himself get lost. He let himself be convinced Malum was the answer. He—"

"No! He can be saved. He can be healed. He could help us!"

Zach walked over to Fenrir with the two purple candles. In his pocket, the two pink pieces of wax from the Land of Gaudium sat cold and still.

"Zachariah, what are you doing?!" Jovie asked.

Zach ignored her and approached Fenrir cautiously. Fenrir didn't move but only shifted his good eye in Zach's direction.

"Hey, Fenrir," Zach said.

Fenrir let out a huff and slight growl.

"Don't be upset. I want you to join me, Fenrir. Can you help me?" Zach asked.

Fenrir growled again.

"No!" Asha said and tried to run to Zach, but Jovie pulled her back.

"Asha, keep still. You will alert the beast," Jovie said. "Zachariah, be careful."

"Here Fenrir, this is proof I trust you to help us. Burra Din will forgive you and welcome you back. Here, you can carry the magi's gifts. The candles: Hope and Faith." Zach carefully set the candles down next to Fenrir's mouth, which was still tied shut. "So I know you miss your friend. I lost people too. But it isn't your fault, and I know that boy loved you very much. Malum wants you to feel lonely, Fenrir. Malum wants you to think you are evil so that you work for him. He's manipulating you. He wants you to feel like trash. Don't you see?"

This time Fenrir didn't growl. He just stared at Zach.

"You can come back, Fenrir. You can join the creatures in the Lumen Hills again. And this time Asha and I will visit you. You don't have to be an evil creature. You can be good," Zach said.

Fenrir huffed softly.

"Jovie, can you release him?" Zach asked.

Silence.

"Jovie?" Zach asked.

"Are you sure this is what you want, Zachariah?" Jovie asked.

"No, Zach. No. He is evil," Asha pleaded.

"I have to know he can be saved. This is what Burra Din is all about, isn't it? Free him, Jovie, please."

"As you wish, Zachariah," Jovie said with worry in her voice.

The frozen shackles disappeared, and Fenrir stood slowly. He reached his massive head up to stretch out his neck. Zach shook nervously. He was so close to Fenrir. If he wanted to, Fenrir could swallow Zach in one gulp. Zach just stared up at him. Fenrir walked closely and brought his one good eye down to

Zach's face and stared. Zach pushed the candles closer to Fenrir with his foot.

"Join us, Fenrir. Protect the gifts. Be good again. That's what your, uh, boy would have wanted," Zach said.

Suddenly Fenrir took a step back and lowered his head to the ground. Zach carefully tied each candle to the loops on Fenrir's collar as his hands shook from fear.

"There. You can help us now, Fenrir," Zach said, taking a step back.

Suddenly Fenrir lifted his head and howled loudly. Zach felt a drop in his stomach. This was a bad idea. And with a kick of his hind legs, Fenrir took off into the woods.

"Noooo! Fenrir!" Zach ran after him. "No! Come back!"

Fenrir kept running. Zach tried to chase him down but with the candles, it seemed Fenrir had his old strength back. Tears streamed down Zach's cheeks and his chest tightened in panic as he watched all his hard work disappear into the trees, realizing Fenrir couldn't change. He dropped to his knees and put his head in his hands. He didn't hear Jovie and Asha coming up behind him until they were right next to him.

"Oh, Zachariah," Jovie said.

"What have you done?" Asha asked.

Zach looked over at her. Asha was shaking with rage.

"How could you do that?!" Asha screamed.

"Now, Asha," Jovie said.

"No!" Asha yelled. She walked over to Zach and pulled him up by his shirt. "How could you do this to Burra Din?! To me?!"

"I . . . I . . . " Zach said.

"What?!" Asha said.

"I wanted to help him! He—" Zach tried to explain.

"He didn't deserve help! He quit on his boy! He quit on BURRA DIN!" Asha yelled.

"Asha! Haven't you ever made a mistake?! How did you feel? Didn't somebody help you?"

Asha let go of Zach's shirt and stepped back from him.

"Yeah! See!" Zach said. "This journey isn't just about the prince, if you haven't noticed. Everywhere we go, it seems we have to do something important. It's like Burra Din wants us to fix something. Didn't you notice that the door led us right to this awful place with no people to save, and the one creature alive within miles of us is Fenrir?! Burra Din wants us to save Fenrir! Don't you see it?!"

Asha looked down as Jovie walked over and hugged him gently. Zach felt a weight in his chest.

"What?!" he said, confused. He reached in his pocket and pulled out the new piece of wax, the last pink magus. It had the word *Misericordia* written across it. He looked up at Jovie. In a panic, Zach pulled the other two pink magi out of his pocket. The pieces immediately began to melt together to make the Gaudium candle, the third gift. Jovie looked at Zach and Asha with a sad but proud expression.

"No! Not yet!" Zach cried.

"You have done it, Zachariah. It will be alright," Jovie said.

"But, we lost. We don't have the—wait, no!"

Asha reached for Jovie, but when he did, Jovie began to fade. She turned into an ethereal aura of light. The pieces of wax melted into one. This time the light of the protector erupted into the sky and burst into sparkles like beautiful fireworks of white. They looked like falling stars dancing in the dark sky. Then the lights came together and shot into the candle in Zach's hand.

"Find joy, Zachariah! You love and are loved," Jovie whispered.

Zach almost dropped the third candle as the passionate light encompassed the pink wax. Then the word *Gaudium* appeared, scrawled across the candle in glowing letters next to Jovie's triangular symbol, and the light faded.

"What just happened?" Asha asked.

Zach looked up at her and shook his head. "I don't know."

"Each magus is important. Three magi make a candle. Each candle is a gift, and you just lost six important magi by giving two candles to that beast! We have lost two candles, two gifts! But because you did that," Asha pointed down Fenrir's path, "we gained a magus. How is that possible?"

"I don't know."

"What are we going to do? Look around you. There is nothing here. We do not know where to go, and we lost our protector already with no idea how to get out of here. I do not know this land. I do not even know what direction to take. Do you?"

"I don't know."

"Stop saying that!" Asha said.

Zach shook his head in defeat and sat on a log. Asha crossed her arms and glared at him, waiting for an answer.

"I don't know why I did that. I guess I thought, I mean, I just wanted Fenrir to get better."

At the sight of Zach's defeated demeanor, Asha's anger faded. Her arms dropped to her side and she walked over and sat next to Zach.

"I know," she said. "When my pita died, I was so angry. I just wanted to run away and hide from the world. Truly, anyone who asked me about him made me so angry. I wanted to punch them because, well, each time they asked, I was forced to think about him and it reminded me he was gone. I really hated that. The only way out of my anger was my maata. She saved me. She helped me see happiness in the world after his death. That is when my maata gave me the parts for my bowshot."

Zach looked over at Asha.

"It is true. That is why my weapon is so dear to me. I understand that you wanted to do the same for Fenrir."

Zach shook his head at his failure.

"You are a good friend, Zachariah," Asha said, awkwardly patting him on the back. "And a pretty decent swordsman for a monkey boy."

Zach laughed, wiping tears from his eyes.

"Let us head back to the river," Asha said.

Zach got up from the log, brushing off his pants as a thought occurred to him. "Asha, why is this candle pink and the others purple?"

Asha thought for a moment. "I do not know."

"Oh yeah, who doesn't know somethin' now?" Zach asked.

"Monkey Boy, let me think. I believe it is because this land is called Gaudium. I remember my maata explaining that word to me once. It is the word for joy and pink is the color for joy in Burra Din."

"Oh, but why are the others purple then?"

"Purple is the color for prayer and meditation in Burra Din. Maybe that has something to do with it," Asha explained. "I do not know for sure. I did not like the stories and bookwork. I like hunting, so I did not always listen."

"Oh, I get that," Zach said. "Let's—"

"Hush," Asha said, wide-eyed.

Then Zach heard it. A loud rumbling. He looked over in the direction of the noise and saw a large mountain between the trees. He squinted his eyes to get a better look. It was hard to see the mountain top because the snow was so thick and there seemed to be clouds of it building in the air. RUMBLE. RUMBLE. He wondered why he couldn't—AVALANCHE!

"Run Asha run!"

Coming down the mountain just near the trees was a large wave of snow. They watched for a split second as the snow clawed over treetops and covered them in a white wave of cold powder. They ran and ran. Asha shot her arrowhead and attached it to a tree. She pulled on the rope and grabbed Zach. They swung forward faster than they could run, but it still wasn't fast enough. Eventually they hit the ground again and tried to run for their lives, but the snow was gaining on them. Zach felt his legs burning and heard Asha crying out as she put everything into saving herself from the onslaught of snow racing down the mountain side in never-ending waves. Seeing a massive rock jutting from the ground, Zach thought they might be able to take cover on its leeward side. It was tall, and hopefully the snow would just build around it not over it.

"Asha!" He pointed at the rock.

They made it and crouched next to it. But before the snow hit, something huge grabbed both of them and raced off! It all happened so fast; Zach had no idea what was going on. Was he flying? Was he dead? He felt something holding him from the back of his cloak and looked up. Who had grabbed . . . FENRIR! It was Fenrir! He had saved them! Zach looked over at Asha, who had her hands over her eyes. He reached for her as they bounced up and down. He grabbed her arm and shook her. She looked at him. He pointed up. Once she realized what was happening, her eyes grew wide and panic shot across her face at the fact that she was being carried off in Fenrir's jaws. Zach held her hand tightly.

Suddenly Fenrir tossed them both in the air. Zach shut his eyes, and when he opened them, he found himself on Fenrir's back with Asha right behind him. He turned and looked to see if she was alright. She wrapped her arms around his waist, and

Zach gripped Fenrir's collar. He couldn't help but laugh out loud at the insanity of it all. And they gripped Fenrir tightly as they rode alongside the avalanche.

PART FOUR
THE LAND OF PAX

DOOR TEN

PONDERO
REFLECTION IN THE LAND OF PAX

"As in water face reflects face, so the heart of man reflects man."
Proverbs 27:19

To their relief and thanks to Fenrir, they had successfully outrun the avalanche. Without him, they would have been swallowed up by the cold wave of snow. After running for a time without comment, Fenrir finally put Asha and Zach down on the forest floor. They immediately noticed clouds parting above them, and the dark land was now penetrated by a beam of sunlight. It felt incredibly warm. Zach looked behind them and saw a trail of green grass popping up along their path where there was less snow. The land must be healing, he thought.

Even Fenrir stretched back his head and leaned up to catch the warmth of the sunlight.

"Beast! Why did you save us?" Asha asked.

Fenrir lowered his head between his paws as if to bow to Asha, and he gave a slight wag of his tail.

"I think he likes you, Asha,"

245

Zach said. He walked over and petted Fenrir, noticing the two candles still attached to the collar.

"Fenrir, are you gonna help us?" Zach asked.

Fenrir stood proudly, showing off the candles so they could see that he had not given them to Malum. Then Zach heard a voice that was deep but no longer dark, "Yes, I shall join your side. Thank you, boy."

"That's awesome! Asha, did you hear that?" Zach asked.

"I could not hear him before. I cannot hear him now," she said, agitated.

"Well, he said he wants to join us. And look! He still has the candles."

Fenrir leaned down. Zach pulled the candles off of Fenrir's collar and waved them around. Then Zach grabbed the pink Gaudium candle and tied all three back onto the leather collar carefully.

"What are you doing?!" Asha exclaimed. "I understand why you did that before, but are you really going to let him carry those for the rest of the journey?"

Zach looked at Fenrir, then at the ground, then up at Asha. "Yes."

Asha grumbled something under her breath, picked up a stick, and started whacking the ground with it. Zach tried to hold back a laugh. It was like she was having a tantrum. She continued to mutter under her breath. Zach could only make out certain words. It sounded like "Fine . . . don't have to . . . candles . . . ridiculous . . . Monkey Boy." Then looking back at Fenrir who had cocked his head and was staring at Asha, Zach realized Fenrir was focusing on her with both eyes. His eye was healed!

"Asha, look!" Zach said.

She abandoned her tantrum and threw the stick over her shoulder. She walked to Fenrir and he lowered his head. They looked at his eyes. Not only was one eye healed but neither were black. Fenrir's eyes now had a brown hue and a slight twinkle to them. His mangy, gray coat was turning a beautiful silky black, and he seemed taller.

"He's healing," Asha said with astonishment.

"Yep," Zach said, satisfied with himself.

Asha noticed and rolled her eyes. As she stood up straight and pushed Zach, Fenrir licked her face with his giant tongue.

"Oh by the Spirit of Burra Din, do not ever do that—"

He licked her face again.

"I think he's gonna make you like him."

Asha stood frozen in disgust as Fenrir fell on his back and kicked up his legs. He looked like he was laughing. Asha wiped the dog's drool from her chin.

"How do we know we can trust him? How do we know he will not switch sides again?"

Fenrir stopped laughing, lowered his head, and let out a whine and a huff.

"He won't."

"But how—"

"He won't."

Zach knew Fenrir was sorry. He had to believe it. He understood Fenrir needed someone to pull him out of Malum's clutches. Zach had been the one to do it. Zach had been the one to trust him. So Fenrir would now be forever loyal and a friend. Asha just narrowed her eyes at the large wolfdog.

"Look, Asha!" Zach said, pointing behind Fenrir.

It was another wooden door. Only this time, the door was the size of a building. Large enough to fit—you guessed it—Fenrir. It had the word *Pondero* inscribed across the top.

"It's big enough to fit, Fenrir! Told you we could trust him!" Zach said.

"Ha! We shall see," Asha said as Fenrir hopped around them, delighted.

"We shall," Zach replied, sarcastically.

Zach was floored by the intense personality change of this wolfdog. This must have been what he was like before Malum got ahold of him, Zach thought as he approached the large door. Just to be sure, Zach decided to climb on Fenrir's back, encouraging Asha to do the same. She did, reluctantly. Then they walked toward the door, and it opened itself this time, confirming—in Zach's mind—that Fenrir was meant to be a part of the journey. Fenrir paused at the door. Zach could sense his uncertainty.

"Good boy, Fenrir. Walk through the light of the door." The dog stood a little prouder and carefully stepped through the gateway.

This time when the travelers stepped out of the door, they were hit by the most beautiful view they'd ever seen. Even Asha was silently mesmerized. They were standing in grass on the top of a rocky cliff. At the edge of the cliff was a straight shot down to a bright blue and green ocean. In the distance a waterfall poured over the edge elegantly into the deep pool below. The sky was a beautiful combination of pinks, purples, and blues as the sun set in the distance. Trees intermittently covered the land on the cliff, and just above a ridge was a temple-like building nestled in the side of a mountain. The temple seemed to have different rooms that were all built along the cliff as if the buildings naturally grew out of its stony side. The air smelled fresh with a hint of moisture from the nearby waterfall. It was refreshing. A cool, comforting breeze blew through the three of them, playfully whipping Asha's braid and Zach's short hair. He watched as the breeze seemed to encircle Fenrir. The warm air was a wonderful change from the bitter cold of Gaudium.

"It is wonderful to see you acting as yourself again, Fenrir," a voice said from behind them.

They turned to find a young man standing amidst the tall mountain grass, wearing what looked like a white kimono with ancient violet designs. The man didn't look much older than 20 but had stark, white hair pulled up in a bun. His eyes were a deep blue, and he had a quiet smile on his face. Just beneath the content look sat the triangular tattoo, only this tattoo was pointed down with two slashes through it. As he stepped forward, Zach noticed a metal sword hanging by his side. It was awkward looking because the man was not very big but the sword was. It looked more like a katana of a giant medieval samurai than of the young man who stood before them. Fenrir bowed as he walked closer.

"Oh do not bow, my friend. All is forgiven here. I am grateful you have rejoined us once again in protecting Burra Din. Welcome to the Land of Pax."

He spread his arms wide, and his cheeks became so full that his eyes almost disappeared, but you could still see the twinkle illuminating them. The young man's voice was soft but confident. Zach immediately felt a sense of calm at the protector's presence.

"The Wind Whisperer," Asha said quietly to Zach.

A gentle breeze blew through a field of lilies surrounding a path that led up to the temple.

"I am Kazuya, the protector of Pax. I've been waiting for you, Zachariah," he said.

"How does everyone know we are coming?" Asha said, pushing Fenrir away as he begged for her to pet him.

"Ah, the wind carries many secrets," Kazuya said, motioning for them to follow him. "And while we do not know everything

249

Burra Din has in mind, protectors are well-educated in the signs of the prophecy."

They walked up the path through the field of lilies. When they arrived at the building that looked like a temple, they found a surprising amount of people coming and going on the grounds.

"Do these people live here?" Zach asked, trying to figure out how this small building on a hill could possibly be home to a village.

"In a way," Kazuya said. "They come here to be healed."

"Healed?" Zach asked. "Are they sick?"

"In a way. They come to be healed within." Kazuya led Zach, Asha, and Fenrir up an ancient stairway to a large courtyard. "I fear you will have to wait out here, my friend," Kazuya said to Fenrir.

Fenrir sat and the ground shook slightly. A group of people, sharing Kazuya's tattoo, in the courtyard waved, and two children shot out from the group. They ran up to Fenrir, who laid his head down and braced himself for the rough love of young children. They hugged him, kissed him, and nestled in his now-beautiful fur.

"I think he will be happy here," Asha said.

"Told you you'd like him," Zach said.

"I still don't trust him."

"Yeah, okay."

Zach watched Asha laugh at the children trying to climb Fenrir's tail. Fenrir immediately relented, taking them for rides back and forth, swinging his tail. When they entered the doorway of the temple, they found a very simple room with a short table and sitting area with cushions. But instead of sitting down at the table, Kazuya walked through the room and out the back of the building to a small backyard filled with flowers and plants of all kinds. There were rows of trees with white blooms. Near the blooms were bright blue fruits that people were picking and putting in baskets. Kazuya handed each of them their own small basket.

"Let's harvest some haskap berries. Follow me."

As they watched Kazuya gently pull the fruit from the trees, Zach noticed how the protector wasn't in a rush to do anything. He walked lightly, almost as if he was hovering above the ground. And everything he did, Kazuya did with great care. Asha and Zach mimicked his actions in picking the fruit. For a few seconds they worked in silence, and then Kazuya spoke.

"I saw Fenrir carrying my brother and sisters on his collar."

Zach was confused at first but then remembered the candles held the spirits of Amal, Vera, and Jovie.

"Can you tell me their stories? The wind only carries small secrets, not lengthy details," Kazuya asked.

"Um, I guess I'll tell it," Zach said.

After trying to sum up their adventures in the last three lands as best he could while picking a basketfull of fruit, Zach took a seat on the ground next to Kazuya.

"So we've been to three lands, collected all three magi in each land. Then they turned into these candles, which are gifts, I guess. And now we're here," Zach said.

"It is a beautiful story," Kazuya observed.

Asha joined Zach on the ground.

"Yeah, I guess so," Zach said, realizing he'd never really thought about it.

"It seems wherever you go, some healing is done, and you seem to learn a thing or two yourself," Kazuya said, having a seat.

"Is that not the truth," Asha said sarcastically.

Zach rolled his eyes at her.

"And do you know where you are supposed to go next in the Land of Pax?" Kazuya asked.

"No, usually Burra Din guides us if we're patient," Zach said, rolling his eyes.

"Burra Din is not exactly straightforward," Asha added.

"Well, have you had time to meditate on your journey?" Kazuya asked.

Zach and Asha just stared at Kazuya for a moment.

"With all due respect, Kazuya," Asha said, "I do not think we have time to meditate or rest or anything. Burra Din is dying, and we must—"

"Meditation gives one strength and balance amongst chaos. How can you bring balance and gifts to the world of Burra Din if you yourself are not fully healed?" Kazuya asked.

Asha looked confused and then irritated.

"We saw some stuff that was pretty rough. Malum has control over parts of Burra Din," Zach said. "I don't think we can wait."

"Where are we off to? For of course, I must go with you as the others did," Kazuya said, sitting next to them in the shade of the tree with his basket on his lap. He began pulling the leaves and stems off the fruit.

"Oh, uh, I don't—" Zach started to say.

"There you have it," Kazuya said. "You do not know where to go. Maybe that is what you must meditate on. Maybe only here in the protection of our temple can you truly clear your mind, find tranquility, find your answers. In order to go on, you must—"

"Stay," Zach said, understanding the paradox.

"Ah, yes. You are gathering the wisdom of our temple already, young Zachariah."

"What's this temple for anyway?" Zach asked.

"This is Iyashi Temple. It is a healing place where people travel from all over to be one with Burra Din. In order to find Burra Din, one must look within. Maybe you were sent here not to heal but to be healed."

Zach raised his eyebrows at the thought. It had never crossed his mind. He felt confused. If this guy was going to keep talking in riddles, he was going to freak out.

"We are healthy," Asha said. "As you can see, we do not need to be healed."

"I see," Kazuya said as he continued to work on his fruit basket. "You may be physically healthy, but are you mentally healthy? You have been under a significant amount of stress as of late. Have you given any thought to the toll it takes on you? I will tell you. If you are not mentally fit, you will not last long in the presence of Malum."

Zach looked up at Kazuya at the mention of his enemy. He tried not to think about the fact that he would eventually have to confront the giant evil warrior.

"Malum is a darkness that does his most profound work, not through physical distress, but mental. As you can see from our renewed friend out there," Kazuya said. "Malum did not destroy Fenrir physically. No, he slowly deteriorated Fenrir mentally. He disrupted the tranquility of our dear friend, filling his mind with doubts and self-loathing."

"Do you think that's what he'll try to do to us?" Zach asked.

"This is hard to know for sure, but that seems to be his way. However, if you come to confront Malum, you should be ready for anything," Kazuya said.

"I agree with that!" Asha said. "Done." She placed her basket of fruit in front of her.

"Yes, Asha. It seems you are finished, but . . . " Kazuya picked up one haskap berry. He pinched the center of the fruit where the stem came from and pulled out another small bit of stem. "You have left half the stem in the fruit in your haste. And unless you like stems in your jam, I would recommend removing the rest as I have done."

Asha's cheeks burned red.

"Oh do not feel embarrassed, my dear. This is what you have come to the Iyashi temple to learn. In doing a task, you must clear your mind of all other things to accomplish the task successfully. You must remove the distractions that prevent you from succeeding. You must find balance, your center."

Asha grumbled and began to quietly and gently pull the remaining stem pieces from the fruits. And Zach, who had realized he'd been doing the same thing, restarted. He liked the Wind Whisperer but found him slightly annoying, almost like an all-knowing sage who calmly walked around filled with answers but forced you to learn them on your own. After they removed the stems from the fruits, Kazuya led them back through the door and down the hall to a kitchen. They placed the baskets on the table. Zach noticed the kitchen was incredibly organized, and the rooms seemed to be divided by large screens.

"I'll show you to your rooms," Kazuya said.

As they walked by one room, Zach noticed a man, legs crossed and eyes closed, hovering above his cushion. He was floating!

"How's that guy floating back there?" Zach asked.

"Floating?" Asha turned her head.

"Yeah, that guy back there was floating!" Zach said again.

Kazuya folded his hands and continued walking in front of them. "He is becoming enlightened. He is quieting his mind and releasing the worries of his heart. He is becoming one with Burra Din."

"Cool," Zach said.

At the end of the hall, the three travelers walked back outside. Fenrir was waiting for them, and they walked down a stone path. The path wove in and out of beautiful gardens. But the centerpiece of the garden was really the lilies. They were bigger than Zach had ever seen. A small stream wound its way around the grounds, weaving around their path. Zach and Asha followed Kazuya over a small bridge to another building.

"Here are your rooms, and the large pavilion over there is for Fenrir," Kazuya said.

Noticing the windows had no glass and the doors were again simply curtains, Zach asked, "Don't you get any bad weather here?"

"No, actually the weather stays consistent. There are extra blankets in your rooms if you need them. You may shower behind the building in the stalls near the small waterfalls. There are fresh clothes in your rooms if you would like them," Kazuya said.

"Thank you," Zach said.

"Please join me in the main hall—where we came from—when you are ready. We can get a good meal. It smells especially spicy today. I am looking forward to it," Kazuya said, walking back to the main temple hall.

Zach and Asha walked into the temple-like house. Fenrir walked over to the pavilion and huffed a sigh of relief as he rested his head on his paws. The center hall stretched beyond to another courtyard, and on each side of the hall was a screen door. Zach took the room to the right and Asha took the room to the left. Zach pulled his bag off his back and set it on the floor inside the clean and modest room. There was a long cushion for a bed, a short table, and a small cushion for a chair. On the table was a pad of paper and what looked like a fancy feather pen of some kind. Zach walked over to the cushion and noticed a white shirt and pants laying next to a blue kimono. The kimono had the triangular symbol of Kazuya all over it in gold. He grabbed the clothes and walked back out to the hall. Hearing the waterfall from behind the building, Zach headed that direction for his shower.

After standing for too long under the water, Zach dried himself off with a towel and dressed in the clothes of the Land of Pax. It was a light fabric and fit perfectly, which would normally be odd, but Zach had come to expect extraordinary things in Burra Din, even perfectly fitting clothes. The fabric must be from Solis, Zach thought. Waiting for Asha, Zach walked through the hall and sat on the steps in front of the building. He took in the beautiful mountainous scenery. The clouds in the sky puffed like marshmallows, hovering around the peaks. The shadows from the clouds created a decorative ring. And the last rays of sunlight broke through the cracks in the large mountain range. As the sun set, small lanterns lit up on the sides of the building and along the temple path.

"Sorry, I fell asleep," Asha said as she walked out of the hall onto the front steps. "Something about this place is relaxing." She stretched her arms and sat next to Zach on the top step.

"Yeah, it's pretty calming," Zach agreed. "It's kind of weird though, ya know, just sitting here and all, waitin' to save the world. I feel like we need to get going."

"Right?! I know! I mean, I know it is important to be patient but I am anxious. I do not want to spend time meditating. Waste of time," Asha said, throwing up her hands.

"Looks like Fenrir doesn't mind," Zach said, turning to check on him. His eyes were closed, and he whimpered slightly as his giant paw jerked.

"Must be dreamin'," Zach said, chuckling to himself.

As he turned back around, he caught the last bit of light behind Asha. She was glowing like some fierce sorceress. Her large bright eyes stared back at him.

"What?" Asha asked.

"Oh, uh—nothing," Zach said, "Maybe we should go catch up with Kazuya."

"Yes, the lantern-lit path leads to the temple, I believe," Asha said.

"Yeah, it seems to follow the same way we came from," Zach said, happy he'd dodged the awkward moment.

When they walked back to the main temple and into the large hall, Kazuya directed them to the dining area. Here they saw lots of friendly people talking softly. Some had already eaten, and some were getting in line for the buffet. Zach noticed that each of their tattoos was boldly designed on their neck. There were even a handful of people whose tattoos were from other lands. One woman's even matched Asha's tattoo.

"Chaya!" Asha said.

"Asha! Oh my girl! It has been too long!" Chaya said.

Chaya, an old woman with thick, beautiful, white hair tied in a bun, dressed in a short red kimono, and who shared the same eyes as Asha, gave her a big hug.

"What in Burra are you doing here?!" Asha asked.

"Oh my girl, what are *you* doing here?" Chaya responded.

"I am on a—well—a quest of sorts," Asha said, looking back at Zach and Kazuya, who waited patiently in line for food.

Zach was listening and waved back.

"Ah, of course you are! You always were an ambitious one. Well, I came here after my husband, Sahil, died," Chaya said.

"Oh yes, I remember you leaving. Did you come here right away?" Asha asked.

"No, I traveled around Burra Din for a time and then ended up here. I love it here! I was very sad when Sahil died. I was lost. But Kazuya found me wandering around Pax and brought me here. I healed my soul and mind and here I am." She hugged Asha again.

"I'm just so happy to see you!"

Zach watched as Asha caught up with her old friend. After getting their own meals, Kazuya and Zach joined them at the table. Asha was completely animated when retelling their adventures. Chaya laughed, and when they found out that Zach was the boy from the prophecy no one doubted it. It was as if the belief in Burra Din was so intense here, no one doubted anything. Zach was impressed and wished he was more like the people of Pax.

After breakfast the next morning, Kazuya led Zach and Asha to a small courtyard on the edge of the mountains. From here, Zach could see over a cliff and then out forever. It was magnificent. He saw three stones with flat tops a few feet apart from one another in an arrow formation in the courtyard. The courtyard was filled with lilies and tall, bright green grass.

"Please join me here on each side," Kazuya said, motioning for them to stand on the stones.

He went through several poses to help them get their balance. Eventually they settled for a standing position. Kazuya told them to watch as he did a series of slow moves with intention and then pushed out his palm. When he shot his hand out, a gust of air blew from his palm and wrapped itself around like a dragon in the sky. Then it turned and shot back into the courtyard, ringing the large brass gong near the temple door.

"That was wonderful! May we learn how to do that?" Asha asked.

"With time and if Burra Din believes you are ready. Here, let us try," Kazuya said.

Zach and Asha balanced on their stones, standing with perfect posture. Kazuya began to guide them through the meditation.

"Close your eyes. Clear your mind. Breathe in and out. Carefully concentrate on each thought you are having and imagine the thought dissolving away," Kazuya said.

How can you "dissolve away" a thought? Zach wondered. He tried to follow Kazuya's directions. Feeling kind of ridiculous, he peeked for a moment.

"You must not peek, Zachariah. Seek within. Find your center," Kazuya said.

Surprised, Zach quickly shut his eyes. Kazuya's eyes were shut too. How had he known Zach's were open? At first Zach struggled to concentrate, but slowly a sense of peace drifted over him. He felt lighter, and the world around him disappeared. He was within himself and could only hear his own breathing. He'd never felt this calm before. Suddenly flashes of his adventures in Burra Din played before him. He saw Asha again for the first time. Her feisty demeanor made him laugh. Amal appeared, and Zach felt sadness creep over his heart. Amal was his first real guide, one of his first real friends. Amal faded into light. Then Vera walked silently through his mind, leaving a trail of beautiful flowers behind her. Zach soared above her on Doragon alongside Asha. They sailed over a beautiful white landscape until they found Jovie with her people in Jovanna, laughing loudly and pointing at them in the sky. From a mountain peak, Kazuya waved, gently surrounded by puffy white clouds.

Then suddenly the sky filled with darkness and Zach lost the image. Everything went black, and the world around Zach became frightening. He saw himself again, but this time he was with his old friends. Floating above the scenario, he was having an out of body experience. He saw himself hanging out with them and making fun of the kids in the class who ate alone. Zach wasn't exactly participating, but he wasn't exactly stopping them. He saw himself sitting in the group unhappy and feeling lonely. Then his vision flashed to another time when he tried to convince one of the boys that the book he was reading for class was actually good. The boy laughed at him, and Zach pretended he was joking. Zach didn't like this version of himself. This was the Zach that did what others wanted him to do. This wasn't the true Zach. Then another image flashed, and he saw himself helping the cold creatures in the Forest of Inspirare, laughing in Consano Lake, sharing supplies with the old woman in Jovie's igloo, pleading with Fenrir, and sitting next to Asha on the steps of the temple watching the beautiful sunset. This was the Zach he liked. This was the Zach he wanted to be. He felt a wave of contentment wash over him again.

Breathing in and out, in and out, Zach realized something else. From the dungeon of Fides to the Gigant mountains, two people had been popping into his head, helping him through his entire journey. His parents. Little things in Burra Din triggered their memory and memories of his childhood. Zach had been so busy trying to stay alive, he hadn't thought to push the memories away. He'd just enjoyed them. Suddenly a wave of air swirled around him. He felt the urge to guide the air. Lifting his hands and grabbing the air as if holding a ball, Zach pushed the ball down and then out. He heard a shot of wind sound, and the palms of his hands shook. The wind whizzed through the air and then a loud GONG! echoed through the courtyard.

"Whoa, how'd I do that?"

"You opened your heart to the gifts you've collected. You are one step closer to healing your own heart, your own soul," Kazuya said.

Asha was staring at him proudly. Then Zach reached into his pocket and pulled out a magus: *Pondero*. This magus was violet like the first ones. Kazuya walked over to Zach and bowed before the magus. Asha hopped down from her stone and looked in Zach's palm. They heard a howl from the other side of the temple. The three of them ran through the hall and found Fenrir sitting, tail wagging, and tongue hanging out in front of a new large door: *Gratium.*

DOOR ELEVEN

GRATIUM
GRATITUDE IN THE LAND OF PAX

"Give thanks to the Lord, for he is good;
his love endures forever."
Psalm 118:1

Zach, Asha, and Fenrir waited in front of the door for Kazuya. After packing a bag and changing his clothes into what looked like a white ninja suit, Kazuya walked down the stairs with Chaya.

"I will do my best to run the temple," Chaya said.

"I am confident in your abilities, Chaya," Kazuya said.

"Yes, dear Kazuya. You have an important job. Protecting the prophecy is more important than anything here," Chaya said.

Kazuya thanked her and walked over to Zach, Asha, and Fenrir.

"Let us be on our way," he said.

A sadness lingered in the young protector's eyes. He was stoic and strong, but Zach sensed his uncertainty as he reached for the door.

"Kaz," a gentle voice said from the side of the courtyard.

Zach and Asha turned to see a young woman walking toward them. She had long, black hair with deep green eyes and porcelain skin. She was about the same height as Zach and wore a lavender kimono. Kazuya looked up and spread his arms wide.

"Kumi! You are back!" Kazuya said.

Kumi looked about the same age as Kazuya.

"Yes, my love," Kumi said.

They embraced and kissed. Zach and Asha looked at the ground. Behind Kumi stood a group of shy children. Kumi leaned her forehead on the strong protector.

"I found the lost children."

Kazuya looked at the children behind her.

"Kumi, I knew you would," Kazuya said.

"Wait, what is happening here?" Kumi asked, looking at Zach and Asha.

"My dear Kumi, the time has come. I must go," Kazuya said.

Tears filled Kumi's eyes. "I understand, my love, but I just returned." She walked over to Zach, quietly staring. "Is this, is this the boy from the prophecy?"

Zach wasn't exactly sure what she was going to do so he just said, "Yes."

"It is wonderful to meet you," Kumi said.

Zach's face turned red. Kumi was beautiful.

"You must go, my love. Save Burra Din. I will be here waiting for you. Do not fear," Kumi said.

Kazuya hugged and kissed her.

"I do not fear. Burra Din calls. All will be well. I love you, my eternal beauty," Kazuya said.

"I love you too, Kaz. Return quickly and safely, promise me."

Kazuya turned and looked at Fenrir's collar.

"Kumi, you know I may not return," Kazuya said.

Zach noticed the candles and felt a heavy weight on his heart for the couple. Kumi, remembering the predicted fate of the protectors, lifted Kazuya's chin.

"We knew this day would come, my love. If Burra Din wills it, you must go. If it is part of Burra Din's plan, we will be together again. I know all will be well."

"Your faith is strong, my Kumi. My heart is at peace, knowing Burra Din watches over us. I will miss you with all my heart," Kazuya said.

He pushed a strand of her hair aside and kissed her one last time. Then, walking away and lingering for a moment to hold her hand, Kazuya turned to Asha and Zach. Zach pulled the door open, and they took one last look at the content people of Iyashi and walked into the light.

. . .

They found themselves on a ragged barren mountainside. It was dark, and the wind whipped violently. Asha and Zach huddled behind Fenrir.

"Kazuya, where are we?" Zach asked.

Kazuya walked to the edge of the cliff silently. He closed his eyes and lifted his hands. Slowly he moved them in and out, balancing on one leg. The wind whipped around him, but Kazuya stood strong and steady. Then he wrapped his hands around an invisible ball and pushed out from himself. There was a loud crack, and the violent wind stopped. Asha and Zach came out from behind Fenrir, who followed them.

"Yes, talking will be easier now," Kazuya said. "We find ourselves on the eastern side of the mountain."

"What shall we do now?" Asha asked.

"I have this map," Zach said as he pulled the ancient-looking map from his bag. He handed it to Kazuya, whose eyes sparkled.

"I have heard of this map, but never seen it. This has the location of the castle. Salvator, the prince. What a blessing."

"So should we head to that spot?" Zach asked.

265

"To my understanding of the prophecy, the prince will return to a place once revered. Those ruins were once a great castle built by the last king of Burra Din who was a descendent of the original tribes of the first gifts," Kazuya said.

"Is it an island? How do we get there?" Zach asked.

"A small port and shipyard sit quietly at the bottom of the mountain. This would be a good place to gather supplies and find a ship," Kazuya confirmed.

"Can you sail?" Asha asked.

"He has wind powers, Asha. I'm sure we can figure it out," Zach said.

She scrunched her nose at him and gave him a friendly shove.

"If we get a small enough ship for the four of us, we can manage. But there may be one problem," Kazuya said.

"What?" Zach asked.

"Fenrir does not like water."

They slowly turned to Fenrir who was now contentedly napping behind them.

"Maybe we will wait to tell him about the water," Zach suggested.

"I think that would be best," Asha agreed. "Now, how do we get down from this mountain?"

"We could climb down or . . . " Kazuya said with just a hint of mischief in his voice.

"Or what?" Zach raised his eyebrows.

"Or we could take a more fun way down the mountain," Kazuya said, flicking his wrist. Suddenly a gust of wind lifted Asha off the ground, twirled her around, and then placed her back down on the cliff.

"Whoa!" Asha said. "What happened?"

"We can take the wind down the mountain?" Zach asked.

"Yes," Kazuya said.

"Let's do it!" Zach said excitedly.

"Are you sure about this?" Asha asked as Fenrir walked over and nuzzled her back. She swatted him aside.

"Asha, it's just like Amal's fire jump," Zach assured her, entertained that this time she was nervous.

"Heh heh," Asha said, gulping.

"You will be safe, Asha," Kazuya said.

And before they could discuss it further, all four of them were lifted off the ground and one by one the wind carried them down the mountain. Hoots and hollers of excitement were heard from Zach, panicking howls and whines came from Fenrir, and Asha just closed her eyes and yelled, "I hate you, Zach!" over and over again. Zach laughed. It reminded him of a giant roller coaster as they seemed to slide down the jetstream along the mountainside, up and down. After only a few moments, the glowing lanterns of the village dock came into view. The wind slowed down and gently set each of them on the ground by the pier. Zach landed and jumped up with excitement. Kazuya landed as if he'd been doing this every day of his life. Asha landed, hair wild, and face flushed from the exhilaration, and Fenrir was gently placed on the ground. However, the hairs on the back of his neck were standing straight up, shoulders tight, and paws clawing into the dirt. He almost looked catlike, as if he dared anyone to try and lift him off the ground again.

"Time for a boat and supplies," Kazuya said, walking toward a small building near the docks.

Fenrir waited outside while Zach and Asha followed Kazuya into the shop. It was an old stone structure that rested up against the side of the mountain. The village was small and seemed to be merely a stopping point for travelers. When they entered the shop, they found they were the only customers. The shopkeeper, a burly, bearded man with gray hair behind the counter, was napping in the corner. Kazuya motioned for Zach and Asha to have a seat at the table. Two plates of vegetables and rice floated over along with two mugs of tea. As they enjoyed their meal, they listened to Kazuya talking with the recently awakened shopkeeper. The shopkeeper seemed to know Kazuya, and the three of them were set to go within an hour. The shopkeeper even had an extremely large dog bone for Fenrir, who was beside himself with delight at the prospect of wrestling the bone into submission. The sleek wooden sailing vessel was equipped with green sails, a deck large enough for just the four of them, and a room below deck with cots and a galley. As they boarded the boat, Fenrir paused. He saw the bone on the boat, but he also saw the water and realized now that they were going to be boarding the vessel.

"Come on Fenrir," Zach encouraged.

Fenrir stood still.

"Burra Din needs you, you courageous beast," Kazuya encouraged.

But Fenrir didn't move.

Then Asha walked past without even looking at him and said, "We will leave you here you big oaf."

Fenrir's tail wagged and he followed Asha onto the boat, licking the side of her face.

"Ugh! You disgust me," she said.

Zach rolled his eyes, and Kazuya laughed.

The shopkeeper had followed them out to the boat to ensure they had everything they needed, but before they set sail he said, "Be careful, I hear the waters are dark in the east. Anyone traveling there will need all the powers of Burra Din to survive the storms brewing in that corner of the world. Where are you all headed, anyway?"

"East," Kazuya said, and with that, he opened the sails and brought forth a wind to guide them on their way.

"May Burra Din bless your journey!" the shopkeeper yelled from the dock.

On the ship, Zach and Asha rushed around, following Kazuya's orders. Fenrir even pitched in, which was extremely helpful due to his size and strength. The only downside was if he gripped the ropes too tightly, his sharp teeth cut the strands. Once they were on course, they sat on the deck of the ship and looked at the endless night sky, illuminated by billions of stars.

"Is it not breathtaking?" Kazuya observed.

"Yeah, it's crazy. I've never seen so many stars," Zach said.

"When there is no other light to distract from their beauty, the stars shine even brighter," Kazuya said.

Zach thought for a moment. His world was full of distractions. It was no wonder everyone struggled to focus. Zach wondered if that's why so many people in his world were unhappy.

"I love sleeping alone in my forest. Happiness fills my heart when I look at the night sky and have no other worries," Asha said. Then she stretched out her arms and laid down, propping her head up on her hand.

"Kazuya."

"Yes, Asha."

"Who were the children back at the temple? Why did Kumi have to find them?"

"Those were the lost children of Tsuki Village."

Zach and Asha sat silently, waiting for him to go on. Neither of them knew the story of Tsuki village. But Fenrir grunted and huffed as if he knew. Kazuya reached over to stroke Fenrir's fur and then continued.

"Tsuki Village was a beautiful place on the ridge of a mountain. It was a saving grace for sailors as it reflected the light of the moon in the dark night, giving sailors the ability to find it amongst the ridge of the mountain. But as has been happening all over Burra Din, the sickness of Malum poisoned the village. The village became a place of darkness where greed and corruption ruled. It also became known as a wealthy village. But the wealth was held at the top by the village counselors who were originally meant to care for the people and determine the laws as an educated council. Then one evening, not too long ago, a group of murderous pirates attacked the town and . . . " Kazuya wiped away a tear. "They took all the treasure of the village and left no one alive."

He paused for a moment. Zach and Asha sat silently as Fenrir let out a small whine.

"Luckily, the families of the village gathered the children together when they saw the pirates approaching and sent them off. They told them the way to our temple, and one of the mothers prayed for Burra Din to send us a message that the children were coming. One day, I was meditating in the courtyard, and the wind carried the message to me. Burra Din encouraged me to listen. I heard the mother's plea, and the people of Iyashi temple decided to send out a group to meet with the children. I wanted to lead them myself, but Burra Din stopped me. When I tried to leave the temple the wind blocked my path, so my dear Kumi led the group instead. Now I know why Burra Din stopped me. Kumi and the group were gone for months. And," he said with a sigh, "they returned just as we were leaving."

Kazuya's face fell.

"You love her deeply," Asha said.

Kazuya looked at Asha sadly.

"Are protectors allowed to fall in love? Be wed?" Asha asked.

"I do not know. I am known as the Wind Whisperer. A protector who works to heal within and bring balance to the troubled. Falling in love with Kumi was just as much of a surprise to me as anyone. The other protectors had not fallen in love. But they all encouraged my relationship with Kumi. Protectors are not immune from the beauties and trials of daily life. We love and we suffer just as you do. And must find tranquility within."

Zach thought of Amal's desperation at the sight of the wraith, Vera's sadness to leave her people, and Jovie's frustration with the Skotovody. Here, Kazuya, the protector who was most focused on calming the chaos of the mind even struggled with his own sense of balance.

"We were set to marry soon. But Burra Din called. Life is full of uncertainties. One must have faith. My life as a protector is dedicated to Burra Din and the prophecy. Kumi understood that, but it does not change how much . . . "

"You miss her," Zach said.

"Yes," Kazuya said.

"She seems wonderful. I mean, we only saw her for a few moments but she seems wonderful," Asha said.

"She really is," Kazuya said. "But I must trust in Burra Din. Burra Din gave me the gift to love Kumi the way I do, so I know that it is real. I must be patient. I know we will be together one day. Even if it is to be in the place beyond. I will wait. I will do my duty. I love her."

The four of them sat silently.

"Do you think we'll all be together after we die?" Zach asked suddenly.

Asha, Kazuya, and Fenrir looked at him in surprise.

"Of course, Burra Din declares it," Kazuya said.

"His maata and pita died," Asha explained.

"Ah, I see," Kazuya said. "I am very sorry, Zachariah. That is a hurt no one should have to bear. But yes, your parents are waiting for you beyond this world or any world. You will be together with them again."

Zach wasn't sure how Kazuya could be so certain, but he didn't question him. He turned his gaze to the night sky and drifted off to sleep, listening to Kazuya and Asha talk. As the ship rocked, Zach had many peculiar dreams. He dreamt he lived in the Forest of Inspirare with Asha, and they hunted together. Then he dreamt of flying through the air with Doragon. They flipped and turned, embracing the freedom of the skies. But mid-dive, the skies turned dark, and Zach felt cold. He was no longer on Doragon's back but standing alone. He couldn't make out where he was, but he heard voices. One of the voices was dark and creepy, Malum.

"Give me the magi! You cannot defeat me! In the end, I will destroy you!"

These words continued to play over and over in Zach's dream in different orders and overlapping until Zach felt like his head would explode. He knelt on the ground and put his hands on his ears. The grating against his nerves and his mind was torture. Then Malum switched tactics and began to attack Zach's heart.

"Your mother is in my grasp. She did not embrace the light before her death. She did not know the goodness of Burra Din. She is mine. You cannot save her!"

Zach screamed as pain shot through his heart. He couldn't take any more. He felt like he was going to faint. The memory of his mother in the hospital bed resurfaced and tortured him. His parents had been his foundation. The thought of her in the grasp of darkness for eternity was more than he could bear. The pain in his chest was so deep, he felt as if his ribs would explode. He breathed deeply and felt water spraying all over his face as he heard a new voice.

"Zach! Zach! Wake up!"

His eyes fluttered open, and he was on the boat again with Asha. She was looking down at him. The panic subsided and he was relieved to see her.

"Hi," he said.

"Get up!" she said. "There's a storm! Come on!"

Kazuya and Fenrir secured the sails and rushed below deck. Fenrir did his best to fit in the tight cargo hold. He sat half out of the door. Zach, Kazuya, and Asha leaned against him.

"I have enchanted the winds around the boat so we may continue our course despite the storm, but I do not know how long that will hold," Kazuya said.

"You think we're getting close to the island. You think Malum is trying to stop us, don't you?" Zach asked.

Zach was drenched from sweat and rain. Kazuya nodded. Asha picked at the strap of her bag, looking nervous. Within seconds, a deafening howl from the wind filled the cargo hold. The boat rocked violently. Kazuya ran up to the deck.

"My enchantment's been broken! Malum!"

Kazuya began ordering them around the boat to keep it from capsizing while he tried to control the wind with his powers. But despite his efforts, the boat rocked violently. At one point, the boat tipped so far to one side, Zach could have reached the sea from the deck. Zach and Asha clung to the side of the boat as it twisted in the water. They could no longer help Kazuya. Any time they tried to move, they lost their balance. Fenrir had also given in and was clinging to the railing. Kazuya stood like a statue in the center of the ship, meditating and trying to become one with the winds, guiding them into a gentle breeze. Then just when Zach didn't think things could get any worse, he looked past Kazuya and saw a monster of a wave. Inside the wave Zach swore he saw a dark pair of eyes and a mouth. The wave crashed over the ship as the mouth swallowed the boat. Engulfed by water, Zach, Asha, Fenrir, and Kazuya were torn from the ship. Zach flung his arms out and tried to fight against the current. He kicked his legs frantically until he reached the surface.

Breaking through the water, Zach inhaled desperately. He couldn't see anything. The rain coming down bounced off the water, blinding him. A creaking noise had Zach twisting to find the boat, which was coming straight for him. Zach dove down. As the current from the vessel pulled at Zach, he kicked away from the ship and back up to the surface. He watched as the boat was torn in two by crashing waves and sank. Trying to stay afloat, Zach looked around for something to grab. Just before he was engulfed by a second large wave, he grabbed hold of a barrel, clinging to a handle on its side. The wave picked him up high above the surface and dropped him back into the water. Zach's body twisted around as he somehow managed to stay with the barrel. As he surfaced, he coiled his body around the bobbing wooden cylinder, holding on for dear life. Coughing up water, Zach tried to catch his breath. Within seconds, he realized the rain had stopped, and the sea was calming.

"Zach! Zach!"

Zach awkwardly turned on the barrel to find Asha floating nearby on a small inflatable boat. Zach swam over to her. She grabbed his arms and plucked him out of the water.

"You've got to be kidding me! Where the heck did you get a boat?" Zach asked.

"My pack."

Zach saw her pack sitting in the boat. Suddenly he was horrified. His pack was lost. He hadn't had time to grab it when Asha woke him up. He frantically patted his chest and was relieved to find that somehow the magus had remained in his pocket through the entire tumultuous swim. Jovie had been right; the magi did have a mind of their own.

"Where's Kazuya?" Zach asked.

Asha pointed to the sky. Zach was shocked to find Kazuya meditating in a cross-legged position, floating in the air. Slowly he came down to the boat and lifted his hand in Fenrir's direction. Zach watched as Fenrir was lifted out of the water. The motionless animal hung in the air, unconscious, along with several boards. Suddenly the boards came together, making a raft. At the end of the raft, a rope secured itself, placing its other end in Kazuya's hands. The gentle wind carefully lowered Fenrir to the raft and sent a breeze through his nostrils. Fenrir lifted his head and coughed water from his lungs. But as he realized he was on a flat raft, Fenrir froze in panic.

"Just lay down, Fenrir! All is well. All is well," Asha said.

Zach was relieved to find that Fenrir was okay.

"So I have good news and bad news," Asha said as she rummaged through her pack.

Turning away from Fenrir, Zach looked at Asha.

"The good news is that I have this boat. The bad news is that everything else fell out of my pack except this pack of soggy bread."

"The map! The candles!" Zach said. "Oh no! Satya! No, the sword is still here. But the map is gone! My entire pack is gone! Fenrir?! The candles?!"

Fenrir leaned up, and Zach saw the collar firmly in place.

Without thinking, Zach jumped off the boat, swam to Fenrir, and climbed on the raft. He stroked Fenrir's back while he checked his collar. All three candles were still in place. Of course they were! The same magic that kept the magi safe had to be keeping the candles safe as well. He turned and shouted the good news to Kazuya and Asha. Then he swam back over to the boat.

"But the map! We don't have the map!"

"All is well, Zachariah," Kazuya said. "We do not need the map. Burra Din will guide us."

"Yeah, but will we make it? We have no food or fresh water. And unless you can magically turn saltwater into freshwater, I don't see us making it very far," Zach rambled, heaving in large breaths and looking around for land. Nothing.

"Have faith young Zachariah. We will manage. Burra Din will help us," Kazuya said.

Zach couldn't stop himself. The weight of his troubles and the desperate feeling of the dream overwhelmed him. He sat back against the side of the boat in silence.

"Let us rest for a bit. When the stars come out, I will read them, and we shall know our course," Kazuya said.

"Oh man, I didn't even think about that. We're all turned around now thanks to that storm," Zach said.

Despair was knocking at the door of Zach's mind. He'd been excited because he thought they were so close. Only two magi away from the fourth gift and the arrival of the prince. Now, it seemed everything was falling apart. He didn't think he could take much more of this. Plus, he still had to face Malum. There was no way Malum was going to just let Zach win. Maybe Malum was right. Maybe Zach should just give in now.

"Zachariah, what troubles you?" Kazuya asked.

"I had a dream, well um, dreams," Zach said, feeling the color drain from his face. Just discussing the dreams made him sick to his stomach.

"What were these dreams about, Zachariah?" Kazuya asked, folding his hands in his lap.

"Malum," Zach said.

"He hears and understands the language of the dark one," Asha explained. "It has been happening this entire journey."

"Ah, I thought that might be," Kazuya said. "Remember what I told you before Zachariah? Do you remember what I said about quieting your mind and meditating? Becoming one with Burra Din? That is the challenge here. That is what my temple is for. The noise you must cancel out is Malum. All distractions, negative thoughts, urgency, anxiety is Malum. He will do everything in his power to keep you from embracing all that is Burra Din. And you, my friend, are getting ever closer to destroying him, so Malum is working ever harder against you."

"The dream was about good things at first," Zachariah explained. "But then the dreams shifted to darkness. I was standing in darkness and my mother, he said he had my mother. He said because my mother did not embrace Burra Din, she would be . . ." Zach rubbed his eyes. "Forever under his power or something like that."

"That's terrible. That cannot be true!" Asha said, turning to Kazuya. "Can it?"

"Why do you think Malum has chosen your mother to use against you? Why not your father?" Kazuya asked.

Zach hadn't thought of that. He wiped the tears away and covered his face with his hands. He was so tired all of a sudden.

"I don't know."

"Did you get to speak to your parents before they died?" Kazuya asked.

Zach glared up at Kazuya. He really didn't want to talk about this. But he didn't have the energy to fight it.

"Yeah, I said bye to them before they left."

"That is not what I mean, Zachariah," Kazuya said. "Did you talk to either of your parents right before they passed through to the place beyond?"

Zach dropped his head in his hands again and, in a muffled voice, said, "Yeah, my mom . . . in the hospital."

"Ah," Kazuya said, pausing for a moment. "That is the key, Zachariah. Watching a loved one pass away can be one of the most tragic events of all the realms. Malum is using that moment against you."

Asha grunted angrily and tossed the package of soggy bread into the ocean. Zach looked up at her.

Enraged Asha said, "I despise evil tyrants."

Kazuya placed a calming hand on Asha's shoulder and continued, "Zachariah, did your mother know Burra Din? Did she understand the lessons you've come to learn here?"

"I don't know," Zach said. "I don't know what my mother believed in. We never really talked about anything like this."

"There is a chance she is in Malum's clutches if she knew nothing of Burra Din or the gifts of Burra Din," Kazuya said, looking sorrowful.

Zach's exhaustion turned to rage. "What do you mean?! My mom's dead. She can't be here, can she?!"

"When someone's body dies, their spirit is released and becomes a part of all realms. Your mother's spirit is still very much alive, Zachariah," Kazuya said.

Zach stared at him.

"So you're saying this evil viking has my mom's spirit hostage?!" Zach asked.

"Malum tries to enslave the souls of all the worlds," Kazuya said.

"What?!" It all made sense. If he could cross over into Burra Din, what kept anyone in Burra Din from crossing over into his world?

"How do we save her?! My mom can't be with Malum forever! What do we do?!" Zach asked, trying to stand in the raft.

"Zachariah," Kazuya said steadily.

Zach stopped and looked at him.

"Look me in the eyes."

Zach took a breath and looked at the protector. He felt calmer as Kazuya focused on him with his quiet, confident demeanor.

"Remember what I told you. You must stay focused on Burra Din. Hope, Zachariah. Have faith and be joyful in the fact that you will not fight this battle alone."

"But how could anyone be joyful about this?" Zach asked.

"Remember, Zach," Asha said. "The prince is coming. If the prince comes, Malum will be defeated. Good will reign. But the prince must come, and the only thing that will work is if we prepare for him by revealing the gifts of old."

"The gifts? How the heck are these gifts of old going to save my mother?!" Zach asked sarcastically as his chest heaved with anger.

But as he stood unbalanced in the raft staring at his friends, he remembered what he'd seen, what he'd done. He had no idea how he'd possibly made it this far. Plus, he'd made so many mistakes. But Burra Din had gotten him here. Burra Din sent the magi and the doors at just the right moments. Burra Din healed its people and watched over its protectors. Burra Din even watched over him. He was only one candle away from the end. Zach suddenly felt a sense of relief spread through him. He slumped back down into the raft.

"You're right, Asha. We're good. Yeah. We're good." Zach was beginning to feel hopeful again. "I'm glad I have you guys. And we have this boat. Let's do this. Let's save Burra Din, and let's save my mom!"

Before he'd even finished his sentence, Zach felt the warmth of another magus in his pocket. He pulled out the second piece of violet wax and showed Kazuya who clapped his hands.

"Hooray!" Asha exclaimed.

Fenrir barked with excitement. The magus read *Gratium* and illuminated Kazuya's symbol. But as they admired the engravings and subtle glow of the magus, the sky darkened again as an unnatural growl erupted from the water. In the direction of the evil grumble, they found the current had increased and their boat was now swirling rapidly to the center of a vortex. They were headed for a whirlpool! Zach stood and for the first time throughout the entire journey, he didn't panic. He placed a hand on Asha's arm.

"Don't worry, Asha. Burra Din has a plan. Hold tight. I think we're supposed to ride this out."

Kazuya began meditating, guiding gentle power from his palms to keep them from capsizing.

"Kazuya, stop," Zach said. "Let go of the boat! Burra Din will control it!"

Kazuya opened his eyes and looked upon Zach proudly. It was almost as if Kazuya had been waiting for Zach to make this decision. The Wind Whisperer let go. Fenrir howled and the boat surged forward. As they came up to the edge of the whirlpool, Zach's stomach dropped. The massive wall of water leading down to the swirling central vortex was the most frightening thing he'd ever seen.

Taking a deep breath, Zach closed his eyes and said softly, "I trust you."

"Look!" Asha said.

Already aware of what happened, Zach opened his eyes. Squinting to try and focus through the violent mist of water, Zach saw it. The biggest door of the entire journey. Whale-sized cursive letters scrawled across its front: *Identitatis*. And it was right in the middle of the ominous swirling vortex.

"Woohoo! I knew it!" Zach cheered.

The boat tipped over the edge of the whirlpool, and they swirled around the massive hole three times before heading straight for the center. The great door opened, and light burst forth into the black sky, illuminating the world around them. Suddenly the whirlpool didn't seem scary anymore. The water was no longer a black, endless pit but a beautiful, blue and green home to wonderful creatures. Ocean life of all kinds flowed through the current and playfully jumped in and out of the water. Zach laughed with exhilaration. Kazuya and Asha cheered. Even Fenrir howled with delight as the small boat tipped over into the portal.

Door Twelve

Identitatis
Identity in the Land of Pax

"For now we see in a mirror dimly, but then face to face.
Now I know in part; then I shall know fully, even as
I have been fully known."
1 Corinthians 13:12

After falling for mere seconds but for what felt like an eternity, the three travelers and their now-loyal beast dropped onto a grassy hillside. Zach lay there for a few seconds, trying to absorb what exactly had happened. He stared at the dark night sky. It was almost completely black save for a handful of stars. He was starting to realize the closer they got to the castle where the prince could be born, the darker it seemed to get. Malum must be concentrating his power nearby, Zach thought. As he rose, he brushed off his pants and walked over to Asha, helping her off the ground. Fenrir was sitting, tongue hanging out, and wagging his tail as he watched them. Kazuya had not fully landed on the ground. He'd been hovering right above it and then pulled himself right side up, landing gracefully on his two feet.

"Wow, that was out of control," Asha said as she pulled her pack onto her back and readjusted her bowshot.

"You said it," Zach agreed. He felt his chest and was relieved to find the two magi were magically in their place. Even though they'd stayed with him this long, he couldn't help but check. He was also happy to find that Satya was still safely in its sheath.

"Are the magi still in your pocket?" Asha asked.

"Yep, I have no idea how they stay in there," Zach said.

"Your faith is strong," Kazuya interjected.

Zach and Asha looked over at him.

"The magi stay with you because you are faithful. They have a mind of their own," Kazuya said, adjusting his sword.

Zach looked back at Asha. They shared a look. Jovie had said the exact same thing.

"Come on, Fenrir," Zach said.

Fenrir hurried over to them, and Zach gave him a scratch on his back as he checked the his collar. All three candles—Hope, Faith, and Joy—were still safe and sound. Zach just had to find one more magus and they'd have all four gifts.

"Now that we're getting closer, I think I better carry these."

Fenrir whined and huffed as he lowered his head so Zach could get the candles.

"It's not that I don't think you can do it, boy. It's just, I'm most likely going to have to battle Malum myself, and I think I may need these on me."

Fenrir gave Zach a look that seemed to say he understood.

"Except, I don't know where I'm going to put them."

"Here, use my belt," Kazuya said.

He walked over to Zach and handed him the long piece of leather. He showed Zach how to wrap each candle with the leather strap and then tied the belt over one of Zach's shoulders, under the opposite arm, and around his waist. Zach felt like one of those military guys with the grenades strapped to his chest. One of those cool guys from the action movies who pulls a grenade off their chest, bites the pin, and then launches it into the perfect spot, blowing something random up behind him as he walks away. Zach stood a little taller when Kazuya was finished.

"Where are we?" Zach asked as Kazuya stepped back.

"Burra Din is generous. We are in the exact place we need to be," Kazuya said, looking around. "This is the island where our ancestors built Salvator castle. The ruins are in that direction."

Kazuya pointed toward the dark southern part of the island.

"Great," Asha said sarcastically.

Kazuya, Asha, and Fenrir began to walk in the direction of the darkness. However, Zach stood frozen. Once they realized he wasn't following them, they turned around.

"You comin' Monkey Boy?" Asha asked.

"Um, do you think Malum is waitin' there alone?" Zach asked, staring at the darkness.

Kazuya shook his head.

"Yeah, me neither. Um, don't you think we need an army or something? I mean, waltzing up to the castle with just the four of us doesn't seem very wise."

"Before we left the mountain village, I sent out messages to the other lands and villages. The wind carries the message. But I do not know if the people will listen or if they will come. Now that the protectors are gone, they will have to be in tune with Burra Din to hear the message. Warriors from Iyashi temple should be on their way. Kumi will lead them," Kazuya said.

"So let me get this straight," Zach said. "We're heading into certain doom where a teenage boy from another land—me—will challenge a dark viking on steroids who can go between worlds and amass an army the size of Texas. And the only backup I have are you three?"

Fenrir grunted disapprovingly.

"No, don't get me wrong. You guys are great. But it's us four against Malum and his army, and you're telling me maybe these other people will show up? Only if they're listening to the wind?"

Kazuya smirked slightly. Zach shook his head and laughed to himself.

"Okay, this sounds about right. Everything I've done so far seemed freakin' impossible, why not raise the stakes?"

"What is a Texas? Is it big?" Asha asked.

"Yeah, pretty big," Zach said.

Asha sighed and rolled her eyes. "Let us be going, then."

"I would not be surprised if Malum's army was already in place," Kazuya said.

"Oh, that's reassuring," Zach said as he followed Kazuya.

"Doing the right thing is never easy," Kazuya said.

"And why is that? Why isn't doing the right thing easy?" Zach asked.

"That is an easy one," Asha said. "Burra Din grants you free will, right?"

"Yeah, I guess so," Zach said.

"Well, when you choose to do good. Burra Din is proud, and Malum is rageful. So Malum sends everything in his power to stop you. Hence doing good is hard."

Kazuya looked upon Asha proudly.

"But when you do evil, Burra Din is disappointed; however, you have been granted free will and may decide what to do. Malum, on the other hand, is thrilled and makes it easy for you to make a mess of your world."

Zach thought for a moment and said, "That makes sense. Geez, Asha, you're pretty smart." Then he smirked at her and gave her a playful shove.

Asha blushed.

"It is not Asha's intelligence that brought her to that conclusion, Zachariah," Kazuya said.

Zach looked up at Kazuya.

"It is her faithfulness. When you are faithful, hopeful, and joyful, everything becomes clear."

"Right, those are the three candles or, um, gifts. So what's the fourth?" Zach asked.

Kazuya just smiled and walked toward the darkness.

Once they reached the bottom of the hill, Zach could make out the ruins of the ancient castle in the distance. From where they stood, a wide, grassy field came up to a winding stream. Then over the stream the ground rose again. Atop a small hill stood the castle citadel remains. Gray stone walls towered high into the sky. However, the left wall was half gone and the stones that had fallen were piled on top of each other. Inside the castle walls, a tower, or keep, was filled with cannonball holes.

"What happened to that place?" Zach asked.

"Unfortunately, when the gifts of Burra Din were forgotten, a war broke out among the people, separating them and causing destruction across the world. That was before the protectors," Kazuya said.

"Do you really think the new prince will be born in those ruins?" Asha asked.

"I do not know," Kazuya replied, "but I believe Malum thinks so. I also know Burra Din brought us here for a reason."

They walked toward the ruins, taking the side of the field near the treeline so as to not be out in the open and vulnerable to attack. When they'd made it about halfway to the stream, they heard a loud, beastly cry and the blow of a horn, which sounded awful—like nails on a chalkboard. Zach, Asha, Fenrir, and Kazuya all made a break for the treeline, taking cover among the brush. The woods on the sides of the field shook violently. Dark warriors and creatures erupted from the treelines and marched quickly into formation. They chanted and waved their black banners as they lined up in front of the castle. Then from behind the several rows of dark black warriors, Malum appeared. The center of the lines moved aside to create an aisle for Malum. He was in no rush and marched arrogantly. Once he reached the first row of warriors, Malum pulled out a long sword with a jagged blade and beheaded the creature standing closest to him. His dark warriors didn't even flinch.

Zach cringed at the sight of blood spewing from the limp body. This whole time Zach had hoped calling Malum a deranged viking would help the ancient warrior seem less frightening in the end. But he was wrong. Malum was terrifying. He looked five times Zach's height and wore a long black cloak with sharp slate armor. The armor was outlined roughly in red. His helmet, gray and shaped like the skull of a dragon, was terrifying. The eyes and mouth of the helmet were completely black, making the red streaks across the face stand out like bolts of bloody lightning. And as he casually kicked the dead warrior aside, Malum sheathed his jagged sword, drew a large ax from his back, and held it in both hands. He tapped the handle in his palm. The head of the ax had a sharp, flat front and a spiky back. It looked like Malum had attached some kind of metal porcupine to the back of the massive ax. You don't come back from getting hit with that, Zach thought. Malum stared into the woods.

"Zachariah Lebouré, I know you hide among the trees. My wrath awaits you."

The warriors grunted in unison.

"Fenrir! I sense your betrayal. It is useless to challenge me. Let us talk. As you can see, my warriors heavily outnumber your small fellowship."

Fenrir growled and Zach shifted. Kazuya put a hand on Zach to reassure him. Zach looked at him and Asha.

"Just wait," Kazuya said.

"Zachariah! Hand over the gifts, the magi. If you do this for me, I will send you home. You may leave this land and all will be well. I may even consider releasing your mother," Malum said.

A sharp pang of guilt shot through Zach's heart. His mother! He tried to jump up, but Kazuya and Asha pulled him back down behind the trees.

"Very well, if it is proof you need, then proof I have!" Malum bellowed.

Malum held up his heavily armored hand, and a large pig-like creature marching on its hindlegs brought forth a small gold box. Malum took the box and lifted it into the air.

"Inside this box sits your mother's soul!"

Zach's heart broke. He looked imploringly at Kazuya who shook his head.

"It is a trick, Zachariah. Do not let him fool you. It is a trick."

Zach clutched his glass sword, Satya, with one hand, and the magi with the other. Malum flicked open the box and a great whoosh was heard followed by the panicked sound of Zach's mother's voice.

"Zachariah! Are you there?! Help me, Zach! Give him what he wants! Help me!"

Zach's eyes burned with tears as a wave of rage overwhelmed him, and he jumped out from the cover of trees. He drew Satya, who glowed, and held it high.

"Let her go!" Zach yelled.

Asha, Fenrir, and Kazuya, after attempting to pull him back into the woods, relented and stood by his side.

"Ah, I see you understand now. She is mine! If you want your mother's soul, you must hand over the gifts, the magi!" Malum said.

Malum held the box higher for Zach to see. Zach heard his mother's voice again.

"Zach! Help me!"

Zach was torn. He didn't know what to do. Then suddenly he felt a strong wind coming from the woods. Kazuya turned to the woods and set a hand on Zach's shoulder.

"I will give you the gifts. I will give you the magi on one condition," Zach said.

Asha and Kazuya looked at him. Zach batted them away. Fenrir whined. Zach hushed him.

"Ah, you have found sense. What is it you wish? What do you desire?" Malum asked.

"If that's really my mom, what was the last thing she said to me before she died?" Zach asked.

Malum hesitated then flicked the box.

The voice from the box said, "I love you, Zachariah."

Zach walked forward a few steps, held his sword high again, and said, "Nope."

Then he ran into battle, screaming his own version of a war cry. He ran alone at first. But within moments, Asha, Kazuya, Fenrir, and the entire body of warriors from the Land of Pax, led by Kumi, burst from the trees. The onslaught of Iyashi temple warriors was a glorious sight. Before Zach could reach Malum, he disappeared within the lines of his troops. Then two Pax warriors clashed with two of the dark warriors. A loud clang rang through the field. The battle had begun.

Zach had never experienced nor could have ever imagined the reality of battle. This was nothing like his video games. It was bloody, beyond frightening, feral, and utter chaos. Men screamed in pain as others turned into monsters. It was like a terrible nightmare. Kazuya blew dark warriors away with his powers and brought many down with his oversized katana. Asha expertly flung her bowshot and coiled it around several dark warriors at a time. Fenrir was ferocious, letting the rage from years of abuse fuel him. He seemed to be unstoppable. And Zach, well, Zach held his own thanks to Satya. He managed to take down a handful of warriors as he searched for Malum. He encouraged himself with the thought that if he found Malum, the battle would end. He could stop the carnage.

Malum towered over everyone and should have been easy to find, but Zach did not see him anywhere. He jumped over fallen warriors and ducked beneath swinging swords. And then they heard another beastly cry. The terrible shrieking horn blew, and a large stomping came from behind the castle. Zach heard the beating of wings as a large dragon shot into the sky with Malum sitting upon a bronze, throne-like saddle. The Pax warriors fled the field to find cover. Even the dark warriors cowered at the sight of their fearsome leader. Zach followed, overwhelmed by the sight of the great beast. He and his men found cover in ruins near the castle. The dragon flew down to the field, setting everything ablaze. Malum even attacked his own dark warriors to destroy the battle ground.

Zach watched as men tried to flee but were too late. It was one of the most horrifying experiences he'd ever witnessed. Men raced for the cover of the ruins, but some who'd been ignited by the dragon's flames ran in circles or dragged themselves along the ground screaming in pain. The sound was unbearable. Fenrir dodged the fire and tried to help the warriors reach the ruins where Zach and the others hid. But it was treacherous. Kazuya tried to throw the dragon off course with his wind powers. But the dragon flew strong. Finally, Malum pulled back, and the dragon hovered above the scorched earth settling near the castle keep. The field was a horrendous site. The long green grass was now brown burnt bits, and the field was covered in ash. Dead warriors from both sides littered the ground. Zach was speechless. All this because he didn't hand over candles?

"Zachariah! Zachariah!" Kazuya said as he came up behind him. Zach turned to him.

"Are you alright?!"

"Yes," Zach answered quietly. "But why?"

"He's Malum, he is consumed with a lust for power," Kazuya said. "We must prepare to hold fast. I believe others will come."

Zach woke up and shook his head. He couldn't imagine enduring that again.

"No! Are you serious?! He has that dragon. There's no way! We have to give him the gifts. We have to—"

"Zach!" Asha said.

Zach looked at her. She walked up to him slowly and hugged him. Then she leaned her forehead on his. Zach was so full of despair that the show of affection didn't even faze him.

"Zach," she whispered. "Malum tried to trick you with your mother's words. They were false, but did your maata tell you something before she died?"

The warriors and Kazuya listened. Zach stepped back from Asha and shook his head. He didn't want to share them.

"Zach, what did she say?" Asha asked, holding his face with her hands.

Zach looked up at her. Her big dark eyes were full of compassion.

"My mom told me, um . . ." Tears filled his eyes. He'd never told anyone this. "My mom, well, she said, uh." Tears fell. "My mom never said anything like it before so I didn't understand. She said . . ."

Now everyone was listening. Realizing Zach needed to be seen as well as heard Fenrir lifted him up on his back. Zach balanced and reluctantly waved at the crowd of warriors looking at him. Kazuya sent a wind that carried his voice. Zach felt awkward. But as he looked at the faces of the beaten-down warriors, Zach knew his next words were not only encouraging for him but for everyone who stood up to Malum. He wiped his eyes and cleared his throat.

"My mom said, 'Do you see that beautiful light, Zachariah? Be that light. Be the light in the darkness, Zachariah.' So um, that guy, Malum. Well, he sucks."

Some of the soldiers laughed and others grunted in agreement. At the sight of the Pax warriors, Asha, Fenrir, and Kazuya, Zach felt more confident.

"Everything about him is dark and it's like impossible. But we can do this. Listen to my mom and be the light!"

Once Zach was back on the ground, Fenrir nudged him with his nose, and the warriors around Zach cheered. Despite the fact they were surrounded by the enemy and waited for the drop of dragon fire, hope trickled through the ranks. After hugging Fenrir, Zach walked over to Asha and Kazuya.

"That was wonderful, Zach," Asha said, tears welling in the corners of her eyes.

"Your mother was a wise woman," Kazuya said.

"Thanks. It's funny though. She never really mentioned the gifts of Burra Din to me before—hope, faith, joy, and . . . well, I don't know that last one yet—but I feel like my mom knew what they were anyway."

"I believe we all come to understand the gifts and Burra Din in our own way," Kazuya said.

Zach sighed, feeling much better.

"Now what do we do?" Asha asked.

"This can only end with me, right?" Zach asked.

Kazuya, who'd been joined by Kumi, and Asha looked at him.

"The only way this ends is with me facing Malum, right?" Zach asked again.

"Yes," Kazuya said.

"Well, then let's do this." Zach pulled his sword from its sheath and walked over to Fenrir. He climbed on his back. "Let's charge the lines and get me to Malum. I will face him. All you have to do is stay alive."

"Zach, how in Burra are you going to defeat him?" Asha asked.

Zach patted his chest where the magi sat and then pointed to the candles. "I don't know, but I don't think I'm supposed to know. Burra Din will take care of me."

Kazuya and Kumi gave Zach looks of approval. Then they returned to the ranks and organized everyone for a charge. Asha stared up at him.

"Don't worry, Asha. I'll see you in the end. I know it. Thanks for being my friend," Zach said.

Asha stepped closer to Fenrir, who lowered Zach down to her height. Asha motioned for Zach to come forward. She grabbed his face with her hands and pulled him in for a quick, innocent kiss. Zach's face burned red. Asha pulled back, face flushed.

"Now, off with you Monkey Boy! Go show that tyrant who's the GOAT!"

The soldier next to her gave Asha a funny look.

"Greatest of all time," she explained to him.

Zach, cheeks bright red and flustered, led Fenrir to the back of the line.

At this point the field was empty. Malum's warriors were reorganized in lines, protecting the castle ruins, and Zach's warriors were behind ruins in the field. Breaking the deathly silence with a cheer, Zach's warriors ran out from the stone walls. And up from the middle of the lines rode Zach on Fenrir's back. With a loud cry, Malum's dragon took flight. The dragon soared high into the sky as the warriors below crashed together. Fenrir took Zach in the direction of the dragon. And as the dragon dove down upon the field, creating a ball of fire in its throat, Zach braced himself.

But instead of a dragon's roar, he heard an eagle scream and opened his eyes in disbelief. There flying above him were the awe-inspiring creatures of the Lumen Hills. Dorogan and Sundara attacked Malum's dragon. The dragon let out a stream of fire. A battle ensued in the sky. Flying creatures from all over Burra Din joined in the battle to stop the dragon. Then from behind them, Zach heard confident grunts. As he turned, Zach was shocked. He saw warriors from every land marching out of the treeline. The warriors from Spés, Fidem, and Pax all wore violet armor with the triangular symbols on their chests while the warriors from Gaudium wore a deep pink and their symbol. Suddenly Zach realized they all matched their gifts, their lands, their candles! Zach couldn't believe what he was seeing. They'd all come. They'd all listened and heard the whispering of Burra Din. They believed in the prophecy, and they all believed in him. Recharged, Zach rode into the fray. He found Malum, who had dismounted from the dragon. Satya in hand, Zach clung to Fenrir as they approached the Overlord of Darkness. Malum, seeing them coming, stood strong with his ax and motioned for the warriors around him to leave Zach alone.

"He's mine!" Malum roared.

The warriors stopped fighting suddenly and turned their attention to the center of the battlefield where Zach, on Fenrir's back, faced Malum. The field was silent save for the shifting of armor.

"This is for whom you left me, Fenrir?" Malum said, approaching Zachariah. "This small child, this weak, misguided otherworlder?"

Fenrir growled.

"It's okay, boy. Just stay right here. I can do this," Zach said.

Zachariah slid down Fenrir's back and approached Malum, who towered over him. As the beast of a man shifted his ax, his entire body of armor rumbled. Zach still could not see his face. Everything within his helmet was fog of endless black, as if nothing but darkness lurked inside the body of armor. Then suddenly, without warning, Malum stepped forward and shoved Zach. He flew several feet away and landed on his back.

"You are nothing! You will never be anything! I may not have your mother's soul but I will have yours!" he roared. "It will be a small trophy next to the gifts but it will delight me in the fact that you, a meaningless peon, would dare to challenge the greatness of Malum."

Zach struggled to get up. But once he gained his balance, he was able to lift his sword toward Malum. Satya glowed brightly and grew to the height of the evil warrior. The dark master laughed balefully.

"You think you can defeat me! Look at you! You are worthless!"

Malum stepped forward and shoved Zachariah again; only this time before he could pull his arm away, Zachariah slashed down with Satya, cutting Malum's hand off. As the armored hand fell to the ground, Zachariah flew through the air, even farther this time. But instead of landing on his back, a gust of wind caught him and helped him land gracefully on his feet. He looked at Kazuya, who was watching. Kazuya winked at him. Zachariah's chest now hurt terribly. Malum had shoved him very hard. He clutched his sternum, and in doing so realized his pocket felt different. He looked inside and saw that the magi had crumbled to pieces. The three candles on his chest were still intact, but the two magi in his pocket had been crushed! He panicked but tried to talk himself down. He still had all the pieces of the two Pax magi; it would be okay. Three magi made a candle, a gift. As long as he had all the pieces of the magi, it would be okay. The magi melted together to make a candle anyway. He'd watched as the three magi melted together to make the candle of Spés, Fidem, and Gaudium. Did it matter if they'd been crushed to pieces before making the final candle, the final gift? He didn't have time to worry about that. He had three candles now, three of the four gifts; he could use them. He had to defeat Malum with the gifts he already had somehow. He would hope, he would have faith, he would be joyful? Yes, joyful! Zachariah started to laugh.

"What are you laughing at?" Malum said. "I have suffered greater injuries than this. This is nothing."

Zach shook his head and laughed harder.

"Whaaaaat?!" Malum yelled and stormed forward faster than Zach's reflexes could respond. This time Zach flew back almost a hundred feet. But Kazuya stopped him from falling again. Malum shot a bolt of darkness from his hand directly at Kazuya. Kazuya fell to the ground and immediately went pale.

"No!" Kumi screamed.

Asha rushed to his side. Kumi held his head up and spoke softly to the fallen Wind Whisperer. Zach, angry at the sight of his friend unconscious on the ground, became serious and focused on Malum.

"I was laughing at you. YOU, MALUM!"

Malum's giant head shifted back toward Zach. He shot a bolt of darkness and it hit him in the chest, pushing him back again. Zach felt his pocket warm. The magi pieces were coming to life! But Malum charged him.

"You—"

Shove.

"Will—"

Shove.

"Hand over—"

Shove.

"The GIFTS!"

Now Zach wasn't sure if he could get up. He touched his pocket. Malum walked over and set a heavy foot on Zach's chest.

"These are mine!"

Malum reached down and ripped the three candles, the three gifts, from Zach's chest strap. Malum had the candles! The gifts of Hope, Faith, and Joy. Amal, Vera, and Jovie!

"No!" Zach yelled.

He could barely breathe. Malum pressed down harder. Then Zach heard the whiz of Asha's bowshot. The arrowhead wrapped around Malum's waist, and he was pulled away. Asha whooped and hollered as she rode Fenrir, pulling Malum down the battlefield. Malum's warriors started to chase after her. But Malum screamed and sent a dark wave of power through the bowshot. It shattered into pieces. Asha and Fenrir skidded to a halt. Malum, enraged, stood and slowly turned toward Zach again. As he flicked his wrist, Asha and Fenrir were launched into the crowd of warriors. Malum still had the three candles. He held them high above his head, showing all of Burra Din.

"Who do you think you are? You laugh, but I destroy!"

Zach slowly stood. Everything inside his body hurt, but he had to get the three candles back from Malum.

"You fight, but I win!" Malum continued.

Zach pulled his sword up and held it high.

"You believe, but I act!" Malum roared as Zach braced himself. "Who do you think you are?!"

And that was the worst question Malum could have asked. There was still a chance. Malum still needed one more candle, the gift of

Pax. Zach, exhausted, gripped his sword with one hand and the crumbled magi in his pocket with the other. Suddenly everything became clear.

"Who am I?" Zach asked. He raised his voice so all could hear. "I am a friend, a nephew, a son!"

Zach stepped toward Malum and the candles in Malum's hand illuminated. Malum looked at the candles and then back at Zach.

"I am hopeful!"

And from the Spés candle in Malum's hand, Zach watched as Amal's spirit shot into the air in a burst of flames and hovered above the battlefield. Zach could see Amal's face amid the ethereal light, smiling down at him. Zach took another step toward Malum.

"I am faithful!"

A floating swirl of flowers surrounded Malum and the Fidem candle as Vera's spirit appeared, gracefully joining Amal. She looked content and proud. Zach took another step.

"I am joyful!"

In a rocket of snowflakes, Jovie's spirit shot out of the pink candle. She twirled in the sky and winked at Zach as she joined Amal and Vera. The three protectors hovered above Zach.

Another step.

"And I am at peace!"

Zachariah lifted the glass sword in the air and brought it down, forcing the blade into the scorched land. Light burst from the ground. He closed his eyes and felt the world around him disappear. Then the power of Burra Din surged through him. He moved in a warrior stance, leaving Satya in the ground. He balled his hands and pushed them toward Malum. The force from his palm hit Malum and sent him flying back across the battlefield. Zach didn't even open his eyes. He set his hands on the hilt of his sword again and stood motionless. For in Zach's mind was a sense of calm, a sense of peace. He heard nothing but the spirit of Burra Din humming through him.

A familiar change occurred in his pocket. The warmth was accompanied by a small weight. He opened his eyes and reached in. He found the three magi melding together in his hand, and slowly the new one's word melted away: *Identitatis*. When they joined together, the word *Pax* illuminated across the last violet candle with Kazuya's triangular symbol. Zach looked up. Malum laid motionless on the ground. He looked over and saw Asha and Kumi stepping back from Kazuya. Kazuya's body slowly turned to light. It wrapped itself around Kumi, who smiled with tears falling down her cheeks. The light seemed to hug her. Then a face formed within the ethereal light and kissed her softly. Kazuya's light erupted into the sky, creating a warrior among the stars. Then with a whoosh the light entered the last candle. The last gift.

"May you be at peace, Zachariah. The prince is coming," Kazuya said.

And with that, the last candle was complete. Zach held the candle in his hand, amazed he'd done it. Then suddenly the candle was pulled from his hand. Zach watched as the candle flew through the air straight into Malum's palm. Now Malum had all four candles. Malum let out a loud evil laugh. He held the four candles in the air once again. Zach couldn't believe it. He'd not only brought three gifts straight to Malum but had created the last one right in front of the evil warrior.

"Give them back!" Zach said.

Fenrir growled and Asha lunged forward. But Malum turned and shot a black bolt of lightning from his hand, pushing Asha back into the crowd.

"The gifts are mine! I possess them! I possess their power!"

Malum flaunted his victory. And his warriors let out a unified grunt. Zach breathed heavily as he watched Malum. Then he remembered something Amal had told him. The gifts weren't things somebody could control or possess. The gifts weren't the actual candles. Each time Zach truly got to know the protectors they turned into the candles. But he didn't get to know them by chance. He'd chosen to get to know them. The moment he'd given in and chosen to ignite hope, embrace faith, share joy, and accept peace was the same moment the gifts had become a part of Burra Din, a part of him. The gifts had never left Burra Din. The gifts were the hope, faith, joy and peace in him, in each person of Burra Din. They weren't things: they were choices. Choices that made Burra Din, or any realm, a better place to live. Choices that made for a better life to live. Zach looked up at Amal, Vera, and Jovie. Who all looked down on him with pride.

"You don't have the gifts!"

"These are interesting words to use before your death. I have won! I possess the power!" Malum said.

"You could have the gifts, easily. But you don't," Zach said, shakily.

Malum grunted at him in disgust.

"The gifts aren't things you can collect or possess. They always exist around you, around us. They're choices we make. And Malum," Zach took a deep breath, "you made the wrong choice."

Malum looked down at the candles in his hand as the last one illuminated and a breeze blew through the field. The wind hit Malum's hand, and Kazuya's spirit danced into the sky, joining Amal, Vera, and Jovie. The candles in Malum's hand were crushed suddenly by a great invisible force. Pieces of them crumbled from Malum's hands as he desperately tried to catch them. But his efforts were in vain as the pieces disintegrated into the atmosphere around him.

"Noooooo!" Malum screamed.

But no one cared, because in the sky the protectors' spirits swirled, becoming one beam of light that erupted into the most beautiful firework Zach had ever seen. Embers from the fireworks floated down from the sky and landed on each citizen of Burra Din. The tiny embers looked like flames dancing above their heads as each person's face brightened with laughter. As the flames slowly dwindled, the entire field of warriors quieted. As soon as the embers faded, Zach heard Malum before he saw him. A rumble in the ground had Zach looking up to find Malum charging toward him like a huffing rhinoceros. But instead of preparing for battle Zachariah stood motionless. He closed his eyes and handed the impossible feat over to Burra Din. And when Malum was feet from Zach, a glowing light ripped through the atmosphere and a beautiful, intricately carved door appeared before him. Malum abruptly slammed right into the door.

Zach's eyes widened as he read *Nativitatis*. Mesmerized, he reached for the handle. The ground rumbled beneath him and Zach stopped to watch as all the dark warriors disintegrated before them. Even the giant dragon that was lying in wait near the castle disappeared in a cloud of smoke. All that was left was Malum, who was now the size of a normal man, standing helpless. Within moments, he exploded into light, and everyone cheered. Zach looked to Asha, who encouraged him to go forward. Zach motioned for her to follow, and she rushed to him. Asha grabbed his hand, and as Zach reached for the handle again, the door stopped glowing. He couldn't turn the knob. Asha tugged at his arm. Zach turned to her.

"You must go on without me. This is the end for me. I do not think I am to follow you. I cannot leave my people. Burra Din wants me to stay here." Zach looked behind her and saw her maata, Aachal, standing in armor. She gave a single proud wave.

"Your maata fought too?" Zach asked. He had no idea Aachal was a warrior.

"She's full of surprises," Asha said.

"I see that," Zach said, turning to Asha. "I don't want to go without you."

"I will see you again, Monkey Boy. Burra Din will make sure of that," she said, giving him a kiss on the cheek.

Everyone cheered. Zach's cheeks burned red, and he was speechless. Asha smiled sheepishly, and ran back to her mother, who shook her head lovingly at her daughter. Zach waved and felt a nudge behind him. He turned to find Fenrir.

"Be a good boy, Fenrir. Don't worry, Asha's with you," Zach said.

Fenrir whined, and Zach hugged him. At the sound of Asha's whistle, Fenrir ran to her side. As Zach looked back one more time at his new friends, he felt that same familiar warmth in his chest. Looking down, he saw the candles had reappeared on his belt, whole once more. Three purple and one pink. He'd done it. Zach had collected the three magi of each land and illuminated each of the four gifts in the world of Burra Din. And despite the fact they'd crumbled in Malum's hands, they'd appeared once again on Zach's chest. Surprised and yet not surprised, Zach reached for the doorknob, walking through one last portal.

NATIVITATIS

"So all this was done so it might be fulfilled . . . "
Matthew 1:22

When Zach arrived on the other side, he was surprised to find himself, not in a castle, but deep within a forest. It looked familiar. Was it the Forest of Inspirare? He wondered. In front of him was a small hut with light flickering in the window. Then he heard a baby cry. Was that the prince? That's odd, Zach thought. A prince born in a small hut in the woods, completely unknown. But he stepped forward. When he got to the door and before he could knock, Zach heard a woman's gentle voice.

"Come in."

Zach opened the door. When he walked in, he saw a baby wrapped in a worn blanket lying in what looked like a wooden storage box. He also saw a woman lying next to the baby on blankets. She looked worn out but completely content. And a tall, exhausted man sat in a chair, smiling up at him.

"You're here! How lovely," the woman said.

The man got up and slapped Zach on the back proudly.

"How did you know I was—ah—Burra Din, right?" Zach asked.

"Yes, of course, and there's someone here who would like to meet you," the woman said.

She picked up the child and turned him to meet Zach. The baby was beautiful and held qualities of all the people of Burra Din. He had the large eyes of Spés, the beautiful dark skin of Fidem, the adorable pointy ears of Gaudium, and the white hair and calm smile of Pax. The sparkle in the baby's eyes reminded him of

Asha. Before Zach could refuse, the woman handed the child over to him. Zach awkwardly held the little one. But when the baby nestled in Zach's chest, he suddenly felt comfortable with the child in his arms. He looked down into the baby's innocent face and saw that underneath the white curls and on the baby's forehead was a tattoo-like mark. Except this one was the combination of all four triangles of Burra Din. This one looked like a . . .

The baby touched the candles on Zach's chest. Zach looked down and pulled each candle off of his belt one by one. He sat on a chair and laid the candles on the baby's lap.

"The magi turned into these. These are your gifts, little guy. These are your friends: Amal, Vera, Jovie, and Kazuya," Zach said softly.

The baby gently laid a hand on the candles. And after a quiet moment and a small cooing sigh, light erupted from the candles. It was a joyful light that shot from the window and traveled like a rocket into the sky. Holding the baby, Zach followed the light out of the hut and looked up beyond the trees. In the sky, in the same shape as the baby's tattoo, incorporating all four of the triangles, was a star. As he stared at the star in the sky, Zach swore he heard people in the distance cheering. This was the sign to all of Burra Din that the prince had been born and the gifts had been remembered. Zach suddenly felt emotional. Then the baby's mother walked toward Zach and wrapped her arms around him.

"Thank you, Zachariah. Please know that a parent's love never ends. Your mother and father will always be with you," she said, taking the baby and swaddling him in a blanket.

The world around Zach faded as he heard his own mother and father's voices in unison, "Be the light, Zachariah. We love you." And Zachariah was at peace.

. . .

"Zachariah! Are you alright?!"

Zach opened his eyes to find Father Joe leaning over him.

"Huh?" Zach was back in his room lying on top of a pile of junk.

"I came back to make sure you were really getting up this time for church because I didn't see you in the pew. I found you here on the floor. Are you okay?" Father asked.

Coming to terms with the fact he was back in his own world, Zach sat up. "Oh yeah, I guess I must have hit my head."

"Here let me help you," Father Joe said as he pulled Zach off the floor.

As Zach got up, he heard something hit the floor—or rather some things. He and Father Joe looked down and saw candles lying next to his feet. Three violet candles and one pink candle. They had the words *Spés*, *Fidem*, *Gaudium*, and *Pax* scrawled across their sides. Suddenly the memories of Burra Din flooded back to him. Zach picked them up and looked over to the wooden tree sculpture, realizing they'd fit right in the candle holders on the Advent calendar. He also noticed the doors of the Advent calendar were all slightly open. Zach carefully placed each candle in the little holes. Then Zach heard his phone buzz with a notification. Zach walked over and saw it was another message from Elizabeth. He set his phone on the bed and decided that he'd go ahead and message Elizabeth back about playing the drums. Because maybe having friends wasn't so bad. Zach grinned to himself as he thought of Asha.

"Looks like you found those candles after all," Father Joe said.

He studied the Advent calendar with excitement in his eyes. Zach buttoned his shirt. On their way out the door Zach looked up at Father Joe.

"I think they found me."

INSPIRATIONS AND MEANINGS

Story Elements

- Zachariah—Zachariah was named after Elizabeth's husband in the Bible. Elizabeth and Zachariah are John the Baptist's parents. Zachariah is struck dumb and silent until the birth of his son, John. He thought they were too old to have children even though the Angel Gabriel told him it would happen. Zachariah also means "remembered by Yahweh." Zach finds out he is remembered by God in the story.

- Labouré—Zachariah's last name is Labouré because Saint Catherine Labouré is one of the saints of silence, which goes with the story behind Zachariah's first name.

- Father Joe—named for Jesus's adoptive father, Joseph. He is a father-figure to Zachariah.

- Mary—named for Jesus's mother. She is mother-figure to Zachariah.

- Elizabeth—named for Zachariah's wife in the Bible story.

- Grandpa Gabe—named for the Angel Gabriel. He provides the Advent calendar just as the Angel Gabriel provided Zachariah with God's plan.

- Burra Din—Indian English word for Christmas. Represents globalization of Christianity.

- Why Latin words? Latin was the universal language for the Catholic Church, but it is no longer used in everyday language.

- Why tribes? Based on the ancient Hebrew tribes under Abraham, who received the knowledge of God and then needed to be reminded of God's gifts to mankind through many prophets and Jesus.

- Why protectors? Based on saints who guide people closer to Jesus.
- Malum—Latin word for Evil

LAND OF SPÉS—Cultural Influence: Germany, India, Pacific Islands, Norsemen

- Spés—Latin word for Hope
- Design of the land—Lie under a Christmas tree and look up. It's all there.
- Amal—Indian name for hope and based on Saint Jude Thaddeus for his hopefulness and understanding. He is also the saint of lost causes, and Zach feels lost in the beginning of the story. St. Jude is also depicted in art carrying a club and an ax to symbolize his martyrdom.
- Benignitas—Latin word for kindness
- Fiducia— Latin word for trust
- Votum— Latin word for hopeful prayer, promise
- Asha—Indian name meaning hope and life
- Aachal—Indian name meaning steady
- Forest of Inspirare—Latin word for inspiration
- Factum Mountains— Latin word for action
- Confido Cave— Latin word for confidence
- Adventurus River— Latin word for adventure
- Lumen Hills— Latin word for light

LAND OF FIDEM—Cultural Influence: Germany, Pacific Islands, India

- Fidem—Latin word for faith
- Design of the land—Gingerbread houses and tropical Christmases

- Vera—Indian name meaning faithful and is based on Saint Therese of Lisieux for her childlike faith. St. Therese is represented by flowers, especially roses.
- Patientia— Latin word for patience
- Humilis—Latin word for humility
- Mollitia—Latin word for resilient
- Barri—Indian name meaning innocent
- Eadrich—Indian name meaning manly and wealthy ruler
- Livi—Indian name for olive branch or symbol of peace
- Tubi—Middle eastern name meaning brightening
- Ria—Indonesian name meaning joy or river
- Alab—Filipino name meaning passion or blaze
- Gardens of Gratia—Latin word for thanks
- Fides/Fideans—Latin word for faith
- Velox Plains—Latin word for swift
- Solis—Latin word for sun
- Consano Lake—Latin word for healing
- Innoxius Stream—Latin word for harmless

LAND OF GAUDIUM—Cultural Influences: Germany, Russia, Ireland

- Gaudium—Latin word for Joy
- Design of the land—Siberian Tundra and Santa's home in the North Pole
- Jovie—Russian name meaning joyful and is based on Saint Philip Neri for her joyfulness and love for people. St. Philip is known for his affability. He is the patron saint of joy and laughter.
- Caritas—Latin word for love
- Animo—Latin word for courage
- Misericordia—Latin word for mercy
- Jovanna—Slavic name for God is Gracious

- Skotovody—Russian term for ranchers or pastoralists
- Mir—Russian word for peace
- Zakhar—Russian name for the Lord will remember
- Bol—Russian name for pain
- Khorosho—Russian name for good
- Umnaya—Russian name for clever
- Krasota—Russian name for beauty
- Pavel (Pavie)—Russian word for small
- Wisps—Celtic legendary faeries who guide one to their fate
- Gigant Mountains and River—Latin for giant
- Bruma—Latin word for snow or mist

LAND OF PAX—Cultural Influences: Japan, Eastern World Healing, India

- Pax—Latin word for Peace
- Design of the land—Mountains of the Eastern Asian Coast and Eastern temples
- Kazuya—Japanese name for calm, harmony, peace and is based on Saint Dymphna for his focus on healing and peacefulness. St. Dymphna created a place of healing for the people of her time.
- Pondero—Latin for meditate
- Gratium—Latin word for grateful
- Identitatis—Latin word for identity
- Chaya—Hebrew name meaning life
- Kumi—Japanese name meaning beautiful
- Somnium Sea—Latin word for dream
- Iyashi Temple—Latin word for healing
- Tsuki Village—Japanese for moon
- Salvator Island—Latin word for savior
- Castle Ruins represent the history of the tribes of Israel

NATIVITATIS—Nativity

- The prince and his family = Jesus, Mary, and Joseph
- The triangle tattoos come together to make the four pointed Christmas star.
- Overall book is about preparing your heart for the coming of Jesus through the lessons and gifts of Advent. The gifts of Advent are symbolized by four candles on a wreath at Christmas time for Catholics. You light one of the four candles each Sunday before Christmas. Light the purple candle of Hope first, the purple candle of Faith second, the pink candle of Joy third, and the purple candle of Peace last.
- Why a dogwood tree? Legend tells a story of the dogwood tree providing the wood for Jesus's cross. When I was a little girl, I was told The Legend of the Dogwood Tree and was shown the beautiful cross at the center of the dogwood tree flowers.
- Why cultural influences from around the world? This represents the globalization of Christianity. Despite our differences, the world comes together to celebrate Hope, Faith, Joy, and Peace.

MERRY CHRISTMAS!

Information on the saints was studied from the sources below. Find out more by visiting their websites.

1. goodcatholic.com
2. catholic.org